An Ethical Compass

DATE DUE

An Ethical Compass

Coming of Age in the 21st Century

The Ethics Prize of the
Elie Wiesel Foundation for Humanity

Preface by Elie Wiesel
Foreword by Thomas L. Friedman

Yale
UNIVERSITY PRESS
New Haven and London

Copyright © 2010 by
Elie Wiesel Foundation for Humanity.
All rights reserved.
This book may not be reproduced, in whole or in part,
including illustrations, in any form (beyond that copying
permitted by Sections 107 and 108 of the U.S. Copyright
Law and except by reviewers for the public press), with-
out written permission from the publishers.

Designed by Sonia Shannon.
Set in Bulmer type by Integrated Publishing Solutions.
Printed in the United States of America
by Courier Westford.

Library of Congress Cataloging-in-Publication Data

An ethical compass : coming of age in the 21st century :
the ethics prize of the Elie Wiesel foundation for humanity
/ preface by Elie Wiesel ; foreword by Thomas L.
Friedman.
p. cm.
Includes bibliographical references.
ISBN 978-0-300-16915-7 (paperbound : alk.
paper)   1. Ethics, Modern—21st century.   I. Elie
Wiesel Foundation for Humanity.
BJ320.E84   2010
170—dc22
2010023426
A catalogue record for this book is available
from the British Library.

This paper meets the requirements of ANSI/NISO
Z39.48–1992 (Permanence of Paper).
10 9 8 7 6 5 4 3 2 1

CONTENTS

ON GOD

FOREWORD

What does a "World-Is-Flat-Guy" like me have to do with a book on ethics? After all, the lofty, abstract world of ethics rarely mixes with the bits and bytes, banks and bandwidth world of globalization, right? Well, my short answer is this: The flat, globalized world has enabled more people to connect with more other people farther, faster, deeper, cheaper than ever before. And as the global financial meltdown in 2008 demonstrated, a breakdown in values and ethics in one country—particularly one as central as the United States—can now have profound implications for scores of other countries whose financial systems are intimately intertwined with America's. The more connected we are, the more ethics and ethical leadership matter, because a moral breakdown in one country, region, market, or institution can affect so many others so much more easily and so much more profoundly. It is for that reason that the essays in this book, *An Ethical Compass,* and the future leaders who wrote them, are so deserving of attention.

It is also for that reason that I salute the important work of The Elie Wiesel Foundation for Humanity. In addition to his lifelong embodiment of ethical leadership and moral courage, Professor Wiesel has quietly operated as an incubator of talent and innovation that would rival Google, Intel, and any other Silicon Valley company. But unlike the technology icons pumping out next-generation hardware and software, for the past twenty years Professor Wiesel has been hard at work trying to improve our human operating system by inspiring the next generation of ethical leaders. Not surprising for a man whom the Norwegian Nobel Committee called a "messenger" of "peace, atonement and human dignity."

I, The World Is Flat Guy, actually got connected with Professor

Wiesel's work in this area via the HOW Guy. I was researching globalization's causes and impacts, pondering a particularly difficult question: "How do people, companies, and countries need to behave in a world that is flat—and becoming hotter, flatter, and more crowded each day? Does behavior matter more now?" In one of our many conversations, the HOW Guy, Dov Seidman, CEO of a company called LRN, which helps businesses build ethical cultures—and which sponsors The Elie Wiesel Foundation for Humanity Ethics Prize—helped me see that the answer lies in the distinction between situational and sustainable values.

Seidman's thesis in his book—simply entitled *HOW*—is that behavior is the real killer app of the twenty-first century. Given that technology has made our lives hyper-connected and hyper-transparent (that is, we can easily see into each other's business and lives and tell others all over the world about what we see, without any editor or libel lawyer), we need to recognize that we are morally interdependent and we need to behave in moral ways, with sustainable values inspiring our behavior. Sustainable values connect us as people to other people. They are values such as transparency, integrity, honesty, and shared responsibility— values that inspire behaviors in us that literally sustain our relationships with one another, with our communities, with institutions, with society, and with our environment.

As I reflected on the painful financial and environmental crisis we are now living through, it occurred to me that, like so many crises, this one stemmed from institutions, leaders, and individuals, in large and small ways, acting on *situational values,* the sort that spark an explosion of short-sighted, selfish, and here-and-now behaviors and actions— rather than on *sustainable values.* Situationally speaking, globalization allowed bankers and brokers to grant subprime mortgages to people who could not possibly service them over the long haul, and then they bundled those mortgages into bonds and sold those securities all over the world to unsuspecting banks and individuals. Situational values said that was possible. Indeed, with globalization, it was easier than ever. Sustainable values would have told the brokers and buyers of those mortgages not to do it—that the whole enterprise was unsustainable. Situational values say it is now really easy for a company in China to buy farmland in sensitive natural environments in Africa or the Amazon and plow them up for soybeans or palm oil. Sustainable values would tell the owners of that land or the governments that oversee it not to let this happen.

That is why in a flat world where more things are situationally possible for individuals and companies, having more people inspired by sustainable values and principles and with the courage to act on them is more important than ever. It certainly is if we want to avoid worse crises in the future and forge a better, more sustainable path of growth, innovation, and human progress. But this, in turn, requires the emergence of a generation of leaders who would personify and exemplify these sustainable values and inspire them in others.

Which brings us back to Professor Elie Wiesel. He is the Sustainable Values Guy. For twenty years, the work of The Elie Wiesel Foundation has devoted itself to helping ensure that the right things, the sustainable things, will happen, not just what the situation allows.

Like a Silicon Valley incubator producing fresh innovations for profitable start-up companies, The Elie Wiesel Foundation, through its Prize in Ethics, has been recognizing and introducing to the world committed, creative, and innovative ethical leaders from our country's colleges and universities. And such innovators in behavior have never been in greater demand. Our world is crying out for ethical leadership.

Today, we not only need a higher percentage of our kids graduating from college—with more education—but also need more of them with the *right* education. And this education must include its ethical component, as Professor Wiesel so eloquently puts it. And given today's crises— environmental and financial—we need to be turning out leaders with the ethical knowledge to treat one another and the world around us with sustainable values and with the moral courage to act on that ethical knowledge.

The 2007 First Prize–winner Magogodi Makhene certainly understands the power of ethical leadership. Of her "tear-gassed childhood" in South Africa during the last throes of apartheid, she writes, "My humanity is inextricably linked to yours, and unless I acknowledge your humanity in defining my own, I will never realize the highest summits of human experience."

That acknowledgment is the core of the African philosophy *ubuntu,* which translates literally to "I am because we are." And it represents a sustainable value, a permanent interconnectedness and shared fate, that we all need to commit to and act from. What freedom was for the Greatest Generation, sustainable values need to be for us, the Regeneration, the generation exemplified by the young authors of these essays. Because without sustainable values governing how we deal with both the market and Mother Nature, we will surely lurch from economic crises to environmental crises. In our globalized world, ethics is not an option; it's a necessity for survival and for a stable world. Elie Wiesel has known that for a long time, which is why his lifelong refrain to his readers and students has been: "Think higher and feel deeper." But that refrain is now more vital than ever.

So look at this book and its essays as if it were a twenty-first-century survival manual, inspiration manual, and recruiting manual. Yes, "Help Wanted"—here and abroad: people who can inspire sustainable values. Fortunately, the applications seem to be flooding in. An America, a world, led by a generation of ethical leaders?—now that's an innovation I'd like to invest in. But then, Elie Wiesel has been doing that kind of investing his whole life—and the rewards are on the pages that follow.

Thomas L. Friedman

PREFACE

The problem of ethics or morality in human conduct is as old as humanity itself. In Scripture, it is embodied by Adam and Eve, who lost their place in Paradise when they stood before the Tree of Knowledge and were compelled to decide whether to obey God's order to ignore the difference between Good and Evil.

The Dead Sea Scrolls remind us of the wars waged between the Children of Light and the Children of Darkness. In antiquity, there were those who believed that two gods in the heavens ruled the world—the god of Good and the god of Evil.

In Dostoevsky's view, man does not choose between good and evil but oscillates between them. For Solzhenitsyn, the frontier between good and evil is located not in geographical space but within the human heart.

What makes us moral? Hereditary beliefs? Unusual circumstances? Epiphanies? Moments of great fear or pain?

On the other hand, what makes someone immoral? Did the SS killers of Jewish children feel guilty at all? Adolf Hitler and Heinrich Himmler, and their fanatical followers, were convinced that what they were doing—building concentration camps and gas chambers—was for the welfare of the world. In their eyes, mass murder was a magnificent moral act. They stood for all that opposes, offends, humiliates, diminishes, and negates humanity. And all means were justified to defeat them.

But what of more recent wars? Can *they* be justified? How do we weigh the destruction of war against the noblest of all commandments— "not to stand idly by"? How many good men and women raised their voices forcefully enough to defend victims of racism and fanaticism in Cambodia, Rwanda, Bosnia, and Darfur?

Not enough. So many tragedies, so many deaths, could have been prevented.

What lessons are we teaching our young people? Have we taught them to stand against indifference? Have we taught them to develop an ethical compass within?

This volume represents for our Foundation an especially happy anniversary—twenty years of the Ethics Prize. Of all the projects we have initiated, none has been more exciting or rewarding than this opportunity to inspire young students to examine the ethical aspects of what they have learned in their personal lives and from their teachers in the classroom.

In the Ethics Prize essays, students draw from their collective memory—that of their parents and sometimes their grandparents—to reflect on a personal experience or perhaps a gnawing, unresolved question from long ago. The conflict between Israel and Palestine. The challenge of forgiving in today's South Africa. The tragedy of Bosnian women. The mothers of the Disappeared of Argentina. The scourge of AIDS.

These young voices are among the best of the thousands of essays we have read with an independent panel of educators. They pose challenging questions to themselves and to all of us about the role of conscience and justice, memory and resistance, in our lives.

Of course, we must bear in mind that the essays that appear in this volume are the work of college students, not professional writers. But they show young people who are remarkably thoughtful and engaged with enduring questions; young people who are sensitive to the sufferings and defects that confront a society yearning for guidance and eager to hear ethical voices.

Listen to the ethical voices within.

Elie Wiesel

ACKNOWLEDGMENTS

Many people have contributed to the success of the Ethics Prize over the past twenty years. Particular thanks go to Professor John Roth, Professors Alan Berger, Judith Ginsberg, Barbara Helfgott-Hyett, Carolyn Johnston, Henry Knight, David Patterson, Alan Rosen, and Stephan Ellenwood, as well as to Ted Koppel and Paul LeClerc. We also wish to acknowledge the early support of Arnold Thaler and the late Billi Ivry.

We are deeply grateful to the Ethics Prize's corporate sponsor, LRN, and to its dynamic founder and CEO, Dov Seidman. Dov is a very special friend to the Foundation and a force behind the Ethics Prize. Thanks also to Dov's team at LRN, especially Kathleen Brennan.

Ileene Smith of Yale University Press and her son, Nathaniel Sobel, a Yale undergraduate, were instrumental in bringing this volume to fruition. As was Foundation intern Lucy Mele. We would also like to thank Foundation staff Leslie Meyers and Alex Heit and intern Ariel Lederman for their invaluable support.

Finally, we thank the thousands of college students across the country who have contributed thoughtful and provocative essays over the past twenty years.

Marion and Elie Wiesel

ON CONFLICT

The Ethics of South African Identity

MAGOGODI MAKHENE
2007
Neumann College

IT HAS BEEN A YEAR SINCE Nelson Mandela raised his fist in celebration, greeting the uncertainty of life after prison. The country is steeped in speculation, thick air breathes anticipation into our living rooms; something is about to happen. My schoolmates compare notes about whose house is best stashed with emergency supplies—foodstuff, cans, books, cash. *What do people stock in preparation for civil war?* My white friends talk about *swartgevaar,* black-danger . . . crazed Africans stealing in the night, demanding that European children leave their Barbie dolls and march to the sea. At home, my township friends mindlessly chant grown-up rhetoric. *One settler one bullet, this land is ours.*

Television news swarms with talking heads, international opinion, censored verbiage—a picture of de Klerk and Mandela accepting the Nobel Peace Prize. *Are we at peace?* My mother's cousin is shot dead by Zulu militiamen; his blood simmers to a boil on his kitchen floor. My tear-gassed childhood knows its end has come. The only life I understand is change; the only identity I claim belongs to a volatile present. Looking in the mirror, I see quiet ripples of contradiction ebbing below the surface, always threatening to rip apart my multipolar world. I am the little black girl in a lily-white sea of faces riding ponies at pink birthday parties; the same little girl whose grandmother cannot spell; the same little girl who calls the squalors of Soweto home. I think first in English, an African who translates a foreign tongue into her own; but I always remember to call upon my ancestors during Mass, where I listen intently to Catholic catechism. My contradictions are important because

3

they shape my identity, and the identity I ultimately choose defines the moral and ethical compass of my adult life.

The difficulty of my childhood cannot be boiled down to a single event. Rather, the challenges spill into provocative questions, forcing the honest responder to shed any surface-level mask worn to meet and greet other faces. Am I a victim when my world bisects dichotomous identities? Do I have the right to point an accusatory finger at friends who are born into an oppressive white South African minority? In forgiving and forgetting, am I betraying my African identity? How do I forge an identity that gives tribute to a torturous heritage without harboring hatred, without adopting the selective humanity of apartheid's architects? Is there redemption in how we identify ourselves? In redefining identity, can a perpetrator become ethical? Is ethical identity cast in committed crimes, or is identity fluid and subjective, allowing us to slide along a transient continuum? Do we all possess—in our darkest hour—the malice that created apartheid?

The earliest indicator I have of life being tipped off axis is the sensation of choking, drowning in blinding clouds of tear gas. Camouflaged bulldozers mow through dust-laced streets. My sunbaked mud cake stands stoically facing the soldiers, mocking their own youth as they hoist poisonous gas in our direction. Eyes water and child play resumes: hide-and-seek. Littered streets strip naked as crowds disperse and children hide from flying bullets. When the crazed dust settles, there is nothing left but the bitter taste of hatred. At the age of four, I am keenly aware that white means toxic. Whites drive frightful Humvees through my hometown of Soweto and tear-gas anything in sight, including my drying mud cake. They bark tall orders at grown men and instill hatred in children. It becomes so easy to stereotype, to judge, to hate. It's us against them. Separation along color lines perpetuates ignorance, which breeds fear and only serves to harbor the human inadequacies that allowed apartheid, "separateness," to thrive well into the twenty-first century. Inevitably, the apartheid regime crumbles, but the battle against separation—an "us against them" mentality—is not as easily won.

As a young South African caught between diametric worlds, "separateness" extends beyond the physical into psychological and metaphysical realms. Everything about life at school is counterculture to what I know at home. My classmates have names like Bianca, Chloe, and Lauren while neighborhood friends call themselves Lerato, Neo, or Kgathliso. Textbooks claim that Jan van Riebeeck found nothing in Cape Town and fashioned that nothing into the Cape of Good Hope; my parents' banned books accuse the Dutch explorer of daylight murder and outright robbery. Other contrasts are less subtle, more difficult to swallow. Despite owning a thriving automobile business, my father is legally barred from buying his family a home outside the government-designated black ghetto of Soweto. My grandparents are subjected to paying disproportional "rent" on a three-roomed shack they will never legally own. By comparison, my white girlfriends live on small plots of paradise in homes that outdo the opulence of Babylon. Amid their wealth and the humbling poverty of my background, it is difficult not to point an accusatory finger at white South Africa. It is hard not to think along identification terms of "us" and "them." The irony is that such thinking perpetuates the premise of apartheid, "separateness."

In identifying ourselves as separate from the evil of white South Africa, the very farce of separation that oppresses my people, the same force against which we struggle, is inadvertently strengthened. The danger of separation is its intrinsic lack of tolerance for the unknown, the ease this provides for blanket blame and the forge of an identity that depends on a foreign evil group, an enemy against whom anger and hatred are "justifiably" targeted. Apartheid as an institution and cultural phenomenon crumbled when the virtual and tangible walls of separation were toppled and identity was no longer defined as "us against them." Separation ended when we recognized that we have more in common than that which divides us. As human beings, we collectively share a common identity that is spread across a broad spectrum, incorporating our lowest, beastlike behavior, as well as the highest expressions of kindness and humanity. From this complex myriad, individuals and societies carve for themselves shifting identities that inform ethical and corrupt, immoral conduct.

Comprehending ethics and morality as subjective to self-identity explains incongruous behavior in individuals and societies. South African Jews' communal apathy toward apartheid perfectly illustrates how human beings can simultaneously subscribe to contradictory moral codes because of the dynamism of identity. As whites, Jews were legally shielded from persecution and enjoyed full citizenship privileges. As a historically oppressed group, with countless members having fled to South Africa in escape of the Holocaust, Jewish South Africans were well positioned to empathize with black South Africa's antiapartheid struggle. But on the whole, South African Jews failed to act in a decisively ethical manner, owing primarily to a shift in an identity that emphasized skin color over historical heritage. The Truth and Reconciliation Commission (TRC) documented the Jewish community's position as "tacit acceptance (at best) or complicit (at worst) of apartheid's institutionalized racism."[1]

As collectively guilty as Jews and other white South Africans are of propping up the apartheid regime, black South Africa cannot forge an identity based solely on a victim-oppressor relationship. In addition to honoring the memory of exceptional white freedom fighters and martyrs such as Ruth First, all South Africans have a larger interest in claiming the past to ensure that history's gross autocracies are never repeated. In varying degree, we are all guilty of endorsing apartheid, separateness, through our acts and thoughts of hatred and prejudice. If we as black South Africans distance ourselves from the collective identity of white South Africa, we implicitly exempt ourselves from the terms of self-identity that led white South Africans into complacency and advocacy of a tyrannical and monstrous police state. To ensure that what happened is never repeated, we must acknowledge white and black identity as belonging to the same universal definition of what it means to be human—a definition that encompasses human failure and achievement. In identifying ourselves this way, we safeguard ourselves against believing that we are without capacity for abusive or oppressive behavior. Indeed, the longtime model government of Zimbabwe has proven that without a national claim of the past's evils, historic victims can form destructive and arrogant identities that fail to recognize that no human being is exempt from immorality without the constant vigilance of self-defining through ethical conduct. Recognizing a common thread of humanness brings us all closer to the fallacies of being human and highlights our collective human potential for societal failure and inhuman behavior. This sensitivity to human failure, even at its worst, and the honesty to admit that we are all capable of inhuman malice without our humanity, is fundamental to the act of forgiveness.

When I ask my family about forgiving and forgetting, it is as though I have exploded a bomb in the kitchen and expected the house to hold still. Everybody has an impassioned opinion, quoting Mandela's vision of a rainbow nation or raising the issue of unrewarded black compromise. Quizzing my grandmother on the subject, I cannot help but think that asking her to forgive some sixty-odd years of exploitation and fourth-class citizenship is audacious. Her response is standard, typical of her generation: "If Mandela can do it, why can't I?" She is quick to point out the need for black South Africa to forgive but is weary of forgetting, because my grandmother has countless memories that will not be forgotten. Memories of dead children, killed by the poverty and violence apartheid subjected her family to; memories of bulldozers and tear gas, the day-to-day melodrama of living under siege—a government subject in an endless policed state of emergency.

But Mandela has done it, Mandela put the memories aside, he chose to forgive. So people like my grandmother, the unsung heroines who labored against apartheid quietly, through the dignity with which they lived their lives, also forgive.

Archbishop Desmond Tutu asks black South Africans to "be nice to whites, they need you to rediscover their humanity."[2] By forgiving, my grandmother and other black South Africans teach others what it means to be human, how a human being can exercise control in defining who he or she is and thus affect the humanity of fellow human beings. In essence, this is a practical demonstration of *ubuntu,* an African philosophy which literally means that I am because we are—my humanity is inextricably linked to yours, and unless I acknowledge your humanity in defining my own, I will never realize the highest summits of human experience. By forgiving, black South Africans allow white South Africans room to grow, to transcend their historic identity as oppressors and find redemption in identity redefinition.

Theoretically, I understand the need for forgiveness, for healing and progression, but in practice, the pain of forgiving has been difficult to overcome. How do we forgive activist Ruth First's murderer—she was a sister, a friend, . . . a mother? Her body lay strewn across the walls, wasted into a million indiscernible smithereens after she opened a fatal parcel bomb. Does her murderer deserve forgiveness? Does forgiving such an act guarantee a change of heart in a self-described killer?

Listening to the Truth and Reconciliation Commission's hearings is a jarring test of faith in humanity and a chilling report of what it means to have an identity without conscience. Watching apartheid's Special Branch policemen run through laundry lists of human rights violations as though accounting for grocery items and hearing grown men weep openly, reliving the torture of imprisonment, make the notion of amnesty for full disclosure seem an unjust and cheap resolution to centuries of oppression. My skin crawls with discomfort as I sit in front of the television, taking stock of the bloodshed and death thousands suffered. I am particularly struck by an unassuming bald man who wears rimless spectacles and leans into a desk-mounted microphone. He states his name, *Wait . . .*, runs through the technicalities of official procedure. . . . *I know this man.* Craig Williams. *Surname Williams?* My mother helps jog childhood memories: Kimberly.

My youngest sister was good friends with a Kimberly, sleepover nights and pony-ride birthday parties. I remember Kimberly's house because of its enormity and my family attending her lavish birthday parties; Van Gogh's sunflowers beaming brightly on the Williamses' kitchen wall. Her father chatted up mine—who knows what dads talk about when you are eight and engrossed with Mickey Mouse? The subject of that conversation grips my mother now, who remembers Craig's probing. *So you have a brother in exile? Where? You support the ANC?* Perhaps he sipped tea here and remarked on his support of South Africa's leading antiapartheid party, the African National Congress.

Maybe tongues slip and volunteer information . . . whatever happened, my mother listens to the man called Craig Williams intently. He confesses to having been a spy for the South African Special Branch Police Unit, to infiltrating the ANC, to being an instrumental player in murders and the delivery of bombs. *Is this the man in whose home my sister slept?* It is difficult to describe the iced hush that shrouds our living room as we hear the firsthand account, confessions of a cunning murderer; more difficult still to comprehend how a man who ignored every rule of human empathy and conscience is subsequently granted blanket amnesty and forgiveness. Is justice served when a perpetrator is shown kindness? Do justice and forgiveness coexist? Is a moral obligation to victims breached when even the most sincere oppressor is granted amnesty or the chance to establish an ethical identity?

As a child of apartheid's terror, I cannot detach my bias in grappling with these questions, but I gain courage and inspiration from other

South Africans who are bold enough to forgive even the most searing scars and suffering. "A white policeman informed the TRC how he, with other police officers, tried to do away with the body of a Blackman they killed before. They put his body in a grill and started burning it. In order to hide this outrageous act, the officers made a barbeque in the same grill. When the police officer finished his testimony, the mother of the victim stood up and embraced the officer and said: 'I only wanted to know what happened.'"[3]

"It was painful, reliving it, but it helped us heal. The truth allowed us to move on, all of us." My mother is not the TRC's greatest fan, but she clings to the widespread belief that the TRC nurtured a nation's wounds, easing us into transition. Asked about forgiving and forgetting, she raises her voice in urgency: "The most important thing is not to forget; this is probably my greatest fear—that children will grow up not know-ing, not remembering how sixteen-, eighteen-year-old kids died in the struggle. I am afraid that our children will forget who we were and what we did. It's good to forgive, because there is no afterlife. The Craig Wil-liams of our times will suffer the consequences of who they chose to be through their own pain. People are forgiven, but they have to live with themselves. Forgiving is not blindness, it is not amnesia. I only hope forgiving will not mean forgetting." My mother goes on to tell me the story of my uncle, her cousin, who was car-bombed in exile. Her sen-tences race through years of emotion, burning her tongue with passion. "I read about Vernon in Citizen Newspaper, something about an ANC terrorist killed—the Boers celebrating an activist's slaughter. You know, I didn't know that was him. I mean, I felt pain for the person the article described as Moeketsi, but that was his exile alias, a security cover I didn't know. So I read this gruesome story about my cousin's bodily remains dangling from a tree and threw away the paper, without mak-ing that association.

"When the exiles returned in the 1990s, I learned how that Citizen story was a piece about my cousin. Nobody in the family wanted to talk about it. There were no details, no information, *nothing*. Then the TRC: his immediate family went to the hearings hoping to learn about his death and betrayers; who had given Special Branch information on Vernon's movements? But there was nothing; nobody came forward to confess a thing. That was the hardest part, not knowing how everything happened, not having the truth because it almost made his murder fictional, a fragment of our imagination. That's why the funeral this year was so important. Everyone was in tears—this is more than twenty years after the man was killed. We buried his only remains, a ribcage, in South African soil. Afterward, his mother told me she felt light for the first time in years because she felt her child was not forgotten. His memory was still alive. We can forgive, but we must never forget." Remembering is the theme of South African musician Thandiswa Mazwai's song "Nizalwa Ngobani"—Who has given us life?

"Nizalwa Ngobani" pleads with young Africans to remember the contributions of our ancestors, unsung heroes and heroines who sacrificed their lives for the liberties we enjoy today. "The world changes, revolutionaries die, and the children forget. The ghetto is our first love and our dreams are drenched in gold. We don't even cry, we don't even cry. Have you forgotten where you come from?"[4] In moving forward, South African youth must reconcile the past with a new identity, acknowledging where we have been as a country without allowing the sadness of our history to dictate who we become.

Today, we learn about apartheid like the rest of the world—in textbooks and museums, where a small fee will transport you into a slice of life under apartheid, complete with signs, "Slegs Blankes—No Blacks!" To some extent, black South Africans continue to live at the margins of society because of economic inferiority. The stark class division is a phenomenal battle, underlying challenges of high crime, unemployment, and intolerable poverty. In the new South Africa, life is cheap. "[The nation's] murder rate, the highest in the world, is more than five times the rate in Brazil, the next highest country."[5] In redefining our identity, have we learned from the past? Our nation is home to one of the world's most progressive constitutions, yet we cannot kill each other fast enough. Have we gained moral ground since dismantling apartheid, or did the violence that littered our news reports during the struggle merely shift gears, finding a new colorblind and aggressive form of expression?

The world has changed since Mandela pierced the sky with a clenched fist, claiming freedom and proclaiming, "Never, never again will this beautiful land experience the oppression of one by another." I am fiercely proud of what it means to be South African—our commitment to an ethical collective identity, our complex diversity, and even our painful past, which we have claimed and defied by consciously choosing who we want to become. Most importantly, my South African heritage has taught me that we are all members of humanity and even on a global scale, we are only as strong as our weakest link. My fondest memory of home is the contagious atmosphere of optimism that enveloped even ineligible voters during the first democratic, free, and fair elections.

I am old enough to appreciate the monumental significance of what transpires, but too young to grasp comprehensively how this single day will alter my life. I see my grandmother, my Koko. She is up by daylight and dresses in Sunday best; walks to a poll station in Soweto; people are swarming everywhere. Koko waits patiently in line—an hour, three, six—my grandmother waits almost half a day to cast her first vote, her first vote in over sixty years. She has raised eight children and paid hefty taxes for schools without books, for roads she'll never use and citizenship in a nation that did not recognize her humanity. For the first time today, she controls a piece of her destiny. She cannot read, so she scrolls the ballot for the ANC colors: black, green, and gold. Carefully, she marks the paper, walks a few more steps, and casts her vote. Her voice is heard. For the first time, she matters, her citizenship counts. My grandmother voted religiously in every election since that first. The ballot box is not a miracle wand, so change has not been instantaneous. Our beloved leader, Nelson Mandela, teaches that "after climbing a great hill, one only finds that there are many more hills to climb. If there are dreams about a beautiful South Africa, there are also roads that lead to their goal. Two of these roads could be named Goodness and Forgiveness."

I remember these things and carry them forward. Most of all, I remember "ubuntu"—that my humanity is inextricably linked to yours, that I am because we are.

Notes

1. Hazel Friedman, "Finding Their Place in the South African Sun," *Jerusalem Post,* April 21, 2000, B05.
2. Quoted in the *New York Times,* October 19, 1984.
3. Clees Flinterman, "Introduction: Annotated Bibliography on the TRC in South Africa," http://www.niza.nl/docs/200406151407561625.pdf.
4. Thandiswa Mazwai, *Zabalaza* (Gallo Records, Johannesburg, South Africa, 2005).
5. John D. Daniels, Lee H. Radebaugh, and Daniel P. Sullivan, eds., *International Business: Environments and Operations,* 11th ed. (Upper Saddle River, NJ: Prentice Hall, 2007).

Deaths in Paradise

Genocide and the Limits of Imagination in Rwanda

JAMES D. LONG IV
2001
The College of William and Mary

WHAT DOES A DEATH IN paradise sound like? Among banana trees and in the glow of the sun. Do you hear a scream? Does blood flow red? Next to a lake, on a hill, or in the red clay valley. My problem is that I cannot hear it. I see bodies bodies bodies tangled twisted and warped in time, lost to history and memory. Maybe I do not hear because the past is muted to my deafness. So we wonder how the past speaks to us; words, images, smells all come out when someone decides to tell the truth. Truth is loud and history cannot speak, yet we turn sideways in the mirror and stare blankly, at our person and our humanity, and simply ask: What do eight hundred thousand deaths in paradise sound like?

First must come the sound of the enemy. His shoes kicking up the dust of the street. You hear the neighbor's baby crying, and feel drips of salt slide down your temple, cheek, and neck. It collects in a pool on the floor. Perhaps you are crouched, hidden. Or maybe you stand in anticipation. I have heard that it depends on whether or not you have resolved yourself to dying. You might even smell the iron from the family down the street. And so he comes. Blade in fist, glint of sunlight off metal, and you breathe fast. There is no knock, no sign of entry. Everything is conspicuously peaceful, and you forget where you are and why you are there. Remembering life must be the hardest part of death. Flashes are all that your cortex can spare, and then the aloneness of it all sets in. The knell has sounded

and everything moves slowly. Where did he come from? You smell his
sweat and feel your own. Tremble, rumble, grumble. Is this the point
where we are cast out of Eden? If I could, I would ask if it hurts. What do
you think? Fade to red, then black.

Genocide means little when an entire population accumulates on the
banks of Lake Victoria, the streets of Kigali, and a church at Nyarubuye.
In the spring of 1994, the small Central African nation of Rwanda became engulfed in chaos. The Hutu majority led by Hutu Power began
the systematic decimation of the Tutsi minority. In Philip Gourevitch's
seminal book, *We Wish to Inform You That Tomorrow We Will Be Killed*
with Our Families, Rwanda's killings come to light in an honest account
of one man's journey to understand the forces, logic, and reasons for
genocide. Gourevitch writes for a Western audience, and his book becomes a story for those who do not know the reality of the killings. In
helping us to grasp Rwanda's situation, he forces us to come to terms
with our own position in the world. The largest ethical dilemma to be
dealt with in the book is genocide as idea. His subject is humanity itself,
a subject predicated upon unthinkable acts of politically motivated violence. Gourevitch's polemic on genocide becomes more than a call for
preventive action; it is a telling story of how we conceptualize history,
memory, and meaning and the mistakes that we make when trying to
evaluate the unthinkable.

In his book, Gourevitch believes it is essential to understand one's
position when measuring the ethics of a situation. He is conscious of his
position, and I believe that when we discuss anything of ethical import,
it is important to know what we are and what we are not. Often in discussions of genocide this is lost. I am someone who knows nothing
about genocide. I have seen pictures, heard stories, watched movies,
and read books. I am sick of reading, watching, and seeing. I want so
badly to understand, to reach out, to comprehend, but I know that I
cannot. I know that many survivors of genocide cannot explain it to the

rest of us. And why should they? Why is anyone responsible for explaining it? I cannot imagine genocide, and so I imagine it. A reality
imagined. Perhaps this is part of the crime.

The ethic of genocide is not obvious. Our knee-jerk reaction is to
condemn it, blame the perpetrator, and memorialize the victim. And yet
it happens over and over, and all we can say is, "Never Again." These
are the words that we came to hear after the horror of the Holocaust.
Most people thought that this was the first account of genocide in history. When the voices of truth rose from the ashes, we blushed and
perhaps felt angry. Philosophers, authors, and others discussed the possibility of collective guilt. Maybe we are all responsible for what happened. In the case of the Holocaust, we either helped to create madness
or we did nothing to stop it. Although we are not all Germans or Nazis,
we are all somehow to blame. If this is true, we must by extension add a
caveat: we were all victims. Somehow, the crimes committed against
Gypsies, homosexuals, Jews, Catholics, blacks, and others were more
than crimes against a single person, race, creed, or lifestyle. They were
crimes committed against humanity, and I am humanity, so I suffer.
Thus we have the structure of genocide. The perpetrator kills enough
of one kind of someone for the linguists to say: "genocide." Many are
dead; we feel guilty, responsible, and even hurt ourselves. Our humanity is shaken, and our minds cannot grasp the unthinkable. We scramble
for answers, and find what we think is a nice explanation: blacks are
savages, Germans are anti-Semites. By this structure, genocide thrives.

"Never Again" means little in the killing fields of Cambodia, orphan-
ages in Yugoslavia, or the villages of Rwanda. What is never again?
Never again will one group try to exterminate another? Never again will
we fail to act to prevent such killings? Of course it will happen again,
again. And again. We have created a language around genocide, a way
of behaving that perpetuates the crime. Gourevitch shows how this language does little in terms of prevention and that how we frame our questions not only detracts from the victims but pays heed to the killers.

Genocide is an idea. It does not exist. It cannot exist. What exists is the death of eight hundred thousand individual Tutsis and Hutus. The Holocaust saw the death of six million single Jews. Perhaps the human mind cannot comprehend one person being hacked to death eight hundred thousand times. So we create a word. Genocide. G-e-n-o-c-i-d-e. What is genocide? How do I explain genocide? Do a certain amount have to die? Do a certain people have to be persecuted? Thus an idea is born. If we can say "genocide," then we can intellectually engage the subject. There is no way to talk about the decimation of an entire population; no words could be transposed onto paper. So we are left with genocide. One single word that means nothing. What is genocide if it is not the death of one person?

I was not in Rwanda when the killings came, but when Gourevitch relates the stories of the survivors I cannot help but notice a trend: the immediacy of life in the face of death. When men wielding nailed, studded clubs came into the homes of Tutsis, the victims did not think about how their people were being killed. They did not envision the complete destruction of their country, the chaos of towns, the bloodstained roads. They did not think about Hutu Power, the history of colonization and decolonization, race identification cards, or the possibility of help from Western countries. They thought about their mothers, brothers, children. They thought about themselves. Their entire world was hiding with them. Do we think if a child sees her parents hacked to death in front of her that she thinks of herself as a victim of genocide? Does the story of Rwanda in the year 1994 become about anything more than the sight of her creators dead on the ground in front of her? When we talk about genocide we lose every single story. We lose death, rape, decimation. The victims are not merely statistics, they are less than that: they are an idea. Genocide does not capture the reality of death or the immediacy of life. As people who do not know genocide, we use ideas to talk about it. When the men with machetes come, the entire universe is focused on oneself and one's family. Not the rest of the country or the world. Victims and survivors of genocide never had the luxury of thinking about genocide.

The structure of genocide not only renders the importance of victims mute but often focuses on the killers, not the killed. We know more about Hitler than any one of his victims. We know the names of the death camps and the books the Nazis read, and in the wake of the war, the Nazis' stories became the focus of the media at the Nuremberg Trials. What happened to the Gypsies and homosexuals? Today, more and more we read of individual accounts of genocide (Gourevitch's book is almost solely dedicated to the survivors), but why still a fascination with the perpetrators? Perhaps we are curious to know why or how such acts could happen. Maybe if I study the Nazis I will come to understand why they built concentration camps. This idea assumes much. First, it assumes that we can ever understand why people do what they do, when it is killing, and on a large scale. Second, it presupposes that if we could understand why, then we might be able to stop it. Will we ever understand, and will we ever stop it? I think that asking these questions is vital after we have survived the bloodiest century in history. We might never unlock the roots of genocidal behavior, and that is not necessarily a bad thing. Knowing its base is not necessary for stopping it. But why would we want to stop it? We haven't yet. It took Rwanda only one hundred days to kill. Maybe if they could work more slowly. Maybe if the language of genocide was preventative instead of reactive.

There we have genocide: a compelling story for a history book. I am not satisfied. I think we should stop talking about genocide. Talking about it so far has done little good. First, we have to accept some inevitabilities: we might not always be able to stop it; regardless, we should try. When describing it, we inherently simplify it, so our purpose should not be to explain it. We must center on the victims and not reduce the importance of one death. We should talk in terms not of collective death but of individual suffering. If we recognize that many have been persecuted, we do not simply have to name a statistic; rather, we can think of

"holocaust" as the criminal act of person against person. States, governments, political parties, and other structures do not kill. A Rwandan kills.
A Rwandan dies. We can never forget that. We also must come to terms
with guilt and the limits of forgiveness. The UN International Criminal
Tribunal for Rwanda is, at some level, whether rudimentary or advanced,
a supreme act of guilt. Should we feel guilty for not acting? Should we
feel guilty for deaths if we did not directly cause them? What are our
responsibilities, outside of Rwanda, in Rwanda after the deaths stop, if
any? I wonder if we, as individuals and groups, know how to grieve. It
is so hard. Should we build more museums or memorials? Should we
expose truth, and to what degree? Should we cry? I have a feeling that
Rwanda does not need any more tears, but how does one stop?

Speak, Memory. Do not go quietly away, where we cannot find you.
We must listen to Rwanda's stories. My cynical part says that we, most
unfortunately, cannot always stop genocide. And the idealist in me says
that that does not matter. We still have to try. But we also have to learn to
deal with it. It cannot and should not be ignored. It will not go away,
blasted genocide. Genocide is nothing to no one. Genocide is dust.
Death is what we are looking for. Death in the clay earth. Death too
early, before its prime, on too grand a scale for the human mind. Yes,
death is imagined. Eight hundred thousand deaths are imagined. But
whose imagination is speaking? Whose imagination came up with all
those bones, skulls, and blood? It must be mine. It cannot be real, can
it? History is not real, only imagined, as is memory. How will human
memory deal with Rwanda? Gourevitch ends his account of Rwanda
with the possibility of hope by telling of Rwandan schoolgirls who
would not separate themselves into Hutu and Tutsi when the killers
came. So they all died, as Rwandans. Earlier, I asked if we were collective victims of genocide. If that is true, why are we still standing? How
has humanity continued? Genocide is an abomination. We have failed
each other, ourselves, and maybe even God. I cannot help but ask myself if God laughed or cried at Rwanda. Perhaps both.

Genocide, the idea, the Idea, cannot be. It has to leave. Rwanda has blood, not genocide. You say genocide, and I say so what. So what? I want meaning. Meaning. If we could not save those in the Holocaust or in Rwanda, cannot we at least give them meaning? I will try to give you meaning, Rwanda. I will not sleep at night. I might break all of the mirrors I own. Yes, yes, how can I look? How can any of us look? Rwanda, I will not say anything, I will not talk, or read, or watch. After all, what is there to say? I will listen. I will keep imagining, because you know what? I do not want to know it is real. When it is real, I can accept it, and I will never do that.

Rwanda. Paradise. Land of drums and sun. I can see it in my mind. Rwanda, the meaning I give you is really my own meaning, and for that I am truly sorry. I know nothing about genocide. And when I think of genocide, I realize that it causes us to question our own humanity. We ask stupid questions: Could I kill? Would I hide or give up? We speak of morals, duty, and ethics. The ethics are these: Genocide is empty, and machetes are a brutal way to kill. I find it curious that in Gourevitch's writing, Rwandans never speak of genocide. We do, though. We think we can understand ideas because that is easier than understanding evil. We lie. "Forgive me, Father, for I have sinned. I have committed the sin of genocide." We lie.

So children are orphans. People walk without arms. So many dead dead dead dead. Eight hundred thousand heads roll in Rwanda, and is that a scratch on humanity or a severed limb? How have we survived? We are definitely bruised. What is left to Rwanda now is history and memory, two things that will not treat it kindly. Is there a bigger picture, a larger lesson to be learned? See, we do not know until we know whose story Rwanda belongs to. How do we tell who owns it? Tutsis, Hutus, Rwanda, Central Africa, Africa, Earth, Universe. Child, mother, grandfather, sister, self.

What does a death in paradise *sound like?* Perhaps a wail. Yes, a low, mournful wailing coming from atop a hill. Lots of crying from the people next door who are burying their dead. Shovel hits earth, over and over, thousands and millions of times. Does it ever stop? Does history ever stop? When do the pictures and words go away? When do the question marks go to be replaced by periods? I would like to see that day. A death is a death is a death is a death. Machetes have no bias. Let us come to that understanding. Let us no longer pretend or ignore. And let us never be too sure of the strength or weakness of our humanity. We can survive a lot, but I wonder when it is just too much. Too much noise. *Can you hear it? Whose name does it call? Start running. Through the streets of the town, trying to navigate the bodies. You stepped on a skull. Shattered. Run up the hill and down again, until you've reached it. Do not be mistaken, Arcadia is still further, but you have left genocide behind. Escaped. Immigration, fascination, and imagination. The universe transcends singularity and you are home. Here, you remember how to breathe and sweat without fright. In the gloaming. Memory spoken and pasts forgotten. Paradise lost and regained.*

One February Morning

TAMARA DUKER
1997
Duke University

SARA BECAME A VEGETARIAN sometime during college. At the time she told our family, we saw it as another step in a process that began in high school—a slow progression toward religious observance. In explaining her decision to me, she pointed out a few of the Torah's provisions for meat eating: the calf was not to be boiled in its mother's milk, and the slaughter was to be conducted in the quickest, most painless manner. There were several others. If so many guidelines had to be observed to ensure the ethical treatment of animals *despite* the fact that they were fated to die, she reasoned, it just did not seem worth it. The ethics involved seemed to override her need to consume meat. She lived her life the way she believed God intended.

Ibrahim's background was also religious. Although I never met him, I have heard profiles of him by several Islamic studies specialists. He was in his twenties, like Sara and me, and, like us, had a strong sense of community. He likely gave part of his construction worker's salary to charity, in accordance with his religion. Three times, he was jailed for supporting a cause in which he truly believed. His life was never easy, but he knew that if he just lived it as he believed God intended, he would be justly rewarded.

On February 25, Ibrahim boarded a public bus in Jerusalem with a bomb and killed himself, Sara, and twenty-three other people. Sara was my sister.

Abraham is commonly accepted as the patriarch of the three great monotheistic religions. His wives, Sara and Hagar, were the matriarchs of the Jewish and Islamic peoples, according to most accounts. Abraham and Sara gave birth to nations in the ancient land of Canaan. Two millennia later, on the very same land, their namesakes, descendants of those same brother nations, die before their chance to give birth to the next generation.

I think of Sara's work with the homeless and hungry, her volunteer work teaching in a Harlem public school, her passion for the quality of the natural environment, and wonder why such a thing would have happened to her. I think also of Ibrahim and his involvement in Hamas—a militant organization, albeit one which provides food for the hungry and social services when local government falls short. Both Sara and Ibrahim somehow ended up in the same place, doing similar things. Circumstances of which they were both aware, although neither participated in creating, pitted them against one another. Sara, through no doing of her own, had become Ibrahim's enemy. And he killed her.

Certainly, religion accounts for differences in the worldviews of its adherents, but do these differences disqualify the possibility of any common ethical denominator? I wonder how someone so frustrated with the poor quality of his people's existence could marginalize the value of another human life so violently. I try to fathom any possible way that his destructive act of terror could be reconciled into a notion of an ethical life. I consider the point at which one may be accountable for his own ethics, when society and familial education have taught only *that* way. Are our differences simply irreconcilable? From where must we derive the conduct toward our fellow man? Does such a program even exist? These are some of the questions with which we must arm ourselves if we seek to establish an ethical worldview that can accommodate peaceful coexistence.

American twenty-somethings are continually cast as "generation X"—alluding to our lack of any significant defining ethos. "Ethos" in this sense refers to a coherent notion of that which can universally be considered "right" and "wrong," despite superficial differences derived from social conditioning. Our parents had at least one common experience—the Vietnam War—from which their generational identity was derived. But we, according to the current discourse, are lacking a cause, a belief, or a common ethos that will shape *our* group identity. In our defense, we cite multiculturalism as our common creed. A natural companion, it can be maintained, to the globalizing technology that serves to blur existing geographical and linguistic borders. Yet this unifying ethos manifests itself most curiously—and, I would argue, dangerously—in terms of our actual behavior.

In our zealous attempts to erase all borders, labels, and divisions, we import a world of cultures, religions, and ideologies and adopt them as our own. But every ideology is accompanied by a conflict. Every culture, a marginalized minority. Every religion, its ancient grudges and disputes. Whether they supported or opposed the Vietnam War, our parents were involved because *they* were being drafted to fight in its front lines. We fight just as vehemently for our borrowed beliefs, but personally, our lives are not at stake.

Such an observation is hardly original. Lenin termed a similar instance "social chauvinism," referring to his perception of World War I. Although it was a war of the bourgeois class's imperialist designs, he held, the war's ranks were filled by the proletarian class, motivated by nationalist rhetoric. So too the ongoing international conflicts that draw international participation, either or both intentionally and accidentally. I see the link most clearly in the world conflict that has affected me the most, the Arab-Israeli conflict. I often consider why suicide bombers, engaged in a territorial dispute originating in their grandparents' generation, are consistently in the eighteen-to-twenty-six-year-old range—never older. Both instances seem a form of one "class" of people—economic or generational—manipulating another, and both have fatal consequences for the manipulated. And so, my generation deals in commodities: we import, purchase, circulate, and consume wars. We buy them from many sources—from the generation of our elders, from coreligionists across the globe, from our imagined homelands—and then integrate them into our personal ethos. Read our university newspapers for the calls to arms and see how we shoot one another down in our angry letters to the editor. Our market is readily identified by sellers we have never met—as is evidenced by the proliferation of terrorist activities in recent years designated to raise *President Clinton's* awareness or *world* sympathies to a cause. And here we are, eager buyers—sending money, organizing rallies, and appropriating slogans from the comforts of our First Amendment rights, opportunities for upward mobility, and democratic political structure.

I would argue that the absence of real borders has transformed all regional wars into world wars: a frightening prospect, when one considers that historically, the young are constantly overrepresented on wartime lists of casualties. Sara's generation. Ibrahim's generation. My generation. So in developing a workable ethos to govern myself and my peers, I cannot help but view our situation with the urgency and immediacy required for a "cease-fire." We need to view our condition within the context of its dire consequences in developing a modern ethical standard that can temper religious differences and national conflicts with a universal human desire to live happily, to work happily, and to die of *natural* causes.

Several thinkers throughout time have addressed the issue of ethics and wartime; Augustine, Aquinas, and Hugo Grotius are but a few. They all expound from an underlying assumption, however, that there exists such a thing as ethical warfare. Drawing from these intellectuals, the Israeli military strategist Yehoshafat Harkabi defines this notion of ethical warfare as a war that possesses a reasonable chance of success. Otherwise, as he contends in his book *The Bar Kokhba Syndrome,* the degree of human suffering would outweigh the rewards of a successful campaign. Yet I am simply unable to reconcile death as an acceptable means to a greater end. For what end could possibly be greater than human life?

Some would certainly cite ideology as one such end. National survival, democracy, and racial equality are but examples of a long list of ideals invoked in justifying the otherwise senseless loss of a valuable human life. Adorned in ideology, each death becomes a "sacrifice." After all, "dying in vain" could perhaps be the one thing worse than death alone in our culture. Yet history has proven that ideologies cannot outlive the people who hold fast to them. And history has further demonstrated that ideologies are as subject to trends as are hairstyles and gender roles. The "benevolent civilization" that rationalized colonialism, South African apartheid, Hitler's "Final Solution," and the supranational concord of the former Soviet Union are all cases in point. Karl Marx portrays ideology as dreamlike "residue" from the lone complete reality—"the concrete history of concrete material individuals materially producing their existence." To these thinkers, ideologies come from within us, and although inescapable, they are not absolute truths that exist apart from and above us. What can be held real and constant, then, is human existence, which perseveres, despite prevailing ideological waves.

Religion is perhaps most frequently offered as the appropriate end worth dying for. But even beliefs regarding martyrdom, messianic redemption, or a paradisiacal afterlife seem a "consolation prize" for living acts of devotion. According to the Judeo-Christian tradition, "The dead cannot praise the Lord, nor any who go down into silence" (Psalm 115:17). Yet even, however, if one were so inclined to deem his religion worth dying for, *killing for* seems a distinction necessarily made.

Then, last, enters the pragmatist's approach. For what progress is truly achieved with the death of one individual? Even with the death of twenty-three individuals? When an agreement is eventually reached between Israel and the Palestinian nation, I will still not be able to say that Sara's death was not in vain or that Ibrahim's "self-sacrifice" was not a needless one. Nor can I truly say that either one, in their death, served God in any way. Because as strongly as they believed, no change in reality came of their deaths. Islam continues. Judaism continues. The sun rises and sets on refugee camps and affluent Tel Aviv suburbs alike. Only Sara and Ibrahim are no longer here to witness it.

My conception of an ethical standard, then, would hold human life at its quintessence. A living human being, after all, can worship any God he chooses, can live on the same land as his ancestors, if he so desires, or can take pleasures in the natural world, the sounds and smells of existence, and the wonders of science.

With this underlying foundation for a functional ethical program established, the next step involves an overhaul of the familiar definitions with which we construct our identities. To draw upon my personal experiences, for example, I was born a Jew. An American Jewish education entails an elaborate socialization, not the least of which is a strong and emotional attachment to Israel as the "promised land." And it was with this proud blinder that I hiked, planted, and studied my way through Israel so many times, for so long. But with the continual exposure to images of stone throwing, tear gas, bus bombs, and the destruction of villages, a different principle of my Jewish education kept resurfacing to compete for center stage. What of the higher standard of ethical behavior to which my proud nation allegedly held itself? Was this consistent with the type of warfare that was clearly pushing the borders between self-defense and violent imperialism? What of the border guards who used excessive violence against Palestinian civilians on their way to work in Israel proper? Was it possible that *my* people, who were themselves victimized so horribly just fifty years ago, could degrade another people so easily?

Clearly, my strong affiliations with Israeli Jewry indicate the extent to which I, too, have made another's struggle my own. Yet this potentially affords me the opportunity to work for a peaceful resolution, if I can use this inheritance proactively. And so I begin to reconstruct my Judaism and my Zionist affiliations. I recognize my strong, and often emotional, attachment to the land of Israel. But I also have learned to recognize that supporting one thing does not—and cannot—necessarily mean opposing another. The stakes today are simply too high. I can support a Jewish national existence, which by definition does not preclude a Palestinian one. And I can call on my peers—the twenty-somethings of the world—to take similar steps in defining for themselves who they are and for what they stand.

It is from this dynamic process that we must begin to elucidate a certain sense of personal ethical responsibility. One cannot be educated in a vacuum, nor does a society exist apart from a socialization process. It is in this respect that who we become is never fully a free and individual choice. Yet the other extreme—writing off acts against humanity as inevitable results of a cyclical chain of learned behavior—is an unacceptable and impotent alternative. What is the point at which we can and must be held ethically accountable for our actions? Moreover, how, as a society, would we even go about holding others accountable for ethical transgressions?

The Clinton administration's recent antiterrorist legislation is an interesting point of departure, for it essentially aims to harness this vague notion of ethical accountability into a legal framework. In allowing private citizens to seek damages from national entities that sponsor individual acts of terror, this legislation operates under the assumption that ethical behavior is not simply an individual issue. It seeks to remedy the world's ethical ills with a dose of preventative medicine, so to speak. Instead of treating individual transgressors as deviants of some natural law, it recognizes the socialization process by allowing citizens to seek damages from the socialization vehicle par excellence—the state. In so doing, it attempts to force an evolution of sorts in the ethical development of those who have not yet been socialized by punishing the strongest sources of socialization. Hoping all along, of course, that large enough financial penalties will force a reconsideration of ethical behavior.

This approach, however, is not to let individuals "off the hook" as

mere products of their environments. The establishment of a cease-
fire requires measured action on the individual level. We must stop
viewing our conflicts as *inherited,* implying a situation beyond our
control, and begin considering them as *adopted,* involving a deliberate
ethical choice. For legitimizing one's own inheritance of a worldview
connotes the selfsame legitimization of another's inherited (and conflicting) worldview. Semantics matter. We must affirm our identities first
and foremost as members of the human species, and refuse to derive
them by negating others.

Daunting as this reexamination and re-creation of ourselves may be,
it is undoubtedly mitigated by our situation in the era of postmodern
discourse. We are encouraged to assess everything within its context,
and absolute conclusions no longer determine a successful inquiry. We
can admire the rosy and detailed nineteenth-century prints of the
"Holy Land" by David Roberts yet question how they might reveal his
Orientalist inclinations. We can listen to the works of Richard Wagner
or use Henry Ford's assembly-line technology while recognizing that
their creators were anti-Semites. Finally, we have come upon an age
where we can dissect everything—we can peel away the layers of our
religious, ideological, cultural, and social identities and separate the
valuable from the destructive, rather than swallowing them whole. Similarly, creating a universal human ethos does not entail the complete rejection of any heritage. Rather, it allows us the freedom to thank our
forebears for the beautiful traditions they have taught us and the lati-
tude to shed the ones that threaten our peaceful future.

The final element of a workable ethos follows logically from the first
two tenets. Once human life is accepted as of central importance, and
once we can place our common humanity as the fundamental source of
identity, then we can begin to attach to each individual life a sacred
value for its influential and irreplaceable potential for action. One person's death cannot exact nearly as many accomplishments as one person's life led to its fullest. As I continue to mourn Sara's death, I mourn

not only for my lost sister but for the environmental research that will never be done, the discoveries never to be made, the nieces and nephews I will never have, the cousins with whom my children will never play. I think about Ibrahim's family, too, and wonder about the high hopes his mother may have harbored for him. Had he fathered children, perhaps their lifetime would have witnessed the realization of their parents' national aspirations and the end of bloody confrontation. It is inconceivable to me that Sara's and Ibrahim's deaths accomplished more than their lives would have.

Indeed, there are elements in all of us that are the same and others that are different. I am thankful for this when I consider that discovering the polio vaccine, electricity, or water purification techniques are beyond my individual scientific capacity. Selfish reasons, if nothing else, should be enough to prevent us from killing one another. There are no guarantees, after all, that the one shot down today would not have discovered the cure to an illness that another's grandchild would later develop. Today, more than ever before, our lives are inextricably intertwined across the globe, and each action can send far-reaching ripples to those whom we may never even meet.

In this way, we can begin to treat every conflict we encounter as if we have something personally at stake, because in some abstract sense, we do. But instead of pursuing our interests by fueling these clashes through our participation in them, we can understand that it is the very existence of conflict itself which threatens us—not any particular side or point of view. It is this personal threat to which we, empowered, may respond by promoting dialogue over destruction and compromise over combativeness. Or more simply, we can refuse to fight. And we can encourage our peers to do the same.

It has been less than a year since Sara was killed, and I am still struggling with a way to honor her conception of an ethical lifestyle without losing my own individual beliefs. While I haven't given up meat eating myself, nor have my community service projects been undertaken to ful-

fill a religious obligation, I nonetheless search for something—anything—
of her ethical Judaism that I can comfortably internalize within my more
secular humanistic worldview. I found what I was seeking in an often
quoted but nonetheless poignant excerpt from Robert Fulghum's *All I
Really Need to Know I Learned in Kindergarten.*

> Share everything.
> Play fair.
> Don't hit people.
> Put things back where you found them.
> Clean up your own mess.
> Don't take things that aren't yours.
> Say you're sorry when you hurt somebody.
> Wash your hands before you eat.
> Flush.

The humanity of his ethical program is based on the simplicity of practicing acts of common decency and of mutual responsibility. Reminiscent, as Sara might have suggested, of the much revered Rabbi Akiva's
timeless principle upon which he believed all of Judaism was based:
"Love your neighbor as yourself." If only her neighbor had let her live
to teach me that in person.

Black and White in the Land of Israel/Palestine
Toward an Ethic of Care

JONATHAN D. SPRINGER
1990
Harvard University

LATE IN AUGUST I OBSERVED a demonstration of Women in Black, a group of Israeli women who protest the occupation of the West Bank and the Gaza Strip. "Women in white" (counterdemonstrators) stand across the street with signs proclaiming the right of the Jews to their own state in the entire Land of Israel. A fistfight nearly broke out between two men who came to support the opposing sides on the day I attended. "Don't tell me about the suffering of those Arabs—I know what it's like to suffer," fumed an elderly Holocaust survivor in white. "Black widows is what you are . . . prostitutes selling yourselves to the Arabs!" he added. "And you're a fascist!" came the reply from a younger man dressed in black, gearing up for a fight.

I had come to support the Women in Black out of concern for Palestinians in the Occupied Territories, but I could muster no righteous indignation against those in white; who was I to challenge a Holocaust survivor? I was torn. Caring for Palestinian human rights seemed fundamentally opposed to caring for the rights of my own people. The Jewish-Palestinian conflict appeared to be a clash of two equally valid—yet mutually exclusive—claims to self-determination. Black or white, weak or strong, it was an apparent conflict of rights, where the one could be attained only at the expense of the other. As a Jew, I had to fight for the Jews, against the Palestinians.

But I could not reconcile myself to having to choose between the

Jews and the Palestinians. I could not forget the innocent Palestinian victims of Israeli violence whom I had seen during the summer. No longer could I abide by a system of morality that demanded pursuit of rights for Jews at the expense of Palestinians. I resolved to search for a moral approach that could address the needs of Palestinians as well as Jews, that could transcend the conflict of rights.

Growing up, I was an unquestioning supporter of Israel: Israeli mother, father who volunteered in the Israeli army, periodic visits to grandparents in Tel Aviv, year on kibbutz after high school, chair of Zionist club in college. . . . Fear of Arabs was integral to my Zionism. My mother described to me how she was sexually harassed by Arabs when she went to visit Jewish holy sites and how Arabs threw rocks at her scout group when they went on excursions. Bent upon destroying the Jews, the Arabs fled Palestine in 1947 with the hope of reconquering it soon thereafter, according to my mother. I learned that the Arabs were not willing to live in peace with the Jews, and so I boasted to my friends that my mother had served in the Haganah (illegal Jewish militia) to defend the Jews in Palestine against the Arab threat. To me, Arab meant Enemy.

I began to question this black-and-white picture in college, when I first met Palestinians. News reports of Israeli oppression of Palestinians in the intifada (Palestinian uprising) were troubling now that "Arab" was no longer an abstraction to me. I was particularly disturbed by a description in the *New York Times* of Israel's policy of "administrative detention," which allowed for arrest and imprisonment of Palestinians without charge or trial for a period of up to three months. This news challenged what I held true about Israel as the only democracy in the Middle East. It also challenged my view of the Jews as underdogs; I had to account somehow for Palestinian Arabs as another oppressed people, who were suffering at the hands of the Jews, no less.

Clearly, something was awry. I needed to explore the incongruity between what I had believed and what I had recently learned. In order to do so, I decided to spend the summer with Arabs in Israel and the Occupied Territories, learning the other half of the story.

After visiting my grandmother for a few days, I moved in with a Palestinian family in an Arab section of Haifa. My first night there, I stayed up late talking with my hosts, Jaffar and UmJaffar. UmJaffar described to me how she had been banished from her village in the Galilee by Jewish forces in 1948. Jews (could they have been from the Haganah, the unit in which my mother served?) rounded up the villagers, sent them off to Lebanon, and, she said, killed eleven young men in order to frighten people in surrounding villages.

Ironically, my grandfather had been injured in an Egyptian bombing raid that same year. Yet it was only as I sat opposite UmJaffar, a Palestinian woman who had been exiled by Jews, that her suffering became as real to me as that of my grandfather. Both were innocent victims, yet I had only understood the victimization of my grandfather. When I began relating to Palestinian Arabs as individuals, I could learn their history of oppression.

The next month, I volunteered to work at a human rights information center. Having begun to learn about the past, I now felt better equipped to face the present—to make some sense of the newspaper reports I had read back home. I visited a man who had recently returned from "administrative detention" and a girl who was paralyzed by an inadvertent shot from an Israeli soldier. I was disturbed by all that I saw: barbed wire, roadblocks, demolished homes. . . . It was as if the entire West Bank was in a state of siege, fearful of the Israeli—Jewish—army.

In light of what I saw, I felt betrayed by my parents for the incomplete education they had given me. When my mother came to Israel to see my grandmother, I asked her to visit me with my Palestinian host family. She had lived in Israel for twenty-four years, yet had never spoken with an Arab. Reluctantly, she came. Sitting on the balcony overlooking Haifa, Jaffar described to my mother particular instances in which the Israeli government discriminates against Israeli Arabs. It was painful for my mother to hear; she barely responded. I knew she felt personally accused. She seemed torn inside between feeling both guilty and justified about Israel's discrimination against Arabs. Afraid that I might forget the Jewish past, my mother gently reminded me as we left: "Don't forget the suffering of the Jews . . . ."

I wanted desperately to retain my faith in Israel, despite the horrible acts that I learned had been committed on its behalf in the past and Israel's grim role as occupier, at present. As my mother kept reminding me, Jews, too, had once been persecuted. Didn't the Jews deserve a state of their own—in order to prevent another Holocaust, if for no other reason? Moreover, I felt comfortable in Israel—sometimes more comfortable in the Jewish state than I felt as a Jew in the United States. That's why I kept coming back to Israel.

I wanted to be a Zionist. Couldn't I somehow bend or stretch conventional notions of the Jewish right to a state so that it wouldn't cause suffering to the Arabs? After all, I had come to learn about the Palestinians out of my care for Israel, as a Jew. I could identify with Palestinian nationalism only because I, too, was a nationalist. Otherwise, I would have gone to do human rights work in some trouble spot to which I had no connection, like Central America.

It was important to me that the Arabs I met knew my motivations for coming to learn about them. Once, this proved dangerous: I saw a little boy in Nablus with a bandage on his head and I asked him (in my limited Arabic) what had happened. When he said "the Jews" (that is, the Israeli soldiers), I told him that I, too, was Jewish, as if to make him aware that Judaism—or Zionism—does not necessarily entail violence against Palestinians. The boy seemed perplexed. After I said good-bye to him, a glass bottle came crashing at me. For him, all Jews—all Zionists—are enemies of the Palestinians. Since I was Jewish, I could never be genuinely sympathetic to him or any Palestinian, the little boy seemed to say.

Maybe he was right, I thought. Maybe my support for Israel necessarily involved discrimination against Arabs. Certainly, the fact that Israel is a Jewish state entails preferential treatment for Jews. The Law of Return, for instance, provides immediate citizenship to any Jew who wishes to move to Israel. Yet the flip side of this law is a prohibition against the return of Palestinian refugees to their homes. Zionism, belief in the Jewish right to statehood, had led certain Jews to banish some Palestinians from their own land in 1948. Forty years later, this same Zionism seemed to involve discrimination against Palestinians in Israel proper and—worse yet—violence against Palestinians in the Occupied Territories.

The physical oppression that followed from this rights-based Zionism was disturbing. More troubling to me, however, was the mental repression in the form of censorship that resulted from supporting the right of Jews to a state. As a student, I took for granted access to dissenting views on all issues and the freedom to form my own opinions. In the Occupied Territories, even this basic freedom of thought was curtailed, as Palestinian reading material was systematically censored. The Israeli government was trying to prevent the Palestinians from thinking certain thoughts, thoughts that might question Zionism. In order to substantiate its own right to exist, Israel had to silence the competing voice proclaiming the Palestinian right to self-determination—at any cost.

In this system of rights-based Zionism, rights inevitably conflicted: justice for Jews meant injustice to Palestinians. Conversely, the plight of the Palestinians could not be improved without worsening that of the Jews. As a nationalist Jew, I therefore would be unable to act upon what I learned during the summer to improve the plight of the Palestinians. What I learned seemed to be useless knowledge. Perhaps it would have been better not to know what I did, for Jews not to be aware of the suffering they must inevitably inflict upon the Palestinians. Maybe I had been better off before I came to Israel, knowing less.

But I could not ignore what I learned during the summer. If protective ignorance and oppression of Palestinians were the costs of Zionism, I had to reevaluate my Zionism.

I now realize that I was led into this deadlock by my rights-based Zionism. Belief in the Jewish right to statehood can lead to violence against Palestinians because it attempts to transcend present reality. The belief in a right to a Jewish state arose from a particular historical situation, but became timeless and abstract. It led, unfortunately, to the denial of Palestinian needs.

Modern Zionism originated as a political movement largely in response to particular incidents of anti-Jewish sentiment such as the Dreyfus Affair in 1895 and pogroms in Russia soon thereafter. When my grandparents came to Palestine in 1920, they did not have a "right" to create a Jewish state; rather, they *needed* to escape persecution in Poland. After the Holocaust, in which six million Jews were exterminated by the Nazis, the United Nations decided that this need for a Jewish place of refuge could be addressed most adequately by creating a Jewish state. In a world without nation-states or anti-Jewish sentiment, however, Jews could survive without a state. Jewish self-determination is not a right, then, but a pragmatic response to a need.

Now, however, Zionism seems to imply a timeless "right" to self-determination. Ironically, Zionism—which arose from historical circumstance—now invokes its abstract status as a right in order to ignore the new historical reality it has created—the Palestinian refugee problem. A rights-based Zionism overlooks immediate injustices in anticipation of some greater goal; the ends will supposedly justify the means. Zionist language of rights permits individual incidents of suffering to be dismissed as unintelligible outside of a larger context.

So long as we remain within this system, Palestinian needs are masked as rights. Since these rights are seen to conflict with Jewish rights, they can be subordinated—denied or taken away. But no one can deny the existence of Palestinian needs. Demolished homes and closed schools do not represent violated rights so much as violated needs: Palestinians need homes in which to live and schools in which to learn. They need reprieve from the Israeli occupation. These needs are concrete, and they must be met.

It is only by caring about needs that we can honestly address the current violence in the Occupied Territories. No longer do we dismiss injustice against Palestinians as the necessary outcome of two abstract, competing rights. There is no more rationalization on the part of Jews that the ends justifies the means. By caring about needs, our primary concern is the minimization of suffering wherever it occurs. If an innocent person is being hurt, something must be changed in the system that brought it about. Instead of shielding ourselves from the pain that we cause others by casting them in stereotypes and selectively learning history, we can seek to address the needs of all.

Concern for needs connotes an ethic of care—a worldview different than that of rights-based morality. Whereas rights-based morality presupposes a constant state of strife in the world, arising from competing rights claims, an ethic of care views all of humanity as interdependent. Unlike rights, needs do not compete but rather strive to be met in harmony with each other. The ethic of care perceives these needs by remaining attuned to the present, rather than by fixating upon a timeless past.

The work of two feminist thinkers—Carol Gilligan and Rebecca Chopp—is useful in developing this ethic of care. Gilligan describes an ethic of care that implicitly calls for the meeting of needs. Chopp provides a practical concept that paves the way toward resolution of conflict: the morality of praxis.

Interdependence of one's own interests and those of others is the central insight of an ethic of care, according to Carol Gilligan.[1] Once we begin to regard the well-being of others as integral to our own, we overcome the paralysis of competing rights, which rationalizes innocent suffering. We cannot be free so long as others are enslaved (especially by ourselves), and we are therefore obliged to learn about the pain endured by others, to be cognizant of their needs. No longer must we bias our own education and censor the thoughts of our "opponents," for together we can learn and validate each other's experiences.

Sensitivity to the present is the other component of this ethic. We have seen that rights-based morality abstracts and universalizes principles from particular historical conditions in order to justify a claim for all time. The ethic of care, in contrast, seeks to respond constantly to changing historical reality, to include the interdependent experiences of all. An ethic of care therefore resists the formulation of eternal principles.[2] We prevent ourselves from formulating utopian dreams, for fear that—like "rights"—they might tyrannize the present by allowing for short-term violence in order to be fulfilled.

This ethic of care involves awareness of our interdependence with others at all times. But this ethic is not satisfied with mere awareness; the ethic of care contains an internal mechanism to move beyond itself, to take part in shaping human relations. To truly understand society in this light involves a commitment to take an active part in the world. Rebecca Chopp describes this interaction of thought and action as the "morality of praxis." Praxis, according to Chopp, is "negatively stated, the realization that humans cannot rely on any ahistorical, universal truths to guide life," and "positively stated, the realization that humans make history."[3] Negatively, this is unsettling: we cannot predict the future and must remain constantly vigilant to secure the needs of all in an ever-changing world. Positively, the notion of praxis is empowering— it demands action.

This action is not simply a translation of abstract notions of justice into the real world, the exaction of retribution against "guilty" parties. Rights-based retribution is informed by a fatalistic view of conflicting rights; it causes more anger and paves the way toward future conflict. Instead, the action of moral praxis is informed by a framework of interdependence, in which the lives of all are improved by ending the pain experienced by a few. Moral praxis therefore entails practical responses to the needs of all as they arise.

In the particular case of the Jewish-Palestinian conflict, moral praxis calls for the creation of a Palestinian state—not out of a "right" to a state but in order to alleviate Palestinian subjugation to Israeli authority. Such a solution seeks to end the current suffering of the Palestinians by providing refugees with much-needed homes and allowing them to govern themselves. Of course, there are complexities involved. In meeting the needs of the Palestinians, those of the Jews cannot be overlooked: security precautions must be taken to ensure the existence of Israel.

An idealist might demand the repatriation of Palestinian refugees from Israel proper to the homes from which they had been banished by the Jews or fled of their own accord. But the morality of praxis would not call for this policy, citing the presence of Jews atop the ruins of (in some cases, inside) the homes of the Palestinians. To displace the "guilty" Jews at the expense of the Palestinians would amount to righting one wrong by creating more displacement that would eventually lead to another war. The Palestinian refugee problem was created in such a cycle of violence, when the Jews satisfied their own need for refuge at the expense of the Palestinians. To continue in this manner would be to fixate upon abstract notions of just retribution for one party, without responding to the needs of another. By addressing the needs of Jews, as well as Palestinians, the morality of praxis attempts to break the cycle of violence in the Middle East.

Eventually, it is possible that the Law of Return would be repealed, that Palestinian refugees would be allowed to return to Israel. The states of Palestine and Israel might ultimately dissolve. Perhaps a new system of government could then evolve, one which would respect the social customs of both peoples and their respective religions. This might entail a binational state, as once proposed by Martin Buber and Judah Magnes, or perhaps an international confederation of local cantons. The eventual outcome cannot be predicted, nor *should* it be predicted, lest it become an abstract, utopian end which is invoked to justify violent means.

Applying the ethic of care to the Jewish-Palestinian conflict yields a moral praxis—a practical solution to Palestinian suffering that addresses the needs of Jews as well. By overcoming a rights-based morality, I can now act on what I have seen this summer. Indeed, I must act: because we can improve the situation, we are morally obliged to do so. No longer am I unable to challenge the Holocaust survivor at the "Women in Black" demonstration. No longer does the history of suffering of my own people prevent me from working to end the suffering of the Palestinians.

This ethic of care may seem to be a healthy personal perspective which is ultimately inapplicable to the political world. But this is true only if the aim of politics is blood and war, for the morality of praxis offers a different aim—peace. By striving to break the cycle of violence perpetuated by rights-based morality, the ethic of care seeks a resolution that will prevent future violent conflict. When global leaders and individuals worldwide internalize the ethic of care, we will be empowered to meet the needs of all through a practical peace. This is no utopian vision, but a prescription for a livable world.

Notes

1. Carol Gilligan, *In a Different Voice: Psychological Theory and Women's Development* (Cambridge, MA: Harvard University Press, 1982), 74.
2. Rebecca S. Chopp, "Feminism's Theological Pragmatics: A Social Naturalism of Women's Experience," *Journal of Religion* 67 (1987):

239–256. The distinction between an ethic of care and rights-based morality is based on Chopp's distinction between feminist theology and "theology proper." Her insights are informed, in turn, by American pragmatism.

3. Rebecca S. Chopp, *The Praxis of Suffering: An Interpretation of Liberation and Political Theologies* (Maryknoll, NY: Orbis, 1986), 36.

The Bosnian Women

SAMI F. HALABI

1999

Kansas State University

A brief foreword: I read *The Iliad, or the Poem of Force* by Simone Weil (1945) when I was eighteen years old and enrolled in an Introduction to Humanities course. The prose, as well as the political and personal conditions surrounding it, affected me deeply. I would not purport to possess the faintest grasp of the beauty and intelligence with which Weil argued against injustice and for common humanity in *The Iliad.* I do claim that this essay is a devotion to that most powerful work; the structure of both the essay and its sentences is inspired by and a tribute to one of the most profound intellectual insights of our century.

It is imperative, therefore, to read this book, and to ensure that it is read. One emerges from it as from a terrible nightmare, crushed by a hatred at once ancestral and constantly present, weighty. Here are men who know each other well, neighbors who greet each other in the street, friends of many years standing who, suddenly, poisoned by patriotic and ethnic fanaticism, become fierce and bitter enemies.

How to explain such cruelty, such sadism, among people who only yesterday lived in brotherhood with their victims of today?

Why, among them, such a thirst to hurt, to

injure, to humiliate human beings whose only
wrong—whose only "crime"—is to believe in
Mohammed rather than in Jesus?
—Elie Wiesel, Foreword to *The Tenth Circle
of Hell: A Memoir of Life in the Death Camps
of Bosnia*

WAR DESTROYS US. NOT in the sense that we may sacrifice valuable
land and infrastructure or fail in our territorial strategies. War destroys
us because it *conquers* us; in the most literal sense we are turned into
war's possessions and language—strategic decisions to the war—makers,
lifeless bodies on a field, or mere shadows of ourselves to the families
of victims. War so infects our very thinking and feeling that it becomes
us and we it. It is in respect to the nature of the soul that we find war's
deepest and most damaging wounds. When Euripides crafted his polemic on war, *The Trojan Women,* he used the lives of Homer's trauma-
tized women to convey this irreparable damage to his audience. Here I
claim that through the experiences of women we can *feel* the gnawing of
war; women, as the vehicle for understanding the trauma of battle and
loss, can instruct us on its evil in essence. I choose women not only because Euripides chose women but because they have the most to lose
from war. War sacrifices their husbands, sons, and fathers while making
the pillage of their persons and honor mere afterthoughts. The "pride"
acquired in battle or the thirst for power is never to their benefit. They
lose everything.

War is the tragedy of *The Trojan Women* even though there exists
only a shadow of a plot and no action. The play opens with the exchange of the divine gods Poseidon and Athena agreeing that Greece
will pay for its disgraceful deeds committed during the sack of Troy.
Through a series of speeches—lament and rhetoric of vengeance by
Hecuba, queen of the Trojans; mad ranting joy by Cassandra, her
prophetess daughter; utter and total devastation to the daughter-in-law,

Andromache; and the trial of Helen—Euripides portrays the suffering of women from the war. He inspects the way war corrupts and infects the spirits of not only the defeated Trojans but also the "victorious" Greeks.

The Trojan Women is perhaps our oldest work against the crimes of war—it is against this backdrop that I investigate one of our most recent and vicious wars—the ethnic conflict between Bosnian Muslims and Serbs. The Bosnian Muslim women are the new Trojan women; the "cleansing," rape, and abject dehumanization of the victims in Bosnia are the recent reminders that we even today ignore a lesson given to us by one of the earliest figures of our civilization.

Many experts will agree generally that ethics is an individual code of right and wrong that is relevant to who a person is and where he or she is.[1] I reject this claim because some of our deeds as humans are immutable as breaches of ethical codes. They are wrong. Genocide and systematic rape, by definition, are ethical scandals.[2] Euripides' primary character, Hecuba, wife of Priam, mother of Hector, queen of Troy, reminds us of the trauma that war imparts to its victims:

> Sorrow, my sorrow.
> What sorrow is there that is not mine, grief to weep
> for.
> Country lost and children and husband.[3]

Friketa, thirty-six years old, Mali Zvornik: "My city is now in Serbian hands, 'ethnically clean.' I am a Muslim. After the outbreak of war, after the cleansing, the killing of children, I came to Mali Zvornik."[4]

Hecuba's lament affects her audience while providing her some small comfort for her losses. Euripides offers her only the reflection of her torments and anguish to dress her emotional wounds. She now *defines herself* in terms of this war; it wraps itself around her—Hecuba ceases to exist outside its reach of death, bloodshed, and loss. As the war reshaped the mind and emotion of Hecuba, so the Serb soldiers

through systematic murder of Bosnian Muslim men and the rape of the
Bosnian Muslim women devastate minute to minute, day by day their
reality.

Heira, twenty-five years old, Bresovo Polje: "We all feel that we lost
everything. We have been abandoned. We have been imperiled. Every
woman, if she is raped, has to feel the same."[5]

The women of Troy echo Hecuba's cry:

> Another: Worse to come.
> A Greek's bed—and I— . . .
> Another: A night like that? Oh, never
> oh, no—not that for me.[6]

Here we understand the destruction of the woman's soul as an unequiv-
ocal wrong—it takes from its victims the ideas, feelings, being that create
their humanity—they are left with a single companion: the war, in their
memories, as they eat and sleep. The war is complete in its annexation
of the person.

But the process is not isolated in the linear relationship between
those murdered and raped. From the effect of war upon the victimized
and beaten springs another destructive force: the capacity for it to in-
fest the beings and lives of those who have *not* been immediately
harmed. It can stretch far beyond its confines to erode and destroy
nearby innocents.

These people are alive, and the war does not place a blade to their
throats yet cuts them deeply. Hecuba, though a victim herself, mourns
the fate of her daughter Cassandra as her own as the prophetess's virginity is sacrificed to Agamemnon.

> Hecuba: My daughter, who—who drew her? Tell
>   me—
> Cassandra. She has had so much to bear.
> Talthybius: King Agamemnon chose her out from
>   all.

> Hecuba: Oh! But—of course—to serve his Spartan
> wife?
> Talthybius: No, no—but for the king's own bed at
> night.
> Hecuba: Oh, never. She is God's, a virgin, always.
> That was God's gift to her for all her life. . . .
> Throw away, daughter, the keys of the temple.
> Take off the wreath and the sacred stole.[7]

Her daughter's plight is as tragic as her own losses. In Bosnia, Muslim women regard their virginity also as a precious gift from their God, Allah. Religion and tradition cherished by Muslim women in Bosnia translate into a strict reservation of sexual relations until they are married. Like Agamemnon's thievery of Apollo's gift, only more brutal, the Serbs wantonly rape the virgins of Bosnia.

Alrnira Ajanovic, eighteen years old, Tuzla:

> For five nights, I was raped by Serb soldiers inside
> the temporary bordello they had set up in my home
> village of Lipje, three men every night. They took a
> knife and cut my dress open. Two pinned me to the
> bed as the third raped me. Then they switched
> places, each watching the others perform. It contin-
> ued for five nights, with different men each time,
> until the sixth, when they heightened the humilia-
> tion by raping me in front of my father. That Chet-
> nik said that he was going to marry me. My father
> kept silent. I didn't want to see my father again for
> one month. I still cannot talk about this with him.[8]

The daughter's sacrifice becomes an element to shred also the soul of her father. Beyond cleaving the connection and understanding between those who love, war's terrors grip coldly all the eyes that befall them.

War does not limit itself to its "victims." In this sense, all of its participants (and as indicated earlier, all cognizant of it) are the victims.
Cassandra alludes to war's intoxication for the conquerors:

> All, all because he married me and so
> pulled his own house down.
> But I will show you. This town now, yes, Mother,
> is happier than the Greeks. I know that I am mad,
> but Mother, dearest, now, for this one time
> I do not rave.
> One woman they came hunting, and one love,
> Helen, and men by tens of thousands died.
> Their king, so wise, to get what most he hated
> destroyed what most he loved,
> his joy at home, his daughter, killing her
> . . . .
> They lie in a strange land. And in their homes
> are sorrows, too, the very same
> Lonely women who died, old men who waited
> for sons that never came—no son left to them
> to make the offering at their graves
> That was the glorious victory they won.[9]

The truth of war is that it hunts and pillages while remaining winner-
less. War is an entity to itself that feeds like a fire on all the fuel supplied
to it. War pervades the life of every Bosnian, Serb or Muslim, whether
war-maker or victim.

Woman, thirty-eight years old, Teslic:

> A Serb, a very rich man, gave a lot of money for the
> Serbian army from the very beginning of the war.
> One day an armed group named Red Caps came
> to his door; they were robbers, they would take

anything from anybody but they called themselves
Serbs. When they came to this Serb's house, which
was the most beautiful in the village, he took a gun
and shouted at the gang leader. The gang left only to
return the next day. The man, his wife, and children
had to flee; they burned his whole house. There are
other Serbian houses which were robbed; there are
no more Muslim houses and now my village is Serbian property.[10]

The triumph of war here is evident. Those who have tried to wage and
support it also find themselves drawn into it with little chance for
resistance.

The conquerors never absolutely conquer and the defeated are
never absolutely defeated, but war issues masks to humans that prevent
them from realizing this fundamental truth. All share a willingness to
demonize, to *dehumanize,* the Other, always careful never to portray
their opponents as human beings, as mothers, daughters, or sisters. No
relationship exists between the two—as if two distinct and disastrously
opposite species were vying for a particularly plentiful forest. War de-
prives humans of the impulse to reflect upon their deeds as looters and
murderers. In fact, war curiously *changes* those deeds into somehow
expected or natural means of conduct. War is an intelligent beast.

Logos, reflection, is Euripides' most dynamic and important tool in
conveying pacifism in *The Trojan Women.* Reflection allows the audience to see the horrors of warfare, to feel the loss of otherwise innocent
people. Hecuba:

But there is something that cries out for God
when trouble comes.
Oh, I will think of good days gone,
days to make a song of,

> crowning my sorrow by remembering.
> We were kings and a king I married.[11]

Bosnian Muslim women now share this cruel exile with the Trojan women 2,400 years ago, and their cries seem no different, lost friends, lost lives.

Ljiljana Trkulja, twenty-three years old, Tuzla:

> Trice: reality ceases in my eyes,
> under the last twinkling of a wandering star
> longing is in the place of reality,
> dashes on the wings of dream
> Uncoil by my sight familiar streets, passersby,
>   childhood,
> again I am where I belong, where my soul
> has been left, my heart bleeds;
> but, human's hatred has done its job.[12]

Euripides sought to instruct the Greeks in virtue. When he composed *The Trojan Women,* the Athenians had just slaughtered the men of Melos and had enslaved the women and children, all for doing nothing more than declaring innocent neutrality. He also composed it at the moment when the Athenians sailed to their total devastation in the central Mediterranean. His support of democratic institutions, moral use of power, and caution to the victors of war are all more than sophisticated warning of "moderation" for heartless aggressors. His entire point in composing the tragedy is to avert the all-out destruction of all humans: the only means to accomplish this simple concept in survival is to know that war is complete and total corruption of the state and of the soul.

Thus armed conflict crushes anyone who feels its reach. When war is evaluated from this perspective, from its equal punishment to the victor and the victim, we see ourselves as humans as a single people in the face of a great torment. To achieve our gains as states and peoples without war, without the application of militarized force, requires a kind of sheer virtue unheard of (and certainly disdained by some of our greatest scholars and leaders) through history; more important, it is a virtue that requires far more effort and devotion than the action of hating. It is of a completely different nature. Euripides, though, invited us to this virtue; he challenged and educated us in the simplest language of human suffering. If we *feel* this suffering, as we must in *The Trojan Women,* we disable the war, for as strong or as weak we defeat the indifference to fellow humans that is the mother of war. Andromache:

> I say to die is only not to be,
> and rather death than life with bitter grief.
> They have no pain, they do not feel their wrongs.
> But the happy who has come to wretchedness,
> his soul is a lost wanderer,
> the old joys that were once, left far behind.[13]

But in Bosnia, the indifference remains. The wanton savagery of the soldiers testifies to their indifference to those most captive to the force of war, its women. There exists only ambivalence as Serbs desecrate the bodies and minds of Muslim women.

Satka, twenty years old, Tuzla:

> I hate the man who raped me because he had no
>   feeling for me.
> I wasn't his girlfriend. It was savagery. I was an
>   honest girl.
> I was a virgin. I gave it to someone who didn't
>   deserve it.
> Someone whom I love deserves it. But not a
>   savage.[14]

The indiscriminate robbery from Satka incarnates the callousness of the soldier who took her "gift."

The words of reason and common experience escape into the same nothingness that has swallowed them since Euripides composed his tragedy. This is the way war becomes loved. By tearing from men and women the compassion with which they conduct themselves toward friends and neighbors, by *objectifying* humans, the war invents itself as the only medium through which to see and hear and touch the "opponent." It nakedly inflates the fear, the vanity, and the self-aggrandizing elements of the social man. When we look at the warlords in the Balkans, their actions seek to inspire through fear the crazed violence of war.[15] If we can destroy that which makes us the same, our condition as humans, then we can create—in mind, not reality—the "winners," the "losers," the "apostates," and the "faithful."

Bosnian Serbs and Muslims lived together as neighbors and friends for hundreds of years. In mere months their brutality cannibalized the society. This is the next step for war, to take the place of friendship, love, cooperation, celebration, and consolation in the *interactions* between the humans it has corrupted. Loved ones, neighbors, and friends die while fissures, oppression, and murder take their war-preferred place as the norms of human exchange.

War feeds itself copiously with the hate it engenders. Seeking to survive and spread, it carefully eviscerates aspiration from those it touches. Each day war's participants modify their purpose in the face of the threat of violence. The war *replaces* decisions they might otherwise be making; more and more of even daily thought is ceded to the war's place in the life of each. Thinking of how to end the war or if it is even possible to end it shrinks away, so that eventually war's circumstances are accepted and no one expects ever again to resume life without war. Aside from the trauma of warfare, its own existence as a state of day-to-day life depletes its victims. Fear, anguish, exhaustion, murder, the

destruction of people—these tirelessly wear down the spirit that continued life would otherwise sustain.

The conquerors in *The Trojan Women* and in Tuzla, Teslic, and
Bresovo Polje respect at no point the condition of weakness or of defeat
for their "enemies." For both societies' women, rape, murder of children and husbands, forced servitude, and violent diaspora depicted in
stories are the reality of a fantastic state of unrestrained terror. Taken
without brief, shining moments where human fortitude prevails, the
tales of war forecast nothing beyond despair for humanity.

Woman, fifty-eight years old, Bijeljina:

> When we left, a Serbian woman came to see us off.
> She was my best friend and we had lived thirty-
> seven years together. She brought me oranges and
> tomatoes for the trip. My elderly mother was com-
> pletely lost and I was desperate.[16]

> Andromache: The love that endures between
>   mother and son—
> You little thing,
> curled in my arms, you dearest to your mother,
> how sweet the fragrance of you.
> Kiss me—Never again. Come, closer, closer.
> Your mother who bore you—put your arms around
> my neck.
> Now kiss me, lips to lips.[17]

Woman, fifty-four years old, Knin:

> During the trip my younger son was lost somewhere
> in the convoy. My other son died before the war,
> so he is all we have. So, here we are, my husband
> and me, and we are not moving from our spot on the

pavement because this is the place where all refugees come, and my son must come here too. If I lose
him now I am afraid that we will never meet again.
They are trying to get me into a bus to take me
somewhere else, but I will not move. I will wait one
hundred more days until I find my son.[18]

The bond between man and wife, dying slowly, for all these women,
awes us with its purity and strength. Most touching is a simple, final
good-bye from a wife to her husband:

Andromache: O Hector, my beloved, you were all
    to me,
wise, noble, mighty, in wealth, in manhood, both.
No man had touched me when you took me,
took me from out my father's home.[19]

Thus the Bosnian Muslim women say their good-byes to their men and
sons and brothers slaughtered mercilessly.

Woman, late twenties, Sarajevo: "I have learned in this short but for
me so long time what sorrow, loneliness and nostalgia mean. And suffering, real suffering. My head is full of nightmares. I see scenes, as if watching a film. I love the two of us, our past happiness, our smiles, our walks."[20]

The instances of warmth occur infrequently in both the narratives
of the Bosnian women and in *The Trojan Women.* This woman's description is perhaps the entire understanding of it all. She speaks to the
surreal nature of her existence during the war, how it twisted her life
and took her husband away. Like the experience of the Trojan women,
the war has meant the complete surrender of her life.

Euripides alone chose to mark the terror of war for his time. Aeschy-
lus decidedly disagreed with him, thinking that only that which is noble
and right of humans should be taught and never that which is flawed.
Certainly, the inheritors of the Greek civilization, the Romans, and their

colossal war-making machine ignored his simple message. As Euripides wrote, the Athenians he sought to educate sailed to their own destruction; they then experienced the utter defeat and destruction by which they had conducted themselves to that very point. When the Athenians fled Sicily, the fear and the devastation that they executed upon small Melos established a new perspective for them. They could now see war from the standpoint of both the victor and the victim—they could look beyond the blindness of which I spoke earlier. Yet it did little. These narratives of women living today testify that the unfolding of history continued to glorify battle and power and diminish the presence of peace.

The Trojan Women is unequaled revelation. Beginning with the musings of gods measuring justice and human conduct, tracing the sorrow, madness, and overwhelming despair of the unparalleled victims urges us toward the natural empathy that may save us from a future of war. The lives of the women in Bosnia give us another chance to realize unforgivable brutality. Their stories must not be trivialized but must be seen as the continuation of a message to which we must bring ourselves to listen. Jean-Paul Sartre also felt *The Trojan Women* as a powerful tool to engage existence.

In his slightly modified version of Euripides' work, he positions Poseidon, the divine force, to deliver the crucial and defining directive of *The Trojan Women*.

> You stupid, bestial mortals
> Making war, burning cities,
> violating tombs and temples,
> torturing your enemies,
> bringing suffering on yourselves.
> Can't you see
> War
> Will kill you:
> All of you?[21]

Notes

Epigraph: Elie Wiesel, Foreword to Rezak Hukanovic, *The Tenth Circle of Hell: A Memoir of Life in the Death Camps of Bosnia* (New York: Harper-Collins, 1996), vii.

1. Edwin M. Coulter, *Principles of Politics and Government* (Madison, WI: Brown and Benchmark, 1994), 116.

2. Robert Jay Lifton, *Sarajevo: A War Journal* (New York: Fromm International, 1993), xv.

3. Euripides, *The Trojan Women,* trans. Edith Hamilton (New York: W. W. Norton, 1967), 17.

4. Julie Mertus et al., eds., *The Suitcase* (Berkeley: University of California Press, 1997), 123.

5. Roy Gutman, *A Witness to Genocide* (New York: Macmillan, 1993), 72.

6. Euripides, *Trojan Women,* trans. Hamilton, 22.

7. Euripides, *Trojan Women,* trans. Hamilton, 23.

8. Gutman, *Witness to Genocide,* 74.

9. Euripides, *Trojan Women,* trans. Hamilton, 29.

10. Mertus et al., *Suitcase,* 28.

11. Euripides, *Trojan Women,* trans. Hamilton, 33.

12. Mertus et al., *Suitcase,* 82.

13. Euripides, *Trojan Women,* trans. Hamilton, 33.

14. Gutman, *Witness to Genocide,* 72.

15. Roger Cohen, "Terror in the Balkans," *New York Times Week in Review,* October 4, 1998, 16.

16. Mertus et al., *Suitcase,* 41.

17. Euripides, *Trojan Women,* trans. Hamilton, 46.

18. Mertus et al., *Suitcase,* 92.

19. Euripides, *Trojan Women,* trans. Hamilton, 42.

20. Mertus et al., *Suitcase,* 93.

21. Euripides, *The Trojan Women,* trans. Jean-Paul Sartre (London: Hamish Hamilton, 1967), 76.

Of Borders, Infidels, and the Ethic of Love

KIM KUPPERMAN
1996
University of Maine–Machias

ONE MARCH EVENING IN 1987 I crossed the border that separates Morocco and Algeria. Borders involve an unreal step through a vertical sheet of particles, an atomic space that belongs to no one.

These arbitrary lines in soil engender the demarcation of culture and politics, a place where identity shifts because of two connected points and where one crisis after another emerges over several inches of map space. At a border you must readjust your logic, shift gears, pay attention. Profound lessons that can change your life occur here. When I crossed that line in northern Africa—and the event was neither extraordinary nor isolated—I was sexually assaulted by an armed border guard. By sundown of the next day I sat at a table eating with a man and his family whom I had met several hours before. In the course of twenty-four hours—one revolution of the earth around the sun—I was victim, then honored guest, roles imposed upon me by the cartography of history. These dramas of crossing taught me, once time had corroded their sharp edges enough for me to contemplate their greater meaning, that the survival of humanity depends on its members' ability to love the stranger passing through their land.

It is not a lesson I learned immediately; at the time I was as unprepared to define love as I was to cross that border. "Love takes off the masks that we fear we cannot live without and know we cannot live within," wrote the American author James Baldwin, words I would read several years after my personal drama in Algeria.[1] Love is a state of grace, he elaborates, and it is in this climate that individuals can pursue their quest for growth. This ethic of love envisions stripping off all masks and being comfortable in this nakedness. Only then can human beings afford to save one another from the assumptions that are nourished, negotiated, and exacerbated by borders, whose very existence indicates that someone will be on the other side, an outsider who must be monitored and ultimately controlled. It is between neighbors—who are for the most part also cousins—where the divisions are at once the most profound and the least culturally distinct and where love is most absent and necessary.

Follow the borders that divide the Thirty-fourth Parallel, give or take a degree, and you will find the same kinds of dramas enacted over and over again with varying frequency and intensity. Only the names and costumes are different. Walk west of Maghnia, where I stood that March night. Zigzag north and south, here in the Thirty-third there in the Thirty-fifth Parallels, and you will walk through the pockets of the coat of history. You will encounter borders whose names are both familiar— Lebanon Syria, Iran Iraq—and places whose names you might not know, like Marjayoun, where Lebanon, Syria, and Israel converge. Further along this parallel you can travel through the Khyber Pass between Afghanistan and Pakistan, into Kashmir, over the northern tip of India, across Tibet into China, and above the Yellow Sea brushing through South Korea. Finally, just slightly north of the Thirty-fourth Parallel, you will hover over Hiroshima.

Part of what I learned as I stepped from one side to the other in that parallel's quadrant had to do with facts and assumptions about myself that I carried to Maghnia. In the customs house there Algeria's president gazed down upon me with disapproval, his eyes behind dusty glass.

The border guard examined me with a similar expression on his face, his eyes carefully fitted with the dual optics of politics and religion. He saw me passing for a European, in particular, for an unmarried French woman traveling with two men in two cars. These facts and the border guard's training and culturalization provided the evidence for

the reputation he accorded me. It was a reputation created from assumptions about nationality and sexuality, and it preceded me. With
the eyes of Islamic fundamentalism he perceived me as unveiled and
unmarried—a prostitute.

Upon scrutiny of my passport, he discovered that I was also American, a nationality that imparts not only a chaotic, unleashed sexuality
but a discomforting imperialism, especially to those peoples who have
revolted against their colonizers. American is also a nationality that Algerians, along with the majority of the world's Muslim peoples, link to
the existence of Israel, whose borders embrace, ironically, both Islam
and Judaism. Quite possibly, and even more dangerous from the border
guard's point of view, I was a Jew myself. Then there were the cars—
packed to the brim with possible contraband and possessed by an
American and two Frenchmen—this could mean drugs. Being an unveiled, unmarried American who spoke fluent French layered me with a
more political meaning, just as my declaration of being a student endowed me—for both the French and Algerian official embodied in the
border guard—with the persona of a troublemaker. In any of these cases
I was a trespasser, a peripheral creature now headed toward the Sahara
Desert, Allah's garden, where the border guard was a gatekeeper in more
ways than Allah himself had ever imagined.

He observed me for close to two hours, and I am sure that he saw a
person who embodied all the evils that his culture, fueled by the intertwined principles of Islam and socialism, warned him to reject. Not to
mention the possibility of our being cousins; unexpected gatherings
of the clan, especially when the family is so dysfunctional, lead to conflict. It is clear from what he did that he was not practicing one of the
Koran's most fundamental calls, to resolve this family conflict. Nor did
he heed the command to shelter the stranger. It is also clear that once he
began to view me as an available sexual object, I perceived all the errors
I had committed upon my arrival here. This was not about being a
provocateur in my own victimization; rather it was about that terrifying

revelation that my education, specifically, what I knew about history, the real story of real people with whom I was trafficking in a variety of commodities, was entirely wrong. This false history can be both deadly and tragic. This realization, of course, did not allow me to go back and end the scene differently. But it did teach me that I cannot love someone I know nothing about.

Of course, neither the border guard nor I had the time to consider things from this vantage point. Our mutual failure to do so led to the event in which I became a victim of his need to express his assumptions as instruments of a more powerful truth. We both came to the meeting at that border wearing selves we did not like or want to see in the other. Because I was the one making the crossing, it was my responsibility to step over with sensitivity to what lay on the other side. Instead, I came unveiled and unmarried. The expression of such honesty sometimes has to happen in small doses. But even if I had lied and said I was married, the border guard had already been molded by a centrifugal power that no longer possessed the responsibility of a conscience. He thrived on the emotional reactions—in particular, fear—of others. Such a person is a puppet in malicious hands and can make you disappear. Such a man derives great pleasure from making you barter for your immediate survival. Such a man actually prefers that you are not destroyed so that you may live with the scar and its resulting congestion—forever. So far, I have painted a very general and one-dimensional portrait of the border guard, with cursory remarks as to why he exists in the first place.

But when I look at the man for a moment—at his dark hair and sepia-colored skin, into his black eyes—I see a carefully cultivated hatred, a disease whose origins are history itself. The only medicine he ever had to battle this disease was his conscience, which had been appropriated by an intrigue of forces, all with one common design, to make him as efficient as possible at keeping the outsider out. Ironically—and dangerously, since this meant he knew how the other operates—he grew into this position by being an outsider himself, by being hated for what the color of his body insinuated about him. When he paid the price of his conscience he knew that in exchange he would be given coffee and good cigarettes and, once in a while, a bottle of whiskey—in other words, coveted goods in a place where shortages are the standard. Most important, he was granted the status that allowed him to confront another person's life, with the power to alter or extinguish that life.

To fully understand this man, first I had to look at his willingness to pay the price and why he might desire this status. What circumstances led him to the proverbial bargain in which he surrendered his soul? If I looked a little closer at the landscape behind this man, about 160 years back there is a colonial scrim being lowered—here, specifically, the French are in charge. The soil of this colonial scene will nourish the birth and shape the existence of this Algerian border guard. There are the colonizers on the veranda, grapevines in the distance, solar experiments in the desert, the languid excitement of the exotic native extinguished, yielding boredom. In this vacuum the virus of hate is nascent. Before they know it the French are fully infected. A plethora of repercussions will be felt, scattered across time, from the Algerian man not being able to vote in French elections to the Berber woman raped by the landowner to the deliberate displacement of entire populations of Algerians, along with the poor and all other dark-skinned foreigners, to the periphery of France's great cities. The relationship between French and Algerian becomes more and more defined by have and have-not. Each side follows suit by erecting complicated mental borders. In this virus-invaded body politic, revolution foments and then occurs. In 1962 independence is granted as though it were something to be taken away at will and restored by the benevolent missionaries of civilized Christian culture.

Revolution, in spite of its current romanticization by popular culture, is a great expense to everyone involved. It lingers in the shadows in those sun-filled vineyards where the motherless children of the French conquest live and hide. It creates dislocated *pieds noirs* who are perhaps more *métis* than their French compatriots can tolerate. It hatches the hatred needed to round up and execute Algerians in a Parisian stadium. It poisons the North African earth. Somehow, though, it is an acceptable price to pay for freedom. Before their expulsion from the dark continent, the French leave an indelible legacy behind.

That birthright is bureaucracy, which is deftly woven, thread by thread, into the tapestry of colonial life. Raise the next backdrop, one hundred years later, to the 1930s. Here is the world of the now modern civil servant, the pride of the Western world's heritage, civilization's great middleman, who has been nurtured and groomed to stamp everyday life with an official seal. The rise of this civil servant occurs at the precise moment humanity emerges from the stasis of a worldwide economic disaster. War, despair, and the redrawing of borders follow, fertilizing the ground for pure hatred. This is the historical fabric of the border guard's birth. It is also the same cloth used to swaddle the infant who becomes the man who shelters me.

Like the border guard, he has been rocked in the same cultural cradle. Unlike the border guard, he is willing to take off some of his masks, just as he consciously welcomes me at his table where we break bread. This man, a father of two daughters, hopes that the baby his wife is carrying will also be a girl. He does not know how to raise a son, he says. Not in the world in which he presently lives, one in which service in the army is mandatory for all male children. Also, he confides, he does not know how to raise a boy to become a man in a place where hate has become holy. This is what makes him nervous, he says, hands shaking as he pours tea. This is tea, he adds, that he has been saving for a special occasion.

When the French say *real* hospitality can only be experienced at an Arab table, they are not discussing a mystical cultural trait with which they are intimate. Nor are they talking about love. In French, as in English, there is a limited vocabulary to describe the state of being a guest.

The word *hôte* was employed to denote both the host and the guest until the word *invite* was commonly used.

The concept of being welcomed is similarly limited by language, which suggests that when the French talk about Arab hospitality, they are revealing the relationship they would like to have with the Algerian. At this table the French colonialist does not want to share a simple meal with another human being. At this table the French colonialist wishes to be absolved—without any kind of self-examination—of all crimes committed against the Algerian. This *real* hospitality that the French reputedly find at the Arab table is there not because it is a moral behavior mandated by the Koran but because the French expect to find it there. This expectation creates schism when it is not fulfilled, borders to be negotiated, complications to resolve, masks to wear. While I would like to believe otherwise, a residue of this expectation was part of my encounter with the man who sheltered me. This man, whose immediate and extended family relied on him for hard-to-procure commodities like daily food and housing, made my well-being a priority. This placed me in a precarious position. His wife, eight months' pregnant, refused all offers of assistance. To stay for any length of time was to burden her; to leave too soon was to insult my host.

While I was being fed and sheltered by this family, I was advised by my traveling companions that the removal of masks is a procedure that requires great equilibrium. Furthermore, they said, it would be unwise for me to relate the story of the border crossing, just as it would be unwise for me to reveal that I am a Jew. For the sake of equilibrium among the three of us I concurred, locking up these facts about myself so my hosts would not perceive them. One more thing about identity, though: because I was an American and, to a degree, a European woman, a strange thing occurred.

Although their idea was to treat me like a sister, the men in this family accorded me a servile respect that was once demanded of them

by French women. Before being female, therefore, a rank that would
have afforded me congress with the women of this family, I was considered French. This mask, the one of the colonial relationship, like my
Jewish one, could not be removed, in spite of the effort to unveil our
other selves.

As I sat at the Algerian man's table, upon which was heaped a hospitality without limits, I sensed how difficult it was for all of us to maneu-
ver in this new territory, one defined by the risk-taking that ultimately
results in love. I still wonder how much of the hospitality was the fulfillment of that colonial expectation or if the endless food was sincerely
offered to facilitate a passage into the alien land of common understanding. Once we arrived in this place we needed a new language, and since
we had not yet invented it, we used the old vocabulary for this new adventure. Old language means the baggage of associations, cumbersome
luggage on a quest for a new vision of love. And while we drew no lines
in the soil around that table, the fact of the table still meant a boundary
was present.

Eventually the hospitality suffocated me. This may sound like the
height of ingratitude, but it is only a response to what became a series of
failed attempts to move beyond that table and navigate in another terrain,
a place not found in atlases. The original invitation, not the elaborate
succession of platters and decanters that followed, was all that was necessary to begin. After sitting at my host's table the first night, perhaps we all
should have moved to an open space where the divisions of a house
could not intrude. Wandering in this symbolic wilderness may have
brought us to a real wild land, a place that could accord us the physical
space necessary to abolish the mental borders. What would it matter
then, in a place removed from neighbors, bureaucracy, the cultural status
quo, if I told my host I was a Jew? In a true wilderness it is more relevant
for him to know that together we have a greater chance of surviving.

To have removed these masks in a borderless wilderness would have
been revolutionary, and the revolution was not planned to happen in

March 1987 in a remote corner of Algeria. Already we were transcending aspects of culture, class, and race; if we had bridged the gap between Muslim and Jew, we could have gone on beyond being defined as such, beyond the boundaries of the original family that produced us. No longer wearing a label, we would have been free of the details that made us different for so long. My traveling companions pointed out that it was easier to lie: just say you're married, don't mention your family too much, don't talk about politics, and this is what we did instead of facing the challenge of love. My cousins in Algeria will never know that I am not their metaphorical sister, that I am really related to them. That they cannot know this means that we all failed to learn the true meaning of our coming together.

This is not the first nor will it be the last failure of this kind. What is astounding is the number of times this cycle has turned, cruelly folding and crushing human lives in its grasp. Over and over again neighbors transgress borders, and over and over again moral standards are invented and reinvented in response to infractions that humans incur among themselves. The witnesses—the prophets, the writers, the philosophers, the artists, and the poets—have constructed their messages about humanity's failure to love in an infinite variety of ways. That is the ultimate tragedy, our inability to decode the repetitive message of history, to know the difference between right and wrong and not apply this knowledge. We lack this skill because we are not taught where the real lessons in history occur, in our own lives. This forces us to keep those assumptions about one another intact and operative. The failure to love evolves from the failure to reconcile the private and public response to those who are marginal and dispossessed, those on the other side of all those borders, those in whom we recognize part or all of ourselves.

Note

1. James Baldwin, *The Fire Next Time* (New York: Dial, 1963), 109.

Justice—For Whom?

Reflections on the Persian Gulf War

THOMAS MURPHY
1993
University of Iowa

"THE WAR IN THE GULF IS . . . a just war."[1] In a speech to the National Religious Broadcasters George Bush invoked traditional just war theory to legitimize the United States' role in the 1990–1991 Persian Gulf War. George Bush, using classical just war criteria, claimed that there *was just cause* for violence, that Operation Desert Storm was conducted with *legitimate authority,* that the coalition had *just intent,* that war was a *last resort,* that there was *reasonable prospect of success,* that the good accomplished outweighed evil perpetrated (*norm of proportionality*), and finally that discrimination was exercised so as to avoid unnecessary harm to civilians (*noncombatant immunity*).[2] By contrast, Alan Geyer and Barbara Green argued that the actions and precautions taken in the war hardly "add up to a vindication of, or by, the just war tradition."[3] These conflicting views about the invocation of just war theory as an ethical ideal raise the question: "What is the meaning of ethics today?"

The narrative that follows is one individual's reflection on justice and the Persian Gulf War. As a U.S. Army soldier in Saudi Arabia, Iraq, and Kuwait I discovered the challenge of applying an ethical ideal (just war criteria) to real experience. Exposed are the tensions inherent in choices made by a soldier. Can I muster the courage to fulfill a contract? What is an individual's obligation to oppose injustice? What is justice? Upon my return from the war, I began to explore the literature on justice and the Gulf War. My experience framed my response to that literature. Few theorists seemed to address the questions I found myself asking, perhaps because my primary viewpoint has been that of a soldier. Therefore, my intention is to expose the reader to the variety of perspectives (cultural and personal) from which justice in war can be analyzed. I first relate my own experiences and then engage in a discussion of justice in the Persian Gulf War. My argument is twofold: (1) George Bush's claim, that the war was just, represents an abuse of just war theory; and (2) additional criteria need to be established to prevent future abuse of the just war tradition—that is, we must ask the question, "Justice—for whom?"

It was a Monday in November, Veterans Day, that I received the telephone call informing me that my National Guard unit, the 209th Medical Company, was being placed on alert for possible deployment as part of Operation Desert Shield. Like many other soldiers in the all-volunteer force, I had joined the military to earn money for college. Many of us came from families that could not afford to pay for their children's education. For many recruits the military represents "the only ticket away from poverty or a career at McDonald's."[4] Before returning to college, several years in the workforce (flipping hamburgers and mopping floors) had left my wife and I with only a bankruptcy, because borrowing money had been the only means we had to purchase food and diapers for our infant daughter.

I reflect now on how foolish I was when I believed the recruiter who told me that the only place I would go if I was activated during wartime was sunny California. There was plenty of sun waiting for us in southwest Asia, until it was darkened by burning oil wells. Before our deployment to Saudi Arabia, the military sent us to wintery Wisconsin to undergo intensive training and preparation, much of which focused on chemical warfare. On the weekends between the seven weeks of rehearsal, I was able to visit with my family. How do you tell a four-year-old child that you may never return? Each shoulder ride could be the last. You cannot hug each other without breaking down into tears. Could she understand that I did not want to go—but that if I refused, I would likely spend seven years in prison? "Please don't go, Daddy, please stay. Who will rub my back? Can I go with you? Who will make me pancakes?" The echo of her voice still reverberates in a guilty conscience.

After we had filed for bankruptcy, the opportunities facing my wife and me were limited. Hoping for a better future, we chose to pursue college educations. For us, the choice to go back to college depended on money from the army. Social mobility, I had been taught as a youth, was the foundation upon which this nation was built. Little did I know the price I would have to pay in pursuit of the elusive "American Dream." For my wife, my mobilization meant facing single parenthood, at least temporarily. Hope for an eventual reunion was the motivation that gave her strength, but that reunion was never certain.

War is not only a matter of statecraft; there is a human dimension to war that must be addressed. I finally realized that the Vietnam Memorial in Washington, D.C., is not only names on a wall: it represents broken families and lost dreams. Do ethics have meaning for families, or are they simply a principle of statehood? Should we tear loving parents from innocent children to make a "New World Order"?

As an anthropologist in training, I was pleased to see the army's efforts to educate us on the culture and tradition of our soon-to-be host country. On the other hand, I listened in disbelief when George Bush deliberately mispronounced Saddam Hussein's name. "Sadam," as Bush mispronounced the name, was the equivalent of a vulgarity in Arabic. It is still difficult to imagine that a president of the United States would tell the leader of another nation that he was "going to get his ass kicked." If the army could afford the cost of briefing nearly half a million soldiers on the importance of understanding another culture, I wondered why our commander-in-chief did not receive a similar briefing. Peace in a multicultural world is dependent upon respect for others. But just war theory does not require that decision-makers respect cultural differences.

Our plane landed in Saudi Arabia early in January 1991. Even at that point, I harbored a hope that we would not have to fight. At 3:00 am on January 17, that hope was demolished. Inside an apartment building built for the nomadic Bedouins, now converted to a military barracks, I was awakened from my sleep by someone calling my name. "Wake up. It started," the voice said, "go to MOPP level two!"[5] A room full of soldiers bustled in voiceless activity as we quickly dressed ourselves in trousers and a blouse, both lined with charcoal. These clothes, we had been told, *should* protect us in the case of a chemical attack.

The silence in the room was broken by a thundering noise resembling a rocket launch. "I think it's friendly," a voice in the darkness gasped. A brilliant flash of light was followed by the sound of a powerful explosion. No one had to give the command to don our gas masks and remaining chemical protection equipment. Outside the building, we could see the burning pieces of what we later discovered was a Scud missile intercepted by a Patriot missile directly above our location. The hours spent in a gas mask that morning and many others are a horror I will never forget.

A few weeks later, we left the Bedouin apartment complex to set up tents in the Saudi desert. One fateful evening I spent on guard duty remains vivid in my mind. I was positioned at the gate of a mobile army surgical hospital, built of tents and located about fifteen miles from the Iraqi border. Terrorism, we had been warned, was a major threat. We were on alert for suspicious activity. A truck that appeared to be American-made pulled off the main supply route and turned down the makeshift road toward our camp. At a point about two hundred yards away, the truck veered to the right, leaving the road. The truck was heading toward the sand berm surrounding the camp. This action was in clear violation of security. Could it be a terrorist? We had a field phone for communication with higher headquarters, but my companion's attempt to contact the command post was unsuccessful. I had to make a choice. At risk were the lives of hundreds of soldiers if, in fact, this vehicle was being operated by a terrorist. However, the make of the vehicle indicated that it was probably friendly—or a terrorist in a friendly vehicle. The truck stopped at the edge of the berm, and a figure emerged, barely visible in the dark. It was my duty to prevent unauthorized entry into this facility. The figure continued to approach the perimeter. This action, whether friendly or not, was unauthorized. My failure to respond could cost untold lives. Not knowing if I had the courage to fire, I sighted my M-16 on this figure. Who was this person? The perpetrator stopped. Is this someone's parent? The rifle was still on safe; I switched it to semi-automatic. The figure turned around and walked back to the vehicle, alleviating the threat. I switched the weapon back to safe. Whether justified or not, decisions by soldiers in combat are embedded in moral ambiguity.

Shortly before the ground war began, I was selected for a remote mission as part of an ambulance relay station inside Iraqi territory. From that vantage point, I witnessed one of the heaviest bombing and artillery attacks in history. "Bombs bursting in air, gave proof through the night" that death was near there. During those sleepless nights, I reflected on the loss of Iraqi lives at the receiving end of that barrage. Were the victims teenagers, or parents like me?

During the first forty-eight hours of the land invasion, we watched tanks, armored personnel carriers, trucks, and other military vehicles roll by in endless lines. We were prepared for five hundred patients that first day. The first was dead on arrival. Inside his wallet, he had kept a picture of his wife and two children. Five other patients arrived that day, far fewer than expected. Could the small number of casualties relieve some of the pain felt by those who lost loved ones?

Soon we were celebrating a cease-fire with a convoy of Iraqi prisoners of war. Cultural barriers were bridged when a nurse gave a pack of cigarettes to one truckload of prisoners. The Iraqis appeared even more grateful than we were to see the end of the fighting. Had the battle seemed just to them?

The struggle that was being fought inside of me was not yet over. Our next assignment took us to Kuwait City. We were the first medical unit to arrive in the capital. It was there that I saw the "Highway of Death." George Bush had promised the Iraqis that if they would leave their weapons behind and return to Iraq, we would not attack. Among the many demolished civilian automobiles there were very few military vehicles. On some automobiles white flags, now stained red, were still visible. Tears flowed as I smelled the rotting flesh of thirty thousand broken promises.

Before the Kuwaitis returned to Kuwait City, the only civilians with whom we had contact were the impoverished migrant laborers and resident aliens. While most of the wealthy Kuwaitis had escaped to Saudi Arabia, these were the people who bore the heaviest burden of the Iraqi occupation. The bruises on a Palestinian I met gave credibility to his complaints of revengeful abuse from returning Kuwaiti soldiers. The Palestinians were unfortunate victims in the path of a "noble cause."

Eerie dark clouds engulfed Kuwait. The once-beautiful beaches of Kuwait City were tarnished with oil. A few soldiers in our unit, including one who had never smoked, were shipped to hospitals in Europe and the United States for lung damage. Environmental damage was an inadvertent side effect of military action. After three weeks in Kuwait, I was anxious to leave. But instead of going home we were sent to Safwan, Iraq, to treat refugees.

In Safwan, we were assisted by the interpretative skills of two Iraqis. One was a Kurdish physician who had seen his wife and two children brutally murdered by Saddam's retaliatory attacks on Kurdish villages. The other, a veterinarian, was a Sunni Muslim from Baghdad who had witnessed his brother's death for avoiding conscription. He had managed to evade detection by disguising himself as a general in the Iraqi Republican Guard. The Iraqis worked long hours for only food and shelter. Our mission could not have been accomplished without their language skills. Instead of rewarding them for their assistance, we were ordered to leave them behind to face almost certain death. Do ethical causes require us to murder our friends?

At the Safwan refugee camp I came face to face with the victims of not only six weeks of war but six months of economic sanctions. To look into the eyes of a hungry child is a soul-wrenching experience, especially if you realize that you are a participant in the cause of their suffering. The children lined the roads when we drove by, only to be forced away by United States Military Police wielding baseball bats. If only the children could have understood how important this "New World Order" was, maybe the pain would not have been so severe.

Finally, the order came to pack up, return to Saudi Arabia, and prepare to go home. In an attempt to use the excess rations that had been stockpiled for the war, we had been receiving double and triple ration orders. As part of our preparation to leave, I was instructed to begin destroying the excess food. A small fraction of the food had been taken to a refugee camp, but transporting all the food would have inconvenienced our preparations for departure. The remaining food we were to burn. I remember laughing when the heated tin cans exploded. We were excited to be going home. Then, they came. Our location had been kept somewhat secret. We treated only patients that we had transported from the refugee camp in Safwan. Direct admission for treatment was prohibited for security reasons. Up to this point, no children had directly approached our camp.

There were three of them. They walked up to the edge of the constantan wire delineating the perimeter of our assembly. Through the curling smoke of burning food, I envisioned the features of my own daughter over the gaunt faces of three Iraqi children. Who the hell did I think I was? Who would ignite food in front of starving children? A suppressed conscience kindled anguish deep inside, an agony of anger and pain. I was angry at myself for not confronting injustice. As I looked at the children everyone else seemed to ignore, I could not erase the painful image of my own daughter. Years of discipline and training could no longer restrain my shame. In open violation of security, I picked up a case of Campbell's soup previously intended for the flames and carried it to the children. The oldest child, a girl of about seven years, began to speak in Arabic. I could not understand a word she said, but I knew what she wanted. Did I dare do it again? I knew I was violating orders. After returning with the second case, the young Iraqi girl again indicated she wanted more. A third time I returned to the stockpile and obtained another case of Campbell's soup, wondering how the youngest child, no more than three, could carry this box all the way back to their home at least a mile away.

I could not restore the food I had already burned. This guilt I must live with. I was reprimanded for breaching security. However, I managed to stop further destruction of the food and to convince the platoon sergeant that rather than burning the food, it was better to leave the food unguarded upon our departure for the children or others in need of it. That young Iraqi girl had awakened in me a new outlook on war.

On my return home, I discovered a blossoming discussion of just war theory. Bush's justification found support among some thinkers. George Weigel argued that "the Gulf War was a justified war according to the classic canons of the just war tradition."[6] Michael Walzer emphasized a "just obligation" to oppose aggression such as Saddam's invasion of Kuwait.[7] In James Johnson's opinion, the Gulf War "showed that it is possible to fight a contemporary war within the bounds of just war principles of discrimination and proportionality of means."[8] Other thinkers disagreed. Bryan Hehir questioned Bush's appeal to the just war sanction: "The function of just-war categories . . . is not primarily to legitimate the policy of states, but to limit their proclivity to reach for the weapons of war."[9] Geyer and Green warned that "moral pretenses to universalism by a great power can be among the most demonic forces of history."[10] Sari Nusseibeh added that "if anything, the war was not a vindication of moral principles but a vindication of force."[11]

As I read the growing literature on just war, I found myself asking, somewhat selfishly, what about the soldiers? The questions that plagued my conscience were left unasked by most scholars. The vast majority of the just war thinkers were mere armchair theorists who had never been on a battlefield. Maybe it was anger that led me to ask such questions as: How can someone comprehend justice on a battlefield if that person has never left family behind, sighted a rifle on a human silhouette, dodged incoming missiles, donned a gas mask, treated battle wounds, looked into the eyes of starving children, or lost a loved one?

On further contemplation, I began to realize that it is not that theorists are inept or insensitive. Rather, they represent a different perspective. Each inquiry is formed by the experiences and the worldview of the person asking the question. That would help explain the multiplicity of responses to the same criteria. An answer is formulated by one's view of justice, good, harm, reason, success, and legitimacy. My perspective, as a soldier, is based on my own experiences. The answer is determined, in large part, by who asks which questions. How can we, then, transcend our own limited perspective?

What injustices are involved for combatants, on all sides? What had begun as a selfish inquiry now began to expand. Justice—for whom? Who bears the heaviest costs of war? Which groups (ethnic and socioeconomic) comprise the combatants? Who stands to benefit from war and who to lose? What is the impact on the Iraqi people? How can we account for cultural differences in ethical discussion? How does environmental damage affect the discussion? How does focusing on gender change the question? What does justice mean for the hungry children in Iraq? In what manner are our actions compromising their future?

George Bush invoked the just war theory as if it represented a universal standard. By wrapping himself and the country in moral rhetoric, Bush endangered the purpose of just war criteria. Just war criteria should limit the role of the state, not provide it with legitimation. As an unenforceable plaint against sheer power, just war theory offers criteria. The fact is that leaders can do as they wish. In ethics, as in other methods of inquiry, who asks the question and which question we ask in a large part determine the answer. If we do not ask "Justice—for whom?" then this question will not be considered. If we do not ask "Who composes the combatants?" then we risk having a war that meets all other criteria except that all or a disproportionate share of those doing the fighting are the poor or certain minorities, an action bordering on genocide.

It can be argued that just war tradition assumes that war is inherently inequitable and consequently that criteria must be considered. However, George Bush was able to use traditional just war criteria while at the same time ignoring the different perspectives inherent in a multicultural world. I would like to see the question of inequity moved from the realm of assumption to the realm of dialogue.

The all-volunteer force results in a disproportionate share of minorities and poor in today's military.[12] More women than men opposed the war.[13] Indigenous women claim that dominant societies' "militarizing" of men disrupts their social order.[14] Decisions resulting in war are made by leaders of regimes which Arab women "never voted for or supported."[15] By portraying Saddam Hussein as Hitler, an action to which many Jewish Americans objected, Bush implied by analogy that the Arab people were Nazis.[16] Iraqis and other Arab nationals were banned from flying PanAm airline.[17] The destruction of Iraqi infrastructure left civilians as well as combatants without basic "life-support systems."[18] There is no Arabic word for "collateral damage."[19] Environmental disaster and consequent tolls on humanity were "willfully ignored."[20]

Stanley Hauerwas stated that "it makes all the difference who is asking the questions about the 'justice' of the war and for what reasons."[21] He concluded that "the Gulf War was conceived and fought by . . . political realists who found it useful to justify it on just war grounds."[22] Jean Elshtain observed that "just war offers no definitive answer to the question 'But was it just?'"[23] An editorial in *La Civiltà Cattolica* claimed that "the theory of 'just war' is indefensible and has been abandoned."[24]

There is danger in asking "Justice—for whom?" We risk taking a position of extreme relativism in which we abandon universal ethical standards, a situation in which might makes right. Abandonment is not necessary, but incorporation is. I seek an expansion, not a denunciation, of just war inquiry. We must give voice to all those who lack power. Let us empower combatants with representation in ethical dialogue. Let us empower women, the lower classes, those from other cultures, minorities, and future generations.

Ethical theorists must recognize their own cultural biases by asking "Justice—for whom?" We must also recognize that the responses will necessarily be varied. The dualistic yes-or-no answer will not be provided by such an evaluation. Can a complicated answer, incorporating a plurality of perspectives, provide a sufficient guide for policy makers? Addressing inequities in the burdens of war would definitely complicate the application of just war theory. Nonetheless, I argue that as a substitute for an ethnocentric ignorance of alternative perspectives, asking "for whom" would in fact assist policy makers in the decision process, which when it involves so many lives should not be made so simple. Replacing simple yes-or-no answers with complex pluralistic answers can help serve as a safeguard against future crusadelike invocations of just war theory, in which the theory serves more as a source of legitimation than as one of reflection.

Ethical thought today is challenged by the variety of perspectives from which choices are made. We must challenge ourselves to transcend our own limited perspectives. Yet at the same time, we must avoid the danger of abandoning ethics in the face of relativism. This is a challenge that is not easily, and may be never, met. We must begin to ask the difficult question "Justice—for whom?"

Each time I look through the curling smoke of other fires, I recall the tears of a four-year-old bidding farewell, the fear of a soldier, the sound of "bombs bursting in air," the rotting smell of thirty thousand broken promises, the friends who gave their lives, and most of all the vision of my own daughter over the gaunt faces of those Iraqi children. Can we muster the courage to share a little Campbell's soup?

Notes

1. George Bush, "Address to National Religious Broadcasters on January 28, 1991," in *Just War and the Gulf War,* ed. James T. Johnson and George Weigel (Washington, DC: Ethics and Public Policy Center, 1991), 141.

2. Bush, "Address," 141–146.

3. Alan Geyer and Barbara G. Green, *Lines in the Sand: Justice and the Gulf War* (Louisville, KY: Westminster/John Knox Press, 1992), 161.

4. Bruce Shapiro, "Hell for Those Who Won't Go," *Nation,* February 18, 1991, 195. See also Michael L. Vecchiolla, "The Gulf War," in Denny Roy et al., *A Time to Kill: Reflections on War* (Salt Lake City, UT: Signature Books, 1992), 241–242.

5. MOPP levels designate the threat of chemical warfare and the protective actions to be taken. Level 4 is the highest, and 0 is the lowest.

6. George Weigel, "From Last Resort to Endgame," in *But Was It Just?* ed. David E. DeCosse (New York: Doubleday, 1992), 19.

7. Michael Walzer, "Justice and Injustice in the Gulf War," in DeCosse, *But Was It Just?* 1–17.

8. James T. Johnson, "Was the Gulf War a Just War?" in Johnson and Weigel, *Just War,* 35.

9. J. Bryan Hehir, "The Moral Calculus of War: Just but Unwise," *Commonweal* 118, no. 4 (1991): 125.

10. Geyer and Green, *Lines in the Sand,* 172.

11. Sari Nusseibeh, "Can Wars Be Just? A Palestinian Viewpoint of the Gulf War," in DeCosse, *But Was It Just?* 80.

12. Claudia Mills, "All-Volunteer Force: Second Thoughts," *Bureaucrat* (Spring 1984), 48–52. Leonid Very Rev. Kishkovsky et al., "A Call to the Churches," in Johnson and Weigel, *Just War,* 154. Peter Heinegg, trans., "Modern War and the Christian Conscience," in DeCosse, *But Was It Just?* 123.

13. Grace Paley, "Something About the Peace Movement: Something About the People's Right Not to Know," in *The Gulf Between Us,* ed. Victoria Britten (London: Virago, 1991), 67.

14. Winona LaDuke, "An Indigenous Perspective on Feminism, Militarism, and the Environment," in *War After War,* ed. Nancy J. Peters (San Francisco: City Lights, 1992), 245.

15. Fadia Faquir, "Tales of War: Arab Women in the Eye of the Storm," in Britten, *Gulf Between Us,* 77.

16. Albert Mokhiber interviewed by Jeanne Butterfield, "Racism and the Arab Community," in Peters, *War After War,* 63.

17. Mokhiber interview.

18. Geyer and Green, *Lines in the Sand,* 143.

19. Francis X. Winters, "The 'Just War,'" *Commonweal* 118, no. 7 (1991): 223.

20. John Vidal, "Poisoned Sand and Seas," in Britten, *Gulf Between Us,* 134.

21. Stanley Hauerwas, "Whose Just War? Which Peace?" in DeCosse, *But Was It Just?* 84.

22. Hauerwas, "Whose Just War? Which Peace?" 88.

23. Jean B. Elstain, "Just War as Politics: What the Gulf War Told Us About Contemporary American Life," in DeCosse, *But Was It Just?* 54.

24. Heinegg, trans., "Modern War and the Christian Conscience," 118.

ON MEMORY

In Times of Darkness

The Responsibility of the Individual

COURTNEY BRKIC
1995
The College of William and Mary

I REMEMBER A BOSNIA Herzegovina that most people in the world will never know. I remember the smell of the pine forests that cover the dark mountains. I remember the minarets of Sarajevo's Begova Mosque and the black birds that dove around them in the grayness of sky. When I was a baby, my parents pushed my stroller over the cobblestoned streets. When I was old enough to walk, I held my mother's hand tightly as we wove our way through the souk, where merchants sold embroidered cloths, leather goods, and filigree jewelry. It was in this market that we bought wild strawberries wrapped in newspaper on a scorching summer day over ten years ago.

America will not know this. Rather, it will remember the marketplace for the massacre of sixty-eight people who had, in the words of Kemal Kurspahic, come to "the saddest place in the saddest city in the whole world: . . . a market where there are no goods to sell and where there is no money to buy, and desperate people, old, women with children, unarmed civilians, search for things they haven't seen for almost two years."[1]

One and a half years ago a Bosnian set fire to his body in front of the British Parliament. There was little mention made of him. A year ago, a Croatian train on which I was traveling had to stop suddenly in the open because of a bitter rain of shells. A Serb from the Krajina region of Croatia was firing grenades at us from his vantage point on a hill almost two miles away. Nearby, an eleven-year-old child who had sought refuge under a pear tree with his family's cows was killed when the tree sustained a direct hit. I do not know his name. I only know that he died at one-half my current age, and that when, hunkered down in the cellar of an abandoned station, we heard the news of his death, the only lightbulb that worked flickered and died. These are the names that will not be remembered. These are the people who die every day.

Today, I am surrounded by friends to whom I can never quite explain how I feel about the war that is taking place. There is no explaining my anger when people talk about the "Bosnia situation" with woeful wags of their heads. Their horror at the televised scenes that enter daily into their living rooms is real. "But," a fellow student told me once, "there's nothing that can be done about it." In one sentence, millions of humans are given up for dead, and ignorance replaces feeling. He believes what he is fed each day by the media. "It is a quagmire." "... Age-old ethnic hatreds." "No one is innocent." The last, at least, is true. No one is innocent; not the people who watch the bodies of Sarajevo's children on their televisions or the United Nations High Command that will not protect the people about whom they devote numerous conferences, cease-fires, and status reports. Everyone has played a role, from those who kill to those who stand by and watch the killing with no effort at protest.

It is the reactions on college campuses that puzzle me most. Universities, once cradles of protest for a gentler planet, are silent. It is hard in some respects to fault them. We are taught from infancy to respect our elders and to bow to the wishes of our governments because we, as mere students and young people, cannot always discern with enough foresight which path of action will prove to be wisest. However, if we accept at face value the words of an authority figure, whether parent, teacher, or newscaster, our minds have failed to function as they should: individually. Time and again we are drilled against questioning authority.

In high school, we learn the difficult lesson of discipline. We learn, unfortunately, that it is often better not to question but to accept without complaint what we are told by those in powerful positions.

To challenge an irresponsible authority and to protect our fellow men and women in times of war or of peace, however, is the most important duty we have as members of the human race. While it is clear that no one can devote him- or herself at every moment to correcting all the world's ills, it is also clear that for every injustice there are individuals who cannot remain silent.

Sophie Scholl was twenty-two when she was executed for high treason in Germany during World War II. A member of the White Rose, a resistance group of students and professors, she distributed leaflets that urged resistance against the Nazi regime. The leaflets stressed what every German citizen could do both actively and passively to undermine the Third Reich. They found their way into the university hallways, into mailboxes, and onto the streets. They were transported from one German city to another, and redistributed. The third leaflet asks the German people, "Is your spirit already so crushed by abuse that you forget it is your right—or rather, your moral duty—to eliminate this system?" Sophie and the other students involved knew the penalties for their actions. Her father had already been interrogated by the Gestapo after unwisely voicing his true opinion of Hitler to a coworker, and all over Germany Jews and intellectuals had been rounded up. Mental institutions had been emptied, the patients murdered to purge any undesirable elements from the Aryan race.

Sophie Scholl was not a member of a wild band of mountain partisans, driven into the hills after the burning of her village. She was not a Jew or a Gypsy or a homosexual. A "nice girl" from a "nice family," she stood nothing to gain personally by her actions. The risks, on the other hand, would not have failed to leap grimly out at her each time she considered her predicament. The concentration camps where some members of the group would finish the last days of their "misbegotten" youth had been operating for years. She surely realized that the punishment for distributing the leaflets would very likely be death.

During 1942 and 1943, Berlin was seized by a feverish uncertainty. The flyers had appeared like the echoes of a long-suppressed conscience. The German people knew to varying degrees what had been happening, despite historical revisionists who claim ignorance. The flyers put into words what many were fearful of voicing themselves. Philosophers, poets, and statesmen from other times found their way into the pages of the leaflets. A passage from Goethe in the first leaflet reads:

> Now I find my good men
> Are gathered in the night,
> To wait in silence, not to sleep.
> And the glorious word of liberty
> They whisper and murmur,
> Till in unaccustomed strangeness,
> On the steps of our temple
> Once again in delight they cry:
> Freedom! Freedom!

Sophie Scholl and others listened and heard the call, making their way to the temple steps.

But when, finally, the threat was removed and the camps were liberated, Sophie Scholl was among millions who would not live to see liberty. The second leaflet states, "Here we see the most frightful crime against human dignity, a crime that is unparalleled in the whole of history."

The instinct for survival in humans is great, as is our overwhelming desire in times of difficulty to blend into the background and go about our own business of living, unnoticed. By not repeating evil and not referring to the realities of an evil time, people have repeatedly and throughout history argued their own warped innocence. The idea that as long as one directly does no evil, one cannot be held accountable for the evil happening around oneself is ingrained in the hearts of many "decent" people.

This, as Sophie Scholl and the other members of the White Rose wished to point out, is the greatest fallacy. Self-protection is important and above all else necessary, but never at the expense of others. When injustice manifests itself, there must be opposition, especially from those not directly threatened.

Else Gebels met Sophie Scholl in jail shortly before her execution in February 1943. In a letter to the memory of Sophie Scholl, she relates that Sophie had a dream in jail. On a sunny day she carried a child to be baptized. The path to the church, located on a mountain, was steep. A crevice in the mountain ice suddenly opened, and she lay the child on the side before plunging into darkness herself. She told Else Gebels, "The child in the white dress is our idea; it will prevail in spite of all obstacles. We were permitted to be pioneers, but we must die early for the sake of that idea."[2]

My grandmother Andjelka Brkic was widowed with two young sons in the early 1930s. At the age of twenty-one she relocated her family to Sarajevo. Young and beautiful, she was approached one day by a man on the street who introduced himself as Jozef Finzi. He had seen her walking alone on her errands and wanted to meet her. Over the next years, my grandmother and Jozef Finzi fell in love. When he was drafted into the army in the late 1930s, it was to her house that he first went on returning to the city.

There had been rumors of concentration camps and the widespread persecution of Jews in Germany before fighting ever began in then-Yugoslavia. The Jewish community in Sarajevo was not forced into a ghetto. Rather, the first Jews arrested were sent immediately on trains to die in concentration camps in other parts of Europe. Jozef, on returning to his city, did not even know if his family was still living or had been rounded up and deported.

In Sarajevo, news of roundups would occasionally leak to the Jewish community. Some were able to escape, forewarned. Jozef's family was not so lucky: on the day that Sarajevo police came to arrest his family, only he was able to escape over the rooftops and through the city to my grandmother's house, as his parents were arrested. They were deported and died, we think, at Dachau.

At the time that Sophie Scholl was engaged in active protest in Germany, my grandmother was concerned with hiding Jozef and keeping her two sons safe. More than this would be asked from her, however, in the coming years of war. Her apartment became a sanctuary for many people seeking refuge in the next two years. Jozef wanted to stay as long as he could, helping friends and what members of his family still remained to escape. His plan was to then join the partisans until he could live freely again in Sarajevo.

My father remembers one night when the police came for their friends and neighbors, the Montiljos. This night, luckily, they and many others had been warned that roundups were imminent. My father tells us how their apartment had been filled with almost thirty Jews who had known to come to my grandmother's apartment for safety. They had listened to the pounding and angry words of the policemen who, on realizing that their quarry had slipped through their fingers, had ransacked the Montiljos' apartment. Huddled in silence, the people down the hall had breathed a sigh of relief when the police finally gave up and left the building.

Jozef Finzi died at Jasenovac concentration camp in the final days of the war. My father remembers the day they came to arrest him, tipped off by an informer. Jozef had been alone in the apartment with my uncle, who was at that time only eleven. My father and grandmother arrived as they were leading him away, and Jozef asked that they forgive him and told them that he loved them. Two years later, he was shot against the barbed-wire fence at Jasenovac, something my grandmother never knew and that my father learned later from Nela, Jozef's only surviving sister.

My grandmother was imprisoned, and my father and his younger brother lived with Serbian neighbors who cared for them until her release. The case prosecutor, who came from the same small village in Herzegovina as my grandmother, advised her to lie to the court. She told them that she had rented a room to Jozef, unaware of his activities. When I was younger, I knew that the mere mention of those times made my father very sad.

In the seventh grade my school class read *The Diary of Anne Frank*, and I began to understand the Holocaust through the words of a girl who at my age had been forced to abandon her bicycle and school friends for a dusty attic and imminent death.

Because my father could explain confusing things in words digestible to me, I asked him about Anne Frank and what had happened in the war. This, however, was something he could not explain in calm and logical terms. He could not assure me that the actors didn't die and that demons didn't exist, as he had for horror movies. This was, he tried to tell us, as real a reality as our own family.

Little by little, and spread over years, my father began to relate the passage of the war in his childhood. There was no meat, and they all grew thin. They had to run for the mountains when the heavy bombing began. Jozef Finzi had lived with them in their apartment. Jozef Finzi had died.

In the mythology of my family, Andjelka and Jozef have risen to measurements larger than life. At some point in childhood, my image of her took the form of a picture of Athena that I had seen in a picture book of mythology. My grandmother, motivated by her love for Jozef and her desire to rage against the injustice of her time, made a clear decision: at great risk to herself, she, like Sophie Scholl, realized that it would be impossible to stand by and do nothing. Currently, the same city in which my grandmother experienced her joys and sadnesses is dying.

Sarajevo faces a third winter in which all of the trees have already been burned for heat and in which Serbian shelling and sniping disappears for days and weeks, only to return with greater force. Concentration camps continue to function in parts of Bosnia. Women are raped and forcibly impregnated. Entire villages are wiped out.

"Ethnic cleansing" is a most pristine term for death. It does not begin to denote the pain caused. It does serve, however, to make the destruction more digestible for Western audiences. They can speak of death and rape in abstract terms. "Ethnic cleansing" removes responsibility from the West's arena: we need not act if the crimes have been overexaggerated. Ethnic cleansing certainly does not sound criminal.

The responsibility of the individual in this conflict is as important, however, as it was in World War II. One problem, however, is our removal from the situation. Sophie Scholl was dealing with the Germany she knew. She was trying to bring about change for her people, in the only country in which she had ever lived. My grandmother had no other recourse than to help Jozef and his family.

Although she made the decision to help him, it was not really a decision: it would have been unthinkable, and even unnatural, for her to turn away the one she loved. She sheltered him even at the risk of her own family. Sophie Scholl died during the war. My grandmother died in the 1960s. Although they acted "heroically," it is wrong to label them thusly. They were human beings who tried to bring humanity into their sphere. They did not ask for accolades and certainly received none in their lifetime.

There is, I think, a great problem in modern humanity: larger-than-life figures such as Oskar Schindler and Sophie Scholl are admired in almost disembodied ways. The general public tells itself, "I could never be that selfless." Or worse, "This is a dog-eat-dog world. If you risk yourself, you may end up like Sophie Scholl." And however brave and noble she was, she died at twenty-two.

It is, however, the responsibility of every individual to speak out. Protest is something that is far more foreign in today's society than it should be. The American media, purposely or accidentally, obfuscates the war in the former Yugoslavia. The American government has spent the last four years giving lip-service to the poor, besieged city of Sarajevo. The United Nations has maintained a low profile in the same four years, except when turning back Sarajevo's residents across the airport tarmac, so that they could be shot right in front of them.

Individuals read about the war in their morning papers. They mourn the dead on the brisk walk to the car, forgetting the war completely as they drive to work. The images of broken children, camp prisoners, and old women forced to cower in dirty bunkers as shells fall around them have failed to make an impression. The individuals in the world are tired of hearing about Bosnia-Herzegovina, as if it were a miniseries that had outstayed its welcome on syndicated television. It is time to move on, they seem to say, to more pressing and relevant issues.

At this moment, someone in Bosnia is dying. They are turning their eyes to the sky, where NATO warplanes turn their underbellies to the suffering going on below. They are dying before their time, remembering the Bosnia-Herzegovina that I also knew. Somewhere else, if humanity has not fallen farther into darkness and immunity to suffering, there is, perhaps, a group of individuals thinking, what is to be done? Kurt Huber, another member of the White Rose, believed: "Perhaps we shall succeed in shaking off the common tyranny in the final hour and together with the other people of Europe in recognizing in that hour a wonderful moment for building up a new humane world in which the nations and states will feel themselves to be neighbors and not enemies."[3] Perhaps we will also succeed in driving back the darkness in Bosnia-Herzegovina and recognize that hour to signal the advent of a humane world where men and women are brothers and sisters, and the safe will speak out for the imperiled.

Notes

1. Kemal Kurspahic, "The Saddest City," *Washington Post,* February 9, 1994.
2. Inge Scholl, *The White Rose* (Frankfurt: Frankfurter Hefte, 1952).
3. Mary Gallin, *German Resistance to Hitler* (Washington, DC: Catholic University of America Press, 1955), 21.

The Secret of Redemption

Memory and Resistance

ALEXA R. KOLBI-MOLINAS
2000
Smith College

In February 1948, Communist leader Klement
Gottwald stepped out on the balcony of a
Baroque palace in Prague to address the
hundreds of thousands of his fellow citizens
packed into Old Town Square. It was a crucial moment in Czech history—a fateful moment of the kind that occurs once or twice in
a millennium.

Gottwald was flanked by his comrades,
with Clementis standing next to him.

There were snow flurries, it was cold, and
Gottwald was bareheaded. The solicitous
Clementis took off his own fur cap and set it
on Gottwald's head.

The Party propaganda section put out
hundreds of thousands of copies of a photograph of that balcony with Gottwald, a fur
cap on his head and comrades at his side,
speaking to the nation. On that balcony the
history of Communist Czechoslovakia was
born. Every child knew the photograph from
posters, schoolbooks, and museums.

Four years later Clementis was charged
with treason and hanged. The propaganda
section immediately airbrushed him out of
history, and obviously, out of all the photo-
graphs as well. Ever since, Gottwald has stood
on that balcony alone. Where Clementis once
stood, there is only bare palace wall. All that
remains of Clementis is the cap on Gottwald's
head.

It is 1971, and Mirek says that the struggle
of man against power is the struggle of memory against forgetting.

—Milan Kundera, *The Book of Laughter and
Forgetting*

THE OPENING PASSAGE OF Milan Kundera's book *The Book of Laughter and Forgetting* (1979) demonstrates the absolute power but also the
absolute fallibility of totalitarian rule. At the root of this political and
psychological paradox is the persistence of memory. Yet given what we
know of Stalin and his legacy, how can I suggest that a system whose
very nature is so violently methodical be considered fallible? The totalitarian state surely knows no bounds on its own behavior, knows respect
for no authority other than its own—where, then, is its weakness? Its
weakness, Kundera reveals, lies in the fact that in a system fortified by
the absence of alternate and dissident thought, that is all that is needed
to topple it. Its undoing is Clementis's hat.

According to Kundera's account, the Czech Communist Party im-
mortalized Clementis, reproduced his picture by the thousands, and
inundated a nation with the image. Only four years later Clementis's
immortality was revoked; he was hanged as a traitor, and his past, as well
as his present and future, was erased. Kundera's selection of this story is
key. It is reflective of the central purpose of totalitarianism: to change,

and control, the very nature and direction of humanity. More important, however, the passage is indicative of the essence of totalitarianism—the pursuit of a goal that, although destructive and even murderous in its means, is unattainable in the end. In terms of power, the neutralization of resistance, and the command of history, Clementis's hat is emblematic of totalitarianism's failure.

Once revealed, the totalitarian's reign is irrevocably undermined. In losing control of the past, its hold on the present and future is doomed. This can be of little comfort to those, like Clementis, who suffer during terror's reign, but the understanding is crucial. Humanity is far more complex than totalitarianism either allows or expects it to be. "Memory," Hans Buchheim explains in *Totalitarian Rule: Its Nature and Characteristics*, "can help us enormously not to overestimate the danger in the long run, and especially not to feel that we are involved in a lost cause. We are not confronting a monster that is destined and in a position, through inner necessity or as a consequence of historical development, to devour us sooner or later."[1] The absolute state has absolute power in that its influence is both morally and ethically limitless, but it is fallible because its objective can never be realized.

Memory, recognizing the significance of the past and the fluidity of history, is this state's greatest weakness and the people's most powerful weapon. The Baal Shem-Tov said that "in remembrance lies the secret to redemption."[2] Although this essay focuses primarily on totalitarian systems, memory exists as the greatest threat to all repression and the greatest universal obstacle to atrocity and genocide. Through Heda Kovaly's autobiography, *Under a Cruel Star: Life in Prague, 1941–1968*, we are able to understand in greater depth the atmosphere evoked by Kundera. We are offered, in Kovaly, a prime example of how the commitment to individual memory facilitates resistance. Similarly, we also learn of the adverse impacts of a deficient national memory, one that does not adequately reflect history or the individual memory of its peoples; for where totalitarianism seeks to narrowly define and limit human existence, memory enables us to retain our complexity and freedom.

As the twentieth century comes to a close, we are presented with a profoundly depressing list of mass atrocities, gross human rights violations, and incidents of extraordinary evil. The struggle of memory against forgetting is the struggle to reclaim humanity, but it does not end once the reign of terror has fallen. In *Lest Innocent Blood Be Shed: The Story of the Village of Le Chambon and How Goodness Happened There,* by Philip Hallie, it becomes clear that even after the fall of a repressive regime, memory remains a crucial part of the healing process. Using the story of a small French village that resisted the Nazis and exhibited an ethical code that was by far the exception to the rule during that time, Hallie demonstrates the importance of the study of courageous behavior and how this memory can redeem our faith in the power of goodness over evil. Together, Kovaly and Hallie present a compelling precedent for the twenty-first century to follow: remembrance and, through remembrance, redemption.

Individual and National Memory

Totalitarianism does not take hold of a nation overnight. Its power feeds on the growing powerlessness of the people—a certain degree of mass bewilderment and passivity, certain negative rather than positive states of the mass mind are required.[3] It is the election of either memory or forgetting that determines the direction, either positive or negative, of a country's collective mentality. While memory forces a confrontation with a possibly uncomfortable past, forgetting permits an individual to look the other way and disregard all that is problematic and troubling.

When individual denial and the suppression of memory occur on a large enough scale, the negative mindset of totalitarianism is born. And when an individual becomes committed to memory, resistance to totalitarianism is born.

In *Under a Cruel Star,* Heda Kovaly describes the insidious takeover of Czechoslovakia by the Czech Communist Party and the party's
subsequent shift to dogmatic Stalinism. In doing so she also documents
the struggle of memory against forgetting and of her own battle for survival. Through each phase of communism (the idealistic rise to power,
the paranoid and ruthless purges, and the self-destructive decline),
Kovaly retained an understanding of truth amid its many mutations.
Although this inner strength did not protect her from persecution, it
ultimately saved her from dehumanization.

Kovaly, an escapee from the concentration camps, returned to
Prague to participate in its triumphant liberation from Nazi Germany in
1945. Once the excitement of freedom faded, however, she, like other
Czech people, was troubled by her memories of Nazi occupation. "We
were, we thought, burdened with obsolete ideas, prejudices, weak-
nesses," explains Kovaly. "Why had we surrendered to Hitler? Why
had we allowed ourselves to be locked up in concentration camps and
prisons?"[4] These were hard questions to ask, let alone answer, as they
challenged the strong liberal traditions of Czech culture. "The war had
uprooted everything we thought we knew about life, people, history,
ourselves. . . . We had listened with only half an ear when our history
teachers discussed torture or the persecution of innocent people. Those
things could only have happened a long time ago, in the dark ages.
When it happened in our time and in a form far worse than we could
imagine, it felt like the end of the world. It seemed to us that we were
witnessing a total break in the evolution of mankind, the complete collapse of man as a rational being."[5]

The loss of personal and national identity was devastating. The
need to rationalize Hitler's rise to power was overwhelming the need
to understand it. In effect, it was this initial suppression of memory,
this refusal to look closely at the deep-rooted fears, hatreds, and prejudices that allowed for the atrocities of Nazi rule, which led to the emergence of the Czech Communist Party. Conversely, it was at this juncture

that Kovaly's enduring sense of memory led to the appearance of her resistance.

For many, the party returned the confidence that the experiences of the war had destroyed. For Kovaly, however, it seemed too easy. "They offered such clear and simple answers to the most complicated questions," she writes, "that I kept feeling there had to be a mistake somewhere."[6] Kovaly distrusted the ideological conversion that many of her peers underwent. Again, Kovaly found it too simple, a misrepresentation of the recent events that had so affected her life. "I was unable to take the advice of people who kept telling me that the only way back to life was to forget. I wanted to say everything, to cover up nothing, to pretty up nothing, to keep things inside me the way they had been, and to live with them. I wanted to live because I was alive, not just because by some accident I was not dead."[7]

Unfortunately, others were not strong enough to reject the party line, and Czech society experienced a subtle but decisive change. Although her husband's high-ranking position gave Kovaly status within the regime, Kovaly's psychological distance from the party afforded her perspective. When one of her husband's colleagues told him, "I consider you a good friend. But if I ever found out you had done anything to hurt the Party, I'd turn against you in a minute and do my best to make you pay for it," she was convinced of the transformation taking place.[8] "When ideology takes the front seat, human relations are pushed aside," she explains. "When every action and thought is geared to the building of a new society, there is little room left for feelings."[9]

To be sure, by 1951 all feelings except the feelings of loyalty to the state were swept aside as the Stalinization of the Czech party reached its height. Soviet advisers were charged to purge party ranks, and Kovaly urged her husband to resign his position as soon as possible. Refusing to stop and recognize where the regime was headed, Rudolf Kovaly clung to the idealism of the original party program.

As the intensity of the arrests increased, Kovaly's memory again began to haunt her even more. "Doesn't it seem strange to you," she asked her husband, "that so many of the people who are being arrested are Jews?"[10] Her husband's response was one of anger and incredulity. Sadly, Rudolf was too dependent on communist dogma and party truths by this point to notice the repetition of history.

Kovaly, however, through her devotion to memory, was removed from the artificiality that dominated Czech society—her conscience did not depend on endorsing it.

Eventually Rudolf, too, was arrested. Kovaly's account of the infamous Slansky trials, within which her husband was implicated, reveals the extent to which the party had been able to shape its members' memories at will. Lisa London, whose husband was on trial with Rudolf, wrote of the man with whom she had lived for sixteen years, raised children, and fought against Nazis in the French Resistance, "I lived with a traitor." Thomas Frejka, the sixteen-year-old son of another defendant, Ludvik Frejka, wrote in a letter to the editor: "I demand that my father receive the highest penalty, the death sentence . . . and it is my wish that this letter be read to him."[11] Even Rudolf's testimony, broadcast on national radio, reflected the power of totalitarian influence. As his confession unfolded, Kovaly realized that "he was simply reciting something he had memorized. A few times he stopped short, as though he were trying to remember his lines, and then he started up again, like a robot."

> How could they have forced him to such testimony,
> my Rudolf who had never, in all the years I had
> known him, ever lied about anything? How could
> they have made him vilify his parents, who had been
> murdered in Auschwitz? What had he suffered be-
> fore he broke down? How had they crushed him?
> At one point I heard Rudolf's voice say that he had

> been trained in espionage in London when, of
> course, he had spent the entire war as a prisoner in
> German concentration camps.[12]

Totalitarian regimes have no respect for the past. It can only be a tool for furthering their future. The party had used Rudolf's talents and skills as an economic adviser for years, but when they were no longer profitable, he was eliminated. A mere execution would not have been enough, however. Not only must the totalitarian state excise the past, but also it must first render it excisable. According to the state, Rudolf's existence, as it was with many others, was malleable and disposable. But for Kovaly the memory of her husband's life and the circumstances of his death could not be modified. Like Clementis's hat, she maintained the memory of his innocence within her.

After Stalin's death in 1953, the grip of the totalitarian communist state faltered. The figurehead of totalitarianism had fallen and with it the totality of its control. Throughout the Soviet Bloc political prisoners were suddenly, and quietly, being released. The three men tried with Rudolf who had been given life sentences instead of death were among those released and rehabilitated. That same year Kovaly was summoned to the Central Committee in Prague.

In typical totalitarian doublespeak, the party attempted to camouflage its past crimes with benevolence. Kovaly was allowed to read a paragraph from a larger volume stating: "The innocence of Rudolf Margolius has been established beyond a shadow of a doubt. He did not in any way harm the interests of the State. On the contrary, a thorough review of his case has concluded that he fulfilled his duties in an exemplary manner. Had his proposals and plans been implemented, our national economy would have reaped considerable benefits."[13]

"Comrade Jerman looked beseechingly at me," Kovaly relates. "Surely such a generous retraction would soften my heart." However, when Kovaly demanded an appropriate remedy, one that reflected the severity of their mistake—an investigation into the accusations leveled against her husband and their public refutation, along with a public investigation into the methods through which his confession had been obtained—it was clear that the party had no intention of officially reforming state history. Still, empowered by their now obvious fear of the truth, Kovaly refused to concede her memories to the party in exchange for a backward apology. "You can keep your rehabilitation," she told them. "The truth will come out. Just wait, you can't prevent it. And then you'll have to account for this too. I've waited eleven years. I can wait a few more."[14]

When Kovaly was offered compensation by the Ministry of Social Welfare, her response was similar. "You murdered my husband. You threw me out of every job I had. You had me thrown out of a hospital! You threw us out of our apartment and into a hovel where only by some miracle we did not die. You ruined my son's childhood! And now you think you can compensate for that with a few crowns? That you can buy me off? Keep me quiet?"[15]

"It is astounding how terrified such men of action are of words," Kovaly recalls. "No act is too sordid for them to carry out, no act disturbs their sleep, so long as it is not called by its proper name, so long as it is not put into words. In this lies the great power of words, which are the only weapons of the defenseless."[16] Kovaly's memory had endured through years of abuse, and now that her abusers were weakening, her memory gave her additional courage.

In fact, the cracks in the totalitarian regime were soon releasing pieces of memory and truth beyond the party's liking. In 1968 the Soviet Union invaded Prague in order to reestablish control. Psychologically, however, communist ideology had lost the ability to dominate. The reemergence of memory had given authority and autonomy to the people who had once allowed totalitarianism to do their thinking for them. "During the invasion," Kovaly writes, "when we lost everything, we found something that people in our world hardly dare to hope for ourselves and each other. In all those faces, in all those eyes, I saw that we all thought and felt alike, that we all strove for the same things. Prague resisted in every way it could."[17] Where once the lack of memory had allowed for totalitarian rule, Czechoslovakia now responded with an arsenal of memories. Although they could not stop the tanks, the seeds of rebellion had been planted. "The spell under which the Soviets had held many die hard true believers was broken for good. There would be no more illusions, no more self-deception about the nature of Big Brother. The grim reign of ideology was over."[18]

In 1993, after the overthrow of Soviet occupation, former political prisoner and current president of the Czech Republic Vaclav Havel echoed Kovaly's sentiments. "It is astonishing to discover how," he said, "after decades of falsified history and ideological manipulation nothing has been forgotten." Maintaining individual memory within a society that seeks to institute a very singular and restricted vision demands an enormous amount of personal strength. But it also, invariably, feeds that strength. Heda Kovaly's memory of World War II and the Holocaust prevented her from becoming an inadvertent conspirator in the totalitarian/communist takeover of her country.

The memory of her husband's illegal trial and execution sustained her when party repression was at its worst, giving her cause for resistance when surrender and even death would have been easier. Finally, once the limitations of the state became evident, Kovaly was prepared to avail herself of its every weakness in order to assert the truth of her memories. Notably, she was not alone. Luisa Passerni writes in "Don't Forget: Fragments of a Negative Tradition," that "memory—or better: memories—can help us to find ways, in the era of equality and cosmopolitanism, to participate in the other, to share his/her being other."[19] The appearance of individual memory on a national scale unified Czechoslovakia—a country on whose divisiveness totalitarianism had once thrived. Even though the country was punished with a military invasion, an ideological one had been rendered obsolete.

Totalitarianism would no longer enjoy the same measure of supremacy as it once had. The mass revival of individual memory had permanently altered the dynamics of the struggle. The struggle of man against power, as Kundera termed it, was an inevitable victory now that the battle of memory against forgetting had been won.

International Memory

In the prelude to his book *Lest Innocent Blood Be Shed: The Story of the Village of Le Chambon and How Goodness Happened There,* Philip Hallie describes how he came to study and write about a small village of French Protestants who saved five thousand Jews from the Vichy government in southern France. Before he stumbled on the story of Le Chambon, Hallie was a professor of philosophy, and a former World War II gunner, who focused his life on a study of cruelty.

> Across all these studies, the pattern of the strong crushing the weak kept repeating itself and repeating itself, so that when I was not bitterly angry, I was bored at the repetition of the patterns of persecution. When I was not desiring to be cruel with the cruel, I was a monster—like, perhaps, many others around me—who could look upon torture and death without a shudder, and who therefore looked upon life without a belief in its preciousness. My study of evil incarnate had become a prison whose bars were my bitterness toward the violent, and whose walls were my horrified indifference to slow murder. Between the bars and the walls I revolved like a madman. Reading about the damned I was damned myself, as damned as the murderers, and as damned as their victims. Somehow over the years I had dug

myself into Hell, and I had forgotten redemption,
had forgotten the possibility of escape.[20]

For Hallie, if only such evil things were possible, then life was too
heavy a burden for him. "The lies I would have to tell my children in
order to raise them in hope—which children need the way plants need
sunlight—would make the burden unbearable," he writes.[21] Without
hope, both children and adults are susceptible to helplessness. A hopeless and helpless populace is a dictator's dream. Once helplessness is
secured within us, action, especially that which puts oneself at risk,
seems a useless endeavor. We lose the resources with which to fight.
Thus even with memory and even with a heightened understanding of
the processes of evil, great crimes will be repeated because few will have
the strength to stop them.

When we remember horror it is essential, then, that we remember
the goodness that was marshaled against it, no matter if it was the exception to the rule, no matter that the "moral brilliance" of a few "does not
light up the darkness . . . as much as it makes that vast darkness seem
darker by contrast."[22] The comparison of evil and good, when evil is
so great and goodness so small, can be a depressing and disheartening
one. But memories of goodness also include the following: they teach us
that just as evil does not appear out of nowhere it also is not avoided
automatically. Instead, it is avoided by conscious decision, by deliberate
choice among competing priorities.[23] It is only with this understanding
that within memory lies redemption.

Hitlers rely on the degradation of humanity. If the Jews were less
than human, it was easy to round them up and allow them to die in the
inhuman conditions of the concentration camps. The people of Le
Chambon remind us that all people, even a precious few, are worth
saving, even at great personal risk. Hallie had devoted himself to a study
of cruelty because he was determined to understand the ordinary processes of extraordinary evil. Hallie strove to never forget but in doing so

was unable to remember goodness and how evil was fought; he saw only its existence and was understandably numbed. The story of Le Chambon and others like it force its students to remember goodness and the limits of evil. Writes Hallie, "I needed this understanding to redeem myself—and possibly others—from the coercion of despair."[24]

It has already been shown that individual and national memory are integral pieces of resistance and survival. On an international level, memory is essential to motivating future resistance. Remembering cruelty and evil in those terms is an important first step—it gives credence to those who were victimized and identifies the guilty. But if the people who attempted to stop cruelty and evil are not remembered as well, then it is more likely that the negative mindsets of state terror will emerge again.

In considering what specific actions must be taken to prevent the twenty-first century from repeating the mistakes of the past, I could write pages and pages more than I already have. I am content to say here only that without memory at its heart, any and every human rights policy will inevitably fail. In her article "Don't Forget: Fragments of a Negative Tradition," Renate Siebert asks: "Is it possible to skip recent history, the history in which our mothers and fathers were protagonists—because it is rotten—and connect to previous traditions? I do not think so. Can 'not forgetting' become an uncomfortable, yet living, radical and accepting tradition? I believe so."[25] The questions Siebert poses are central to this essay. In Heda Kovaly's memoirs we find that a shortage of individual and national memory invites the mindlessness, and brutality, of totalitarian rule.

Fortunately, we also find that in memory exists the key to courageous resistance. International memory presents a challenge to the greater world community. We, too, have a responsibility to remember because the implications of all repression—the Holocaust, ethnic cleansing, and genocide—are universal. Without the development of memories of courageous resistance alongside the bad, then extraordinary evil may remain unchecked in the future. The knowledge that goodness exists and that it is successful counteracts evil's influence. In Philip Hallie's account of the village of Le Chambon, the existence and power of goodness are demonstrated. More important, in the act of recording the story of Le Chambon, Hallie demonstrates the potential of its memory.

There are many who would argue, however, that memory effects a prison in the past. These people believe that memory is too easily turned into an obsession, an obsession that leads to vengeance and violence. They contend that reconciliation and progress depend on letting go. History proves otherwise. The legacy of the twentieth century alone shows us that remembering is a constant process and one that ensures both mourning and healing. Thus, to stand in the way of memory is to stand in the way of progress. The collective histories of the Czech Republic and of Le Chambon illustrate in real-life terms that memory is in fact at the heart of goodness and the resistance of and battle against evil.

Clearly, memory is both a unifying and empowering social agent in all societies. Undeniably, the struggle of people against power will not be complete absent the victory of memory over forgetting.

Notes

1. Hans Buchheim, *Totalitarian Rule: Its Nature and Characteristics* (Middletown, CT: Wesleyan University Press, 1968), 109.
2. Philip Hallie, *Lest Innocent Blood Be Shed: The Story of the Village of Le Chambon and How Goodness Happened There* (New York: Harper Perennial, 1994), 6.
3. George F. Kennan, "Totalitarianism in the Modern World," in *Totalitarianism,* ed. Carl J. Friedrich (Cambridge, MA: Harvard University Press, 1964), 23.
4. Heda Margolius Kovaly, *Under a Cruel Star: Life in Prague, 1941–1963* (New York: Penguin, 1986), 63.

5. Kovaly, *Under a Cruel Star*, 64.

6. Kovaly, *Under a Cruel Star*, 55.

7. Kovaly, *Under a Cruel Star*, 72.

8. Kovaly, *Under a Cruel Star*, 81.

9. Kovaly, *Under a Cruel Star*, 81.

10. Kovaly, *Under a Cruel Star*, 103.

11. Kovaly, *Under a Cruel Star*, 139.

12. Kovaly, *Under a Cruel Star*, 141.

13. Kovaly, *Under a Cruel Star*, 171.

14. Kovaly, *Under a Cruel Star*, 173.

15. Kovaly, *Under a Cruel Star*, 175.

16. Kovaly, *Under a Cruel Star*, 169.

17. Kovaly, *Under a Cruel Star*, 191.

18. Kovaly, *Under a Cruel Star*, 191.

19. Luisa Passerni, "Introduction," *International Yearbook of Oral History and Life Stories*, Vol. 1: *Memory and Totalitarianism*, ed. Luisa Passerni (Oxford: Oxford University Press, 1992), ii.

20. Hallie, *Lest Innocent Blood Be Shed*, 2.

21. Hallie, *Lest Innocent Blood Be Shed*, 7.

22. Hallie, *Lest Innocent Blood Be Shed*, xiii.

23. Fred E. Katz, *Ordinary People and Extraordinary Evil: A Report on the Beguilings of Evil* (Albany, NY: SUNY Press, 1993), 14.

24. Hallie, *Lest Innocent Blood Be Shed*, 12.

25. Renate Siebert, "Don't Forget: Fragments of a Negative Tradition," in Passerni, *Memory and Totalitarianism*, 167.

Memory, Loss, and Revitalizing Democracy
The Mothers of Plaza del Mayo

TRACY KE
2006
Duke University

We still Sing, We still ask. We still dream. We
still wait.... In spite of the blows aimed at our
lives by the resourcefulness of hatred that
banished our loved ones into oblivion....

Make them tell us where they have hidden
the flower that used to adorn the streets, living out a destiny. Where, where have they
gone?

—Victor Heredia

Disappear: To cease to appear to be visible;
to vanish from sight. To cease to be present,
to depart; to pass from existence, pass away,
be lost.

—*Oxford English Dictionary*

EVERY THURSDAY AFTERNOON at 3:30 pm, the Mothers of the Plaza
de Mayo march in front of the Argentine presidential palace. They cover
their heads with white handkerchiefs, embroidered with the names of
their *disappeared* sons and daughters. The Mothers, who first came to
the square as housewives searching for their lost loved ones, have created a political space for themselves as activists, confounding the Argentine government with their persistent unmasking of the truth behind

its contrived political facade. What began as a private work of mourning has transfigured the corpses of the *disappeared* into epochal emblems, the unresolved reminder of a messianic energy that refuses to be subdued.[1] Through the Mothers, the imperative to mourn the dead has indeed become living energy, which, like Walter Benjamin's angel of history, looks back at the pile of debris, ruins, and defeats of the past in an effort to redeem them. Their work is shaped by a sensitivity toward memory and time, for in the aftermath of war and military totalitarianism, the most powerful voice threatens to be that of forgetfulness. Their presence represents an insistence on engaging the past so that they might seize hold of a reminiscence as it flashes up in a moment of danger,[2] such danger being represented today by the attempts of the Argentine government to draw a veil over the Dirty War. Not only do the Mothers resist forgetfulness, but their resistance has blossomed into a political theory that addresses loss as central to revitalizing liberal society. The Mothers offer a vision of utopia as a living, participatory democracy whereby totalizing structures are countered by dissidence and dialogue.

The promised utopia under constitutional government, the Mothers argue, is impossible without the remembrance of the country's dystopic past. It is imperative that the *disappeared* be made *reappeared* within the realm of the political, for if they are banished into the blind spots of history, so too is any hope of realized utopia for Argentina.

Beyond Forgetfulness

We make the road by walking.
—Antonio Machado

The literary theorist Idelber Avelar noted that the "neo-liberalism implemented in the aftermath of dictatorship is founded on a passive forgetting of its barbaric origins."[3] How then, can one use memory to incorporate a dystopic reality into the march toward utopia? The Mothers have embraced this challenge and provided an answer. In the dialectic of triumph and defeat, they have, as an organization, allegorized what survives of the defeated and given voice to those who feel alienated from political structures impervious to their needs. In an effort to reveal the disappearances the junta tried so hard to erase from memory, the Mothers march in weekly processions, wearing white masks and white handkerchiefs to represent the silenced conscience of the *disappeared*. They demonstrate in the streets of Argentina, joined by young students and international human rights activists alike, demanding the return of their sons and daughters. They engage the international community, writing and publishing their own newspaper, *Madres de la Plaza de Mayo,* and appealing to the United Nations for answers. The Mothers have created an alternative space for remembrance and solidarity through their radical, often impetuous politics. It is a politics that refuses to be alienated at the same time that it refuses centripetal power. Marguerite Guzman Bouvard, whose book *Revolutionizing Motherhood* illuminates many of the themes presented in this essay, details their struggle: "Because they were not admitted into the chambers of governmental power, they claimed the geography of dissent, the Plaza de Mayo, where Argentina proclaimed its independence from Spain in 1816. . . . In defiance of a regime that caused people to retreat into their homes, they take to the open spaces of streets and parks, shouting the truth in a country rendered mute by fear."[4] In doing so, the Mothers challenged centered discourse and centered power to be hospitable to truth and memory; they became "vehicles of the political" against a government reflexively concerned with its own existence.

From Vocation to Invocation

But what of invocation, of that which signified that something irreplaceable has gone,

> perhaps fled or been rendered ineffectual,
> with the result that the world has been dimin-
> ished? What is at stake is not mere recogni-
> tion of loss, but how one works through it.
> —Sheldon Wolin, "Political Theory: From
> Vocation to Invocation"

The Mothers of the Plaza de Mayo was born in 1977 into a nation torn asunder by terror and violence. Their voices resounded with a special urgency precisely because such voices had never been heard in Argentine politics. "These women came out of the shadows, out of a cultural, historical and social invisibility, and into the center of the political arena to challenge a repressive government."[5] The disappearance of a son or daughter was a devastating personal tragedy for the Mothers, one that undermined the familial space, the very foundation of Argentine society.

Searching for their children at police stations, hospitals, and army barracks proved fruitless, long days of waiting answered by a disappointing "Come back tomorrow." But these women stubbornly refused to forget the injustice done to their children and became "self-proclaimed custodians of a history of terror and oppression."[6] By invoking remembrance, the Mothers revealed the power of truth against the grain of premeditated, protean, and ultimately vacuous government. By illuminating the disjunctive, the Mothers defied their identities as victims. Instead, as Bouvard points out, they spoke out truth to the world, claiming what Vaclav Havel called the *power of powerlessness*. Without the reassurances of power, status, or education, these women bravely inherited the call of a different kind of revolution.

Similarly, the political theorist Sheldon Wolin wrote of invocation as a response to a certain kind of loss. Invocation is associated with *recalling*, and its genealogy suggests that some time is *missing*—an appeal to that which has departed. Wolin was very much concerned with how to memorialize loss theoretically. He was worried that, in a culture that measures life by such notions as progress, development, innovation, and modernization, loss tends to be an experience we are advised to *get past*. Echoing Havel, Wolin wrote, "Loss belongs to history, while politics and life are about what is still to be done. Perhaps it is that loss is related to power and powerlessness and hence has a claim upon theory."[7]

Before the Dirty War, the Mothers simply embraced a vocation as home keepers and family guardians. But the move from "mother" to "Mother" would be instantaneous once these women chose to reclaim their children from the junta. They would have a claim upon invocation once they decided that they would not allow their children to disappear from memory. In the beginning, the Mothers simply marched counterclockwise along the plaza, interrupting the unquestioned sphere of dominance at the seat of Argentinean governance. Slowly, they grew bolder, holding up white cardboard figures of their children's bodies, the physicality of which had been so brutally destroyed. Once separated from their proscribed vocations, society would scorn them, treat them as social pariahs. The government, growing ever more fearful of their influence, terrorized anyone who associated with the Mothers. By the end of the junta, three of the fourteen founding Mothers had *disappeared* themselves. Their offices would be ravaged numerous times. In one particularly brutal instance, policemen on horseback attacked the Mothers in the middle of a march with iron chains. But these women refused to disband, for they had suddenly become something more than singular mothers—they entered into the realm of the political that had rendered them invisible for so long. By recalling the cross-grained ideologies of their children, they moved from vocation to invocation by discovering vocation's conscience.

These women did not forsake their vocations as individual mothers, but they transfigured that solitary occupation, so lonely and powerless in the aftermath of the disappearances, into a process of collective recovery. Their courage in not only recognizing loss but working through it on a political stage is what makes them revolutionary.

The Disappeared

The Argentine government has long tried to erase the memory of the Dirty War, characterizing the disappeared as dangerous dissidents and violent subversives. The government-controlled media tried to convey a sense of guilt among families of the disappeared by a barrage of slogans, such as "How did you bring up your child?" or "They must have been mixed up in something."[8] As Bouvard would write, "The junta intended to create a link between political dissidence and social deviance in public opinion and isolate the families of the disappeared."[9]

While there were in fact extremist groups during the rise of the junta, many of the disappeared were university students, community organizers, and young professionals who had no clear political affiliations but who were strongly motivated to improve the lot of the forgotten and the misunderstood. These young activists sought to *reappear* life in a country morbidly closing in on itself through their passion for change, whether that meant teaching kindergarten in a shantytown or organizing laborers to demand cleaner drinking water. They were social reformers who wished to create far-reaching change.

In March 1976, the triumvirate of General Jorge Rafael Videla, Admiral Emilio Eduardo Massera, and General Orlando Agosti formed an alliance that would overthrow the last vestiges of the Peronist government in Argentina. They would suspend congress and install their own supreme court appointees. The military junta banned all political parties and political activities; interest groups would no longer have any say in policy making. Union leaders were imprisoned, and labor strikes would be met with military force. The new ruling militia viewed all forms of alternative solidarities, however passive, as subversion. "It put out the

doctrine of ideological borders, assigning the military the task of pre-
serving the 'moral and ideological health of the nation.' . . . Task forces
were created to capture and interrogate all members of suspect organizations, their sympathizers, associates, and anyone else who might oppose the government."[10] The military junta aimed to protect what it
called Western civilization, and its definition of the enemy was "omi-
nously and deliberately loose."[11] Under the semblance of normalcy,
thousands of people were dragged from their homes, their places of
work, and the streets by plainclothesmen in fleets of unmarked cars.
"Their families and friends were hurled into a limbo of terror and nightmare while the country continued to conduct its business as though
nothing had happened."[12] By carrying out these raids anonymously,
not only would the identities of the disappeared be obliterated, but
their very disappearances would go unacknowledged.

Witnesses were intimidated. Neighbors would turn up their radios
in order to block out the sound of the abductions, in fear that they might
be next. No one would speak to what he or she saw as the entire country was induced into a tragic passivity. The fear and silence imposed on
the people of Argentina were meant to make them disappear as citizens.
"Isn't this just what the junta wanted," reflected Hebe de Bonafini, the
Mothers' leader, "to appear all powerful and to make the people feel
impotent?"[13]

Against helplessness, the Mothers adopt a politics of hope, preserv-
ing and protecting the struggle of their *disappeared* sons and daughters.
They realize that their subversive energy is necessary to revitalizing the
struggle for human rights. A politics of hope esteems opposition to its
policies; it realizes that the lack of opposition at least sterilizes, and at
worst destroys, politics itself. Through their courageous insistence on
being seen and heard, the Mothers realize that the point of their struggle
is not necessarily to arrive at a particular end result; the point of their
struggle is not to subdue or *disappear* the *other* but to *acknowledge* and
be *acknowledged*. Whereas the hegemonic political discourse in Argen-

tina would like to put a "final stop to the fixation with the past," the Mothers cry out that their vanquished loved ones cannot afford to have their histories relegated to oblivion.

Mourning the Disappeared

"Bring Them Back Alive!" the Mothers chant. While it is clear that all of these women realize that they will likely never see their children again, they refuse to presume them dead; instead, they carry forth the wounds of the *disappeared*. For the Mothers, pain is their driving force, a source of their spiritual strength. "Contrary to the normal process of grieving, during which the agony of loss slowly moves away from the center of one's concerns," the Mothers have separated mourning from healing.[14] Mourning is different precisely because it refuses to tritely memorialize and embalm loss—it demands that loss be given a space in the dialogue. "It is not that they do not wish to heal, to recover what is irrevocably lost, but rather, they see their healing as a result of the significance of their mission."[15] The Mothers strive to keep their children's dreams of reform alive so that such atrocities never recur. "Let there be no healing of wounds," they argue. "Let them remain open. Because if the wounds still bleed, there will be no forgetting and our strength will continue to grow."[16] For the Mothers, the physical annihilation of the *disappeared* does not mean the death of their children's dreams. They believe themselves to be permanently pregnant with dissident energy, and therefore see no contradiction between "Bring Them Back Alive!" and the fact that most of the disappeared have been assassinated. Their chant serves as a reminder and a provocation. "We have given another meaning to death," the Mothers have said. "To die for a cause has a different meaning, because it's a death that kills the body, but doesn't kill the idea. Then it is as if one remains. That is why we are not afraid of death."[17] The Mothers inform the present that it is the product of a past catastrophe; they, like Benjamin's philosopher, are convinced that *even the dead* will not be safe from the threat of despotism if old wounds are not mourned and, through mourning, reawakened.

Radicalizing Motherhood

In refusing to bury the dead, the Mothers refuse to retreat into their private concerns, upholding a vision of democracy that is necessarily contradictory, radical, and cross-grained. As the Mothers themselves have realized, to transform a system is always revolutionary. Bishop Kurt Scharf, a former member of the Resistance against the Nazi regime in Germany, once said about the Mothers, "People come to me and complain that the Mother are too radicalized and I answer, 'How many imprisoned children have they found? The fate of how many disappeared have they clarified? Was Captain Astiz condemned and the perpetrators of the kidnapping condemned?' They should continue becoming radicalized."[18] But many have dismissed the Mothers as simply intransigent, unable to move forward in time, as though democracy was something we progress *toward*. In truth, the Mothers' preoccupation with the impact of the past reveals itself in a thoroughly future-oriented enterprise: "Theirs is an attempt to catalyze a continuous past into the future, seeking to recapture a lost past in hope that it could be restored."[19] To restore the past is not to romanticize history but to remember present civilization as contemporaneous with past barbarism. As Wolin writes in *Politics and Vision:* "The past is never wholly superseded; it is constantly seeking to be recaptured at the very moment that human thought is seemingly preoccupied with the unique problems of its own time."[20] In a country where political imagination was suppressed, the Mothers assumed the role of the political theorist— capturing the old so that it might be distilled into the new. Democracy, the Mothers argue, is not isolated but alive, associative, and argumentative. History and democracy are both permanently open to interrogation, for there is great danger in dialectic collapsing into nondialectic positivism. Within totalitarian regimes, oppositional forces are banished, disappeared, and relegated to be the debris of progress itself. The Mothers work to separate this debris from the totalizing whole, refuting the neutralizing insistence of tyranny. The past histories of loss and defeat, they assert, are the lifeblood of the political.

The Mothers' confrontational politics is a way of redefining power to be the recovery of spaces that influence our political lives. Through their continual repetition of the truth and by defining their political vocabulary that unites the public and private spheres, they have forged a space for themselves in political awareness.[21] From gathering in the open spaces of the plaza to speaking in front of an international audience in Geneva, the Mothers thrust themselves into the arenas of political power—striving to shape dialogue and reawaken human consciousness. They have claimed this arena for their children from a "government that sought to eliminate them and then deny their very existence, a place where their children receive a social and political existence."[22] Refused entry to established political institutions, the Mothers gathered in the streets, the parks, and the churches. Denied access to the means of communication, the Mothers traveled throughout the world on speaking tours and gained the attention of parliamentary commissions from Israel, Spain, and Italy. For the Mothers, radicalizing democracy is about a return in time and in memory—a transgression against the grain of existing political structures. "We are transgressors," they claim. "We are revolutionaries because we do not accept things so easily. We are carrying on a different kind of revolution, of women with a different point of view who do not hide."[23]

The Mothers and Liberal Democracy

The military junta justified its tactics to the people of Argentina by laying claim to *crisis*. It claimed that Argentina needed a new beginning, a purging of cross-grained ideologies in order to become a new nation, rescued from the problems of its predecessors. The idea of *crisis,* however, according to Wolin, is deeply invested in its etymology from ancient Greek: *krisis* referred to a condition so grave as to force a turning point. But contrary to the junta's claims, a turning point is defined by opposition. When the junta installed itself, the turning point never materialized: at the very moment of change, the voices of dissent were *disappeared.* In the place of progress was stasis. The advance of modernization, however, is continually made possible by accompanying displacement and replacement of ideas and voices. The alleged goal of the new establishment was to preserve Western civilization as an end in itself. In reality, the voices of dissent and perturbation cannot be silenced in order for there to be a new beginning. Political space would collapse and be rendered obsolete precisely if it becomes artificial and manufactured, a totalizing structure that can recognize no alternatives.

The Mothers' work is labeled as being "radical" because it poses tensions that run against a totalitarian regime that presents itself as the end-all of politics. What the Mothers are practicing is a return to the very source of liberal democracy, the essential radicalism that is inherent in a "government of the people." It is the vital energy at the center of all living politics, asserting that individuals must not lose their political memory, for then they might discover that the real source of power is within themselves. Democracy today has a ubiquitous currency. It is vitiated. Individuals and governments constantly invoke democracy but disavow it just as we disavow the violence of our past. We forget that the democracy is rooted in the robust associations and solidarity of the public sphere. The *disappeared* were *allowed* to disappear because civic society fell apart at the moment of totalitarianism. That was precisely the aim of the junta: to use fear and silence to make all Argentinean people *disappear* as citizens. As the Mothers would write, "They meant to *disappear* our national identity."[24] The recovery of national identity, the Mothers argue, can only begin with the courage to critique and engage in politics, to remember that past trauma was antecedent to the current political state. For Wolin, as it is for the Mothers, danger lurks where there is no notion of opposition, of a turning point. It is when a system seems stabilized and crisis proof that it is the most prone to tyranny.

> It is as though the sole motor of change is the one embodied in the system itself; that the system sets the terms and the limits of change so that setbacks do not disrupt the perpetual motion machine. . . . In the official rhetoric, loss is integrated into a system that is presented as too complex, too universal, and too interconnected—in short, so overpowering yet exquisitely sensitive as to forbid any challenging actions.[25]

This is precisely why the Mothers must remain outside the system. They refuse to live in a "utopia" where loss has been systematized and made innocuous, a utopia whose existence depends symbiotically on the perpetuation of an underlying dystopia. While the military junta in Argentina was dissolved and constitutional government reestablished, the officers of the junta remain in power. Former Argentine president Raúl Alfonsín promised the Mothers that he would prosecute the generals and soldiers responsible for the disappearances during his election campaign, but once in power, he pardoned or promoted most of the offending individuals. The Argentine government, now under President Néstor Kirchner, has continued to mete out generous sentences for Dirty War crimes because it does not want to strain relationships with the powerful military. As much as it claims democracy, the Kirchner regime, like its predecessors, is peculiar because it systematically excludes many of its members from the advantages of "utopia": the labor forces are exploited by the growing commoditization of culture, and Argentina's ageless divide of the state versus the underclass is more marked than ever. The Mothers march on because they realize that an ideal future does not come naturally *after the revolution*. Democratic society must continually struggle to find a space of liberty and justice for itself. Democracy's power is in its ability to recapture lost ideals and to rediscover the lost vocabulary of dissidence. Nevertheless, for the Mothers, what is at issue is not just the vapid notion of dissent itself.

It is the status of democracy as standing opposition and the importance to it of the continuous re-creation of political experience.[26] The Mothers' vital insight is of democracy as inherently "circumstantial, episodic and fugitive: democracy is an ephemeral phenomena rather than a settled system."[27] As it is for Wolin, the actual weakness of democracy is not the consequence of formal attack but of a judgment that democracy can be managed and, when necessary, ignored.

Often, these strategies are couched in terms of managerial efficiency and political stability, the very justifications Kirchner's government now gives for mitigating formal punishment for the guilty. The Mothers' critical role is to crystallize fugitive democracy, a state that must constantly be sought as a moment of experience, a perpetual recovery of memory and loss so as to extend to the wider citizenry the benefits of social cooperation and achievement.[28]

The Mothers of the Plaza de Mayo work tirelessly to revitalize the dying political dialogue in Argentina. Their best hope is to keep the memory of trauma alive so that loss is not systematized but challenged. Day in and day out, the Mothers work to separate the silence from oblivion, and dissidence from departure. With aims such as these, the Mothers are destined to be oppositional, destined to exercise a radical politics that unmasks the brutality of Argentina's past. Their initial goal of bringing back their children has evolved into something much greater than their individual longings. Their work has transformed them into allegorical figures, temporalized tropes of mourning and loss. To mourn the death of dissidence is to keep the possibility of utopia alive, for if dissidence is shaped into a form of political power, then it becomes a space where power emerges from powerlessness. As long as the memory of the Mothers of the Plaza de Mayo is kept alive, there is hope for Argentina.

Democracy is an inherently disavowable reality.[29] The Mothers' subversive energy works to prevent the neutralization of the spirit of the demos. Kirchner's government, like the military junta before it, has tried to embalm public discourse with the rhetoric of stability and nationalism. The Mothers perceive that democracy is embalmed precisely to memorialize its loss of substance.[30] Substantive democracy—equalizing, participatory, and communal—is necessarily antithetical. The Mothers of the Plaza de Mayo will always be a radical force precisely because they embody the instability and challenge of democracy. By invoking the cross-grained, they are the source of revitalization that will allow the *new* to be born out of the *old.*

Notes

1. Walter Benjamin, *Illuminations: Essays and Reflections,* ed. Hannah Arendt (New York: Schocken Books, 1968), 263.

2. Benjamin, *Illuminations,* 255.

3. Idelber Avelar, *The Untimely Present: Postdictatorial Latin American Fiction and the Task of Mourning* (Durham, NC: Duke University Press, 1999), 2.

4. Avelar, *Untimely Present,* 2.

5. Marguerite Guzman Bouvard, *Revolutionizing Motherhood: The Mothers of the Plaza de Mayo* (New York: SR Books, 1994), 59.

6. Bouvard, *Revolutionizing Motherhood,* 59.

7. Sheldon S. Wolin, "Political Theory: From Vocation to Invocation," in *Vocations of Political Theory,* ed. Jason Frank and John Tambornino (Minneapolis: University of Minnesota Press, 2000), 3.

8. Bouvard, *Revolutionizing Motherhood,* 176.

9. Bouvard, *Revolutionizing Motherhood,* 176.

10. Bouvard, *Revolutionizing Motherhood*, 20.

11. Bouvard, *Revolutionizing Motherhood*, 23.

12. Bouvard, *Revolutionizing Motherhood*, 24.

13. Bouvard, *Revolutionizing Motherhood*, 124.

14. Bouvard, *Revolutionizing Motherhood*, 152.

15. Bouvard, *Revolutionizing Motherhood*, 152.

16. Bouvard, *Revolutionizing Motherhood*, 153.

17. Bouvard, *Revolutionizing Motherhood*, 155.

18. Bouvard, *Revolutionizing Motherhood*, 49.

19. Wolin, "Political Theory," 20.

20. Sheldon S. Wolin, *Politics and Vision* (Princeton, NJ: Princeton University Press, 2004), 24.

21. Bouvard, *Revolutionizing Motherhood*, 14.

22. Bouvard, *Revolutionizing Motherhood*, 254.

23. Bouvard, *Revolutionizing Motherhood*, 196.

24. Bouvard, *Revolutionizing Motherhood*, 20.

25. Wolin, "Political Theory," 17.

26. Wolin, *Politics and Vision*, 602.

27. Wolin, *Politics and Vision*, 602.

28. Wolin, *Politics and Vision*, 588.

29. Wolin, *Politics and Vision*, 25.

30. Wolin, *Politics and Vision*, 17.

Toward a Civil Society
Memory, History, and the Enola Gay

1995
Dartmouth College

THE UNITED STATES IS A nation that has always had a particular sense of destiny. From the religious reformers who carved a life out of the New England forests to modern voices who call for foreign intervention, the American people have believed that the United States has a special mission to be a lighthouse of freedom and hope for other nations.[1] This mission is revealed in history and is especially clear in conflicts; the national vision was articulated in the Revolutionary War, tested and strained during the Civil War, undermined during Vietnam. World War II, a war fought to "save civilization," was another time to put values to ultimate tests and live with the sacrifices. The conflict is woven into our national identity like a star on the flag.

Fifty years have since passed and—though memories never sank far beneath conscious thought—the anniversary is a chance to pull up stories and memories from the deep past. The power and resonance of a fifty years' memorial was clear on June 6, 1994, when D-Day made headlines again, this time not for war cries or the thunder of guns but for speeches and the thunder of applause. Men and women who survived the fire of war in their youth have raised children and seen them through Vietnam, witnessed the unfolding of the arms race, the fall of the Berlin Wall, and the phoenix-like growth of Japan. As they begin to tell war stories to their great-grandchildren, they realize that World War II will soon pass into history. Their memory will be entrusted to their children. This anniversary, then, is a national ritual for telling and listening, as well as a dynamic moment for questioning and reflecting. But as we exhume conflicts fifty years gone, we find they were never laid to rest, only buried alive as the rest of the twentieth century bulldozed past. We find the passions and convictions of fifty years ago living quietly in those who were there. Then we find, buried beneath volumes of historical text, breathing softly beneath the rationalizations and justifications, the deep moral ambiguities of wartime. And as we look at history through our only lens, the present, we gain new information and insights, which translate into new conflicts. The current generation of scholars and students are inheritors of World War II, and where past and present overlap is where new conflicts burn most brightly. No legacy is more loaded than that of the atomic bomb. Freeman Dyson compares the legacy with the rules of an imaginary city he recalls from a childhood book: "It is a law of life in the magic city that if you wish for anything you can have it. But with this law goes a special rule about machines. If anyone wishes for a piece of machinery, he is compelled to keep it and go on using it for the rest of his life."[2] As any newspaper will tell, the Smithsonian's upcoming display of the *Enola Gay* is the epicenter of the conflict.

"The Nation's Attic"

The U.S. government placed the stewardship of national memory in the hands of the Smithsonian Institution in 1826. Funded through private endowment and federal money, the white stone buildings flank the Mall in Washington, D.C. They are intellectual and cultural corridors connecting the Washington, Lincoln, and Vietnam memorials, where American history is enshrined, to the Capitol, where today's history happens. An act of Congress in 1946 created the National Air Museum. The 1966 statute—amended to include the space program—charged the museum to "memorialize the national development of aviation and space flight; collect, preserve and display aeronautical and space flight equipment . . . ; serve as a repository for science equipment and data; and provide educational material for the historical study of aviation and space flight."[3] National achievements in the air hold a special place in American consciousness; the Wright brothers and the Apollo 11 mission have become symbols of American ingenuity. The museum itself is a unique experience. For my own family and thousands of others, our annual pilgrimage there is as much a part of Christmas as the tree. I recall my own dizzy awe walking beneath the wheeling planes and towering rockets.

With the fifty-year anniversary coming up in 1995, the National Air and Space Museum (NASM) decided to display the B-29 Super Fortress that dropped the first atomic bomb. The Smithsonian has been the *Enola Gay*'s legal guardian since July 1949, though the museum asked the air force to house it. With limited hangar space, new technology, and an assignment in Korea, the air force squeezed the *Enola Gay* out into the rain and wind. Its restoration, started ten years ago, has taken twenty-five workers and a million dollars to complete. Museum visitors will see a shiny sixty-foot section of the front fuselage hanging in the gallery. Curators worked simultaneously on an exhibit to explain the role of the *Enola Gay* in the end of World War II. Following standard operating procedures, the museum staff submitted their work-in-progress, originally titled "The Crossroads: The End of World War II, the Atomic Bomb and the Origins of the Cold War," to an advisory committee.[4] The panel of experts includes well-known historians from the military, government, science, and academe. During that same period, NASM directors met with officials of the Air Force Association to discuss the exhibit and—on request—to provide a copy of the script. John Correll, the editor-in-chief of *Air Force Magazine,* wrote an article in the April issue that was harshly critical of the exhibit, thereby bringing the issue to broad public attention.

The April article ("War Stories at Air and Space") and follow-up articles articulate the veteran's criticisms both specific and sweeping.

Correll claims that the exhibit takes the Pacific war out of context, depicting "the Japanese in defense of their home islands, saying little about what had made such a defense necessary" and thereby making American offensive moves appear "brutal, vindictive and racially motivated." Second, the article accuses the exhibit of "imbalance," meaning that the exhibit is designed to evoke more empathy for the Japanese than for the Americans. He noted, for example, that a greater number of photos were devoted to Japanese war dead than American. The article also describes how the "emotional center" of the exhibit—artifacts, pictures, and text from "ground zero"—is designed for "shock effect" and will leave the most lasting impression on the visitor. Finally, he blasts the museum for its handling of perhaps the most contentious detail: the number of casualties projected for the invasion of Japan. Correll also saves a good deal of artillery for the current Smithsonian administration, whom he accuses of "politically correct curating."[5]

Due in part to grass-roots organizing by veterans, the controversy crossed the street to Capitol Hill. On August 10, 1994, a bipartisan group of twenty-four House members signed a letter to Robert McCormick Adams, the Smithsonian's executive secretary, calling the exhibit a "historically narrow revisionist view." On that same day a group of six House Republicans met with Martin Harwit, NASM's director, to voice similar complaints. Congressional pressure reached a pitch when the Senate passed a resolution threatening to cut congressional appropriations, which currently make up 85 percent of the museum's budget. Pressure to change the exhibit continued from the press and veterans' groups. By late September, the museum officials sat down behind closed doors with the American Legion and sandpapered the script. Then it was the historians who were outraged: they, too, flung the accusation of "revisionism."

The treatment of the debate to drop the atomic bomb was at the center of their criticism. The earlier scripts contained historical documents that questioned the necessity of dropping the bomb. The newly edited script, however, reflected the "inaccurate but understandable belief that the atomic bomb saved [American soldiers] from being sacrificed in an invasion of Japan." According to the historians, the Smithsonian exhibit was propagating "feel good national myths."[6]

The historians attacked the Smithsonian and the veterans' pressure groups in evocative terms. "It was a humiliating spectacle, scholars being forced to recant the truth," wrote Kai Bird in a *New York Times* column, calling up the tragic specter of Galileo. Similarly, more than a hundred historians signed a letter to the new secretary of the Smithsonian that likened the recent script changes to "historical cleansing."

The use of this phrase draws a subtle link to the "ethnic cleansing" in Bosnia, implying that historical truths—like the Croats—are being wiped out in an internationally criminal act.[7] Finally, the historians accuse the Smithsonian of being "PC," that is, "patriotically correct."

Although the threads of the past intimately bind those who remember the past and those who study it, the two camps are no longer in dialogue with each other. The debate has ceased to be a debate. The rhetoric has reached a strident pitch, and both sides are mobilizing; witness the resolutions passed by the Senate and the Organization of American Historians. Both sides find the values most central to their identity at stake. For a historian, what could be more important than intellectual integrity? For a veteran, what could be more essential than defending the values for which they risked their lives? To sound the depths of the conflict, we must look beneath the media rhetoric.

"Thank God for the Bomb"

What do the veterans mean when they ask the museum to display the *Enola Gay* in its proper context? How would they tell the story? Many would begin their story some years before the war, when the country was reflecting on the empty victory of the Great War and pacifism was in vogue.

Suddenly, bombs, fire, smoke, and lolling ships: Pearl Harbor. Two thousand Americans, eighteen ships, and 292 aircraft were destroyed in the Japanese sneak attack.[8] Though the military losses were far from crippling, the event was a profound psychological turning point of which we are constantly reminded. President Franklin D. Roosevelt, in his speech to Congress asking for a declaration of war, forever tied Pearl Harbor to the terms of Japanese surrender: "unconditional." Pacifism blew away like a feather in a tornado, and the country mobilized for war. A desire for revenge burned brightly among other motivations: the Japanese would pay a hundredfold for catching America with its pants down. It was a playground morality, for all of its depth and seriousness.

Other Japanese military actions incited the emotions of wartime America. A nation with colonial ambitions, the Japanese were aggressively pursuing their goals in East Asia, invading China, Manchuria, and several South Pacific islands. They often treated their newest imperial subjects ruthlessly, and the American press covered the events. Americans were horrified by the "rape of Nanking," in which the Japanese looted, burned, raped, and murdered freely in the Chinese city.

The sense of outrage became all the more intense when American soldiers came face to face with Japanese military strategy. Because of practices such as *kamikaze* missions (a suicidal flight into an enemy ship) and *hara-kiri* (ritual suicide chosen over dishonor), many Americans considered the Japanese to be "fanatics" who would never surrender. Surrender was dishonorable for Japanese soldiers; they held Allied soldiers to the same standards and treated them brutally. In short, the Japanese pursued the battle with a total commitment to victory and a complete disregard for what the Western world accepted as "rules of warfare." This strategy was powerful. Where the Japanese did not win, they forced Allied troops to pay in blood for every inch gained.

Hatred for Japan was strong. The press filled the national vacuum of understanding for this Eastern culture, often portraying the Japanese as less than human. Polls from the era reveal that 10 to 13 percent of the American people wanted to see them wiped out as a race.[9] This psychological tactic is as old and as common as warfare. When the enemy is perceived as inhuman, annihilation of the enemy becomes acceptable, even justified.

As hatred and contempt for the Japanese evolved, so too did American bombing policy. During the European war, the United States refused to join England in the policy of area or "morale" bombing, in which noncombatants became targets. Instead, the U.S. Air Force established a doctrine of precision bombing, based on both ethical and military considerations.[10] In the Pacific theater this doctrine began to crumble under new pressures and new leadership. Weather and geographical considerations made daylight precision bombing less effective than nighttime area bombing. On his own authority, General Curtis LeMay, the results-oriented head of XXI Bomber Command, ordered the firebombing of Tokyo on March 9, 1945. When the mission's success became clear, the war machine in Washington applauded his bold action. Bomber Command swept ethical considerations for noncombatants under the carpet with a simple reclassification: Japan had no civilians. Said LeMay, "All you had to do was visit one of those targets after we'd roasted it, and see the ruins of a multitude of tiny houses, with a drill press sticking up through the wreckage of every home. . . . Had to be done."[11] By the summer of 1945, key military decision makers were comfortable with ninety thousand to a hundred thousand civilian casualties in one night. The most immediate "context" of the atomic bomb was the situation in early August 1945.

Thousands of servicemen were preparing to invade Japan in November. Many came directly from the European theater, while the others were already initiated into the terrors of Pacific warfare. The conflict had reached a grim plateau; it would clearly be a fight to the finish. The American military men were determined to whip Japan into unconditional surrender, though they knew they would die in the process. "We

were living under a death sentence," said John Useem, a Navy lieuten-
ant scheduled for the fourth wave of the invasion. Useem describes
taking a thirty-day leave in the summer of 1945. "I went back to the
University of Wisconsin, where I got my degree. Someone offered me a
job when the war ended. I laughed because I knew I wasn't coming
back."[12] On August 7, when news of the atomic explosion over Hiroshima reached American troops, they were ecstatic.

The sense of relief was tremendous. Surely the war would end! Eight
days and one plutonium bomb later, the Japanese surrendered. The
apparent cause-and-effect relationship was enormously powerful, burning into the hearts of American servicemen and their families. Harry
Truman reinforced this connection, announcing in his radio broadcast
of December 9 that he had dropped the bomb to save American lives.
The atomic bomb appeared to graciously restore the lives Americans
were preparing to sacrifice, just as God had restored Isaac to Abraham.
"Thank God for the bomb."

Why would the veterans want to see the museum tell this story?
They want to invite the listener (in this case, the museum visitor) to
walk in the shoes of a young G.I. stationed in the Pacific. As the events
of the war unfold, the visitor is moved along with them. A veteran-
designed exhibit would evoke shock at Pearl Harbor and outrage at
the treatment of American POWs in Japan. Historical displays, then,
become tools for drawing out particular emotions. When listeners become emotionally involved in a narrative, they are leaving themselves
open for the story to *change* them.[13]

This process of listening and transformation is a major function of
narrative. Clearly, then, when the historians make ground zero the
"emotional center" of the exhibit, the veterans are deeply uncomfortable. According to their experience, the listener should feel enormously
relieved on August 6. The "emotional center" should be an impromptu
barracks celebration as G.I.s realize they will live to see their families
again.

Displaying the *Enola Gay* in a veterans' "context" would serve a moral purpose. The exhibit would explain how decent American citizens could be overjoyed that sixty thousand Japanese civilians had perished in an instant. If visitors are successfully emotionally involved, they will perceive how, if *they* were in a similar situation, they might also say, "Thank God for the bomb."

For the Record

One asks the question: "Why did the United States drop an atomic bomb on Hiroshima?"

The most common answer is: "To save a million American lives." Historians have probed this question and found answers very different from the one above. The final decision to drop the bomb lay with President Truman. Therefore, they have examined the criteria by which he made his decision. When military advisers briefed Truman about a possible invasion of Japan, how high were the casualty estimates they quoted? Archival research revealed that the figures discussed in the Oval Office never exceeded forty-six thousand.[14] The historians want to clear the historical record. They traced the etymology of the phrase "a million American lives" to a 1946 *Harper's* article by Henry Stimson, secretary of war, and found no factual evidence beneath it.[15] Truman's memoirs, too, exaggerated the casualty estimates. Some veterans imagine that this clarification implies a judgment that, if only forty-six thousand were going to perish, then Truman should have chosen invasion over bombing. No historian has ever made this claim. Rather, the historians are interested in the questions behind the numbers: Were Truman and Stimson laboring to relieve their guilt and justify the bombings to themselves and to the public?

The historians leave behind the question "How many American lives did Truman believe the bomb would save?" to ask, "Was saving American lives his primary interest in dropping the bomb?"

Those who would answer "yes" to this question must prove that Truman believed the war could end *only* through invasion. The historical record will not back them up. On the contrary, Truman seemed to have thought peace was at hand; he was aware of Japanese diplomatic interest in peace, the possibility of continued firebombing over Japan and entry of Russia into the war. Why, then, did he need the bomb? Historians have concluded that a host of concerns motivated Truman in his authorization of the bomb. Some scholars focus on his relatively weak position as president. As of August 1945 he had yet to emerge from Roosevelt's awesome shadow; using the atomic bomb would show his allegiance to FDR's "unconditional surrender" doctrine. Historians tick off the other motivations: to intimidate Russia, to establish U.S. power in the postwar world, to allow for the bureaucratic momentum of the Manhattan Project, to use a God-given weapon. Besides establishing these motivations, historians want to present the voices of dissent from the Truman administration and the Manhattan Project.

The historians have an enormously difficult task in helping the veterans and the public incorporate this newly articulated information into their understanding of the war. Many read it as an affront, an accusation, a judgment. If historians dug up a wealth of factual information on the life of Jesus, some of which seemed to contradict the Gospel, surely Matthew, Mark, Luke, and John would be angry. For fifty years the Americans of World War II have arranged the facts in a certain way. Over time the disparate voices and memories have become more unified, and the veterans tell their story with the power of a collective voice. Bound up within this traditional narrative are historical events, strong emotions, and moral justifications. The story represents the veterans' self-understanding.

It is their identity, which they, in turn, have identified with the sacred destiny of the United States. And when historians give the whole story a shake, to test its factual foundation, the storytellers fear they want to tip over the whole structure.

What do the historians want the visitors to experience? In keeping with their professional values, the historians want to create in visitors an attitude of objectivity, of questioning. When the historians researched World War II, they tried not to identify themselves with a particular nationality; according to the rules of objectivity, history written solely from an "American" perspective would be propaganda. Thus, the historians invite the visitors to suspend their own national or political identity to consider the events. With evidence from both Japanese and American perspectives, visitors can make rational, objective judgments. If visitors become successfully involved in this exhibit, they will lose any preconceptions they may have had about the *necessity* of historical events. In this creative state of questioning, the visitors may arrive at new understandings or judgments about the role of the *Enola Gay* in the end of World War II. This opportunity for questioning, however, comes at the cost of an empathetic understanding of the American experience in the Pacific.

Values in Conflict

A deep division at the heart of this conflict separates moral experience from moral reasoning. Veterans want new generations of Americans to learn *why* they believed their actions were right. Historians ask visitors to consider *whether* historical decisions were right. Both perspectives are firmly grounded in valid human experience. The veterans' stories have a stamp of authenticity that comes from life lived. Their words are forged in blood and mud, sleepless nights and letters home.

The historians speak from the authority of rationality and luxury of detached reflection. These two perspectives are in conflict, as the words of my grandfather show clearly. When I asked him if the historians' new numbers and theories were true, he said, "Yes, the evidence is correct, but I can't agree with it, because of my experience. For the historians, the facts are absolute truth and again, I can't agree."[16]

If we look at this dispute carefully, we find serious challenges to any ideal we may have about universal truth. The veterans make the case that the bombing of Hiroshima was subjectively right.

The historians argue that it is objectively questionable. We cannot escape either perspective. We are bound to enter the emotional world of a combat soldier *and* face these two questions: Was the use of the bomb a military necessity? Is the deliberate targeting of noncombatants morally acceptable in any situation? How can we reconcile the two points of view? Moral relativism is an easy and unacceptable solution that prematurely seems to resolve the conflict. A more rigorous view of the conflict asks us to grasp the paradox and internalize it. Living with paradox requires careful thought and constant energy. By allowing ourselves to be "caught in the middle," we see more clearly the moral possibilities within ourselves as human beings.

It seems a small thing to ask of people: to recognize and learn from conflicts over values. Yet it is an exercise in which American society is out of shape. If we consider the venom of the last elections or the protests that lead to body bags in Planned Parenthood, we see individuals and groups unable to resolve value conflicts in peaceful ways. In the Smithsonian debate we are disappointed to find similar symptoms: two sides no longer listening to one another.

Given the diversity of human experience, we will always find ourselves among people who hold conflicting values. Living in a democratic society means that we agree to resolve those conflicts peacefully. Isn't that the civilization Americans fought to save fifty years ago? Didn't those veterans risk their lives to preserve a society that produced people who disagree with them? Listening and learning from other value systems, allowing for complexity and depth, are vital skills. This debate, then, is an opportunity to sharpen our sensitivities. It challenges our historical sense, sparks careful study, and prompts us to recognize the ultimate well-spring of moral judgment: our own awareness.

Notes

1. Robert Bellah and William McLoughlin, eds., *Religion in America* (Boston: Houghton Mifflin, 1968).
2. Freeman Dyson, *Disturbing the Universe* (New York: Basic Books, 1979), 4.
3. John Correll, "War Stories at Air and Space," *Air Force Magazine,* April 1994, 29.
4. Martin Harwit, *"Enola Gay* and a Nation's Memory," *Air and Space Magazine,* August–September 1994, 20.
5. Correll, "War Stories at Air and Space," 24–27.
6. Kai Bird, "The Curators Cave In," *New York Times,* October 9, 1994, 15.
7. Martin Sherwin and Kai Bird to Ira Michael Heyman, unpublished letter, November 16, 1994.
8. Richard Rhodes, *The Making of the Atomic Bomb* (New York: Simon and Schuster, 1986), 392.
9. John Dower, *War Without Mercy* (New York: Pantheon, 1986), 53.
10. Recent scholarship, particularly that of Ronald Schaffer and Michael Sherry, implies that this doctrine, often cited to lend moral superiority to the AAF, is little more than a myth. Conrad Crane, *Bombs, Cities and Civilians* (Lawrence: University Press of Kansas, 1993), 4.
11. Crane, *Bombs, Cities and Civilians,* 133.
12. Interview, John Useem, December 26, 1994, Washington, DC.
13. Walter Davis, a scholar who studies Vietnam veterans, noted the importance of the relationship between a veteran and his audience. "The healing of the combat veteran is inextricably connected to our capacity as a community to hear what the veteran has to tell us and to be changed by it." Jonathan Shay, "Binding Up the Wounded National Theology," *Religion and Values in Public Life* (Fall 1994): 1.
14. Martin Sherwin, *A World Destroyed* (New York: Random House, 1987), Appendix U: "War Planners Casualty Estimates," 342.
15. Bird, "Curators Cave In," 15.
16. Bird, "Curators Cave In," 15.

ON CONSCIENCE

Tatyana's Glory

ALEKSANDR SENDEROVICH
2003
University of Massachusetts–Amherst

ON A RIDE FROM MOSCOW to Petersburg, a lone traveler can hardly forgo the opportunity to awaken before his compartment mates, and, after beating a queue to the washroom, after asking for a glass of tea from the train manager, to prop himself on a windowsill of a speeding train. One then can savor the final hour of travel, when other commuters roll out of bed and prepare to disembark at the train station of Russia's second capital city. In that hour, the nocturnal landscape of endless forests and lakes gradually changes as the train enters the universe of industrial suburbs, the viscera of a big city turned inside out. It is then, on a concrete fence of some monstrous chemical plant, that an enormous inscription, adorned by swastikas on each side, appears. "Beat the Yids!"

"Rescue Russia," indeed, is the second half of the infamous slogan that the author(s) of the inscription decided to leave out. Undoubtedly, such was an intentional act—the two-part mantra, oft-seen and oft-heard, is familiar to the Russian eye and ear. A traveler looking out of a train window, presented with the inscription's first half, will instantaneously conjure up the image of its obviated double. Such a sight, replete with images of *pogromschiks* and Black Hundreds chanting the mantra in its entirety, does not leave any doubts about its intended purpose.

The author(s) of such inscription was (were) clever: nothing will ever be done about his (their) work placed in a spot visible yet not easily reached. Occasional passersby, who try to cut a bit of distance by walking across the tracks to the plant, would never stray those crucial feet from their route to do away with the graffiti. Our lonely traveler, even if he is revolted at the sight by his window, may want to erase these offensive letters—yet, he cannot stop the train. Our passenger may after all be the only one who would feel his heartbeat race, a spark of conscientiousness cross his mind, making him question the ethics of his indifferent gaze. But in these circumstances, he is powerless: he quietly returns to his compartment, packs his suitcases, and prepares to leave the train. The loud inscription will remain undisturbed, facing no protesters and supported by its chief ally: silent apathy.

One cannot stop the train on its speedy route from one city to another, but one can stop one's car on a highway. At the end of May 2002, a twenty-seven-year-old Muscovite, Tatyana Sapunova, spotted a cardboard sign with "Death to the Yids!" (*Smert' zhidam!*) written on it.[1] The sign was set on the side of a major highway, where many drivers are locked in the traffic jams of their daily commute. When traffic stalls at rush-hour, drivers can do little other than to wander their gaze and entertain it in any available way, often by reading all signs that come into view, so as to let the time pass by more quickly. How many such drivers were there in the twenty-four hours that the sign stood still (but yelled loudly) on the side of a highway? Did they react, whether approving or disapproving of it, or simply ignore what they saw?

For the passenger on the train from Moscow to Petersburg the offensive sign that comes into view is remote, inaccessible. Of course, he can always pull the stop lever with which Russian trains are equipped, but the presence of many other passengers on the train makes this impossible. Somehow, our traveler can be exculpated for his inaction because of a sheer lack of an opportunity for him to do anything. It is harder to explain why so many motorists could not consider stopping their car on a side of a highway, crossing onto the side of the road, walking out of their car, and doing away with the sign.

Except for one person. Noticing the sign, Tatyana Sapunova decided to stop her car, walk over to the sign, and do away with it. Yet, as she started pulling at the sign, it exploded. "Sign [poster] terrorism" was the term coined by officials a few days later to describe what is a much subtler phenomenon: those who make it their mission to entice violence against parts of the population also need to punish those who refuse to stand by. Explosives attached to the sign were not meant so much for the Jews—perpetual others in Russia's long and steady history of anti-Semitism; rather, they were meant for the likes of Tatyana, regardless of how few such persons might be.

In her memoir, written clandestinely and first published in the West, Nadezhda Mandelshtam speaks about the ethics of lying during the years of Stalinist terror: "Must one lie? Is it allowed to lie? Is 'lying to save oneself' justified? Is it good to live in the conditions where one does not have to lie? Is there such a place on earth?"[2] Further, writing about the 1930s when lying was both acceptable and inevitable—by the purged to exculpate themselves, and by the executioners to justify some historical necessity for fighting the "enemies of the people," Mandelshtam asks: "But how will the historians reconstruct verity if everywhere onto each particle of truth laid themselves heaps of monstrous lies? Not prejudices, not mistakes of time, but conscientious and thought-out lies?"[3]

On one hand, Nadezhda Mandelshtam rightly predicted the debacle of untangling the truth about that dark period of Russian history that historians now face. What truth lies in made-up accusations? How are historians to treat fabricated witness reports? How much can the victims' own words—elicited under torture and sleep deprivation—be trusted?

Yet, on the other hand, Mandelshtam's prophetic words suggest a larger paradigm about Russian culture. Indeed, it is a culture infused with Soviet-style lying. In its post-Soviet age, the Russian language remains a tongue of double-speak, with familiar words meant to defamiliarize the speaker's intentions, a language where nothing can be taken at face value. Details about the explosion on the Moscow highway that injured Tatyana expose a great deal of denial and lying. Most perplexing is the fact that for more than a day the "Death to the Yids!" sign stood no farther than one hundred yards from a police station. Interviewed by the newspaper *Izvestia,* the chief policeman of that district, Nikolai Vagin, justified the inaction of his unit:

> We did not receive any reports from citizens about this sign even being set up. We did not know about its existence until the moment when the explosion occurred. That is why I had no basis to send my colleagues to search for the sign.
>
> In addition, it is a controversial matter: Is the installation of this sign a crime? I think that from the legal point of view the slogan "Death to the Yids" is not an enticement to ethnic conflicts. Anyone is called "Yids" these days.[4]

The astonishing proximity of the sign to the police station casts a shade of doubt onto the first part of the policeman's answer. There is a great difference between not noticing a violent poster and deciding not to notice it. Such an attitude seems to be embedded deep within the Russian tradition, stretching even beyond the decades of the Soviet experiment. For example, one cannot really say whether the czarist government and the local authorities encouraged pogroms in Russia's western provinces known as the Pale of Settlement. Yet it is clear that they did not exactly oppose such violent outbreaks against the Jewish population, choosing "not to notice" what was their legal responsibility to act upon. The second half of the policeman's statement is even more problematic. The policeman's words are words of double-speak. He knows that the installation of such a sign is a crime under a law that prohibits statements in public that may incite interethnic violence. His attempted analysis of the meaning of calling anyone a Jew in Russia is unnecessary: the term used on the poster, *zhid*, is blatantly clear about its genesis. This term's origins in meaning, derogatorily, "a Jew" cannot be separated from its intentions. Our policeman knows precisely the extent to which the law has been broken by the sign's author(s). He also knows well that what would come under the scrutiny of investigation would be his and his colleagues' inaction. Here, if one is even a high-ranking official responsible for public order, truth takes its usual back seat. A well-evolved culture of lies, lies entangled with apathy and in-action, offers our policeman many ready precedents to defamiliarize the situation the way he is able to. If there is such a thing as Russian national memory, it does not include the admission of crimes against the Jews. The years of Soviet experience, when crimes against whole groups, exemplified most crudely by relocations of entire populations such as the Chechens and the Crimean Tartars, as well as by the evolution of political anti-Semitism—most notable in the "anti-cosmopolitanism" campaign during the late years of Stalin's reign, only exacerbate this memory. The policeman on the side of the Moscow highway is thus capable of speaking in a highly elusive tongue that disguises its inten-tions and is both understood and seemingly not understood by its in-tended recipients—the country's population.

Indeed, even graver than standing by in inaction is standing by in ad-mitting to past crimes—by extent, standing by in inaction and in oppo-sition to the work of public memory, a memory in need of reconciliation of past with the present, a memory demanding that painful traumas be exposed and cured in order for a country's healthful recovery.

I first heard about Tatyana's brave act inside a foreign-language center in Oxford, where I was spending an academic year, in a spa-cious room where I often came to watch live broadcasts of Russian news. My gaze was far removed from events that were occurring some three time zones away. Yet it was impossible not to conjure up reflections on another event in which I had participated just a few days before, when, after a friend announced that a guest lecture by Gennady Zyuganov was to happen that afternoon, I found myself in a large auditorium, silently obliterating the rest of the audience in my mind, staring solely at the leader of Russia's Communist Party.

I did not know whether to laugh or cry during Zyuganov's "lecture." I knew that a man speaking in code words and formulaic phrases could have been any other previous leader of the Communist Party of the Soviet Union. Nothing in his speech was new; everything that he said about the past Soviet glories and the future redemption in international communism has been said before. A "lecture by the leader of Russia's socialism" announced to Oxford students was a farce. Zyuganov knew well that he was not going to give a lecture; he knew that his speech would not have been different from any of the myriad speeches declaimed triumphantly from podiums of the Communist Party congresses. He knew that he was going to lie.

Zyuganov lied even before his arrival in Oxford, he lied throughout his "lecture" about the glories of his party and its contributions to the bright past of the Soviet Union, and he lied while answering questions. One question from the audience pierced me sharply. A student spoke of the German school programs that pay a great deal of attention to de-Nazification of the country, programs that educate German children about their country's shameful past. He then wondered if some degree of de-Sovietization was appropriate for the Russian schools in order to make the future generations live up to their country's own dark experience.

In a manner of speech familiar to him from the decades-old culture of party propaganda, Zyuganov stayed away from answering the question directly. What followed instead was yet another excursion into communism's lasting contribution to Russia's past and the necessity of its resurrection in the country's future. He spoke of the USSR's progress and evolution under wise communist leadership despite the "few mistakes" that were made. Zyuganov failed to explain what these few mistakes were, but it was not hard to extrapolate: death of millions of camp prisoners, murder of kulaks, death of more than a million Jews whom the Soviet government chose not to inform of advancing German danger, failure to disclose the Chernobyl disaster for more than a week during which many lives could have been saved. These were indeed some in the long list of Zyuganov's untold few minor infractions.

Zyuganov's failure to admit to his party's crimes against its own people, his continuous veneration of Stalin as Russia's great leader, and his incessantly formulaic language extend to the country as a whole. Political freedom gained with the demise of communism is a hard pill to swallow for many Russians: the new social order does not offer many ready answers, does not invite everyone to take their appropriate niche. In a society abruptly delivered from "unfreedom," nostalgia lurks beneath, nostalgia for the image of the past glories that Zyuganov and the likes of him continue to feed, cunningly, to the destitute. Gennady Zyuganov knows that he lied to the students in Oxford. He knows also that he lies to the millions who choose to listen to him and vote for the Communist Party in national elections. He understands well that his lies adorn already existing fabrications produced in the Soviet Union, obscuring any possible historical truth in further layers of contradiction. The policeman on the side of a Moscow highway is also aware of his lies that seek to exculpate both his inaction as well as the long-standing tradition of prejudice and persecution. Both men lie because they can do nothing else: they are schooled in prevarication; they are not capable of exposing the truth regardless of how acutely they are aware of it.

One cannot begin to get over a personal trauma if the cause of that trauma itself is not exposed and understood. For a country in need of a cure, a continuous embellishment of the original trauma in further lies is an injection of poison.

Tatyana Sapunova is not Jewish; her action was not done in defense of her people, unless it was the Russian people and their morality that she was defending against another ethical failure. Tatyana resists a status of the hero, saying that any normal human being would have acted the same in her place. For her it does not matter whether the poster aimed to entice violence against Jews or any other people. If she saw a sign "Death to the Azeris!" she would have removed it anyway, says Tatyana. In this, Tatyana's action is one of civic heroism.

The doctor who treated badly wounded Tatyana after the explosion, said, unwaveringly, that he would have done the same had he encountered the sign. One's hypothesis about a possible action in a particular set of circumstances should always be doubted; yet the fact that the doctor was willing to state this opinion alone is a testament to the change that Tatyana's sacrifice is beginning to bring to Russian society.

Tatyana is shy, she does not seek attention, and she refuses to admit that her deed was anything but commonplace. Yet it was not. In a country where the culture calls for silence and gazes shift the opposite way of potential trouble, Tatyana's action was the first contemporary example of ethical consciousness.

The shattering explosion and its popular resonance were the birth pangs of a civil society.

I often imagine Tatyana driving her car along the infamous highway and the first ideas that come into her mind when she reads "Death to the Yids!" on the side of the road. I often wonder if she is reluctant to stop, if she wavers a bit, but I always conclude that the thought of stopping is the first to occur for this woman. Tatyana stops her car. She says that she will be back in a minute to her elderly mother and her little daughter, both sitting in the back seat. She climbs the side of the road and pulls the sign before the explosives attached to the poster go off.

I cannot help but think about Tatyana's car as a microcosm of Russian society in flux in the fledgling post-Soviet years. An elderly woman,

a young woman in her twenties, and a toddler moving along the highway of change—three crucial generations gathered together at once.
Tatyana's mother spent most of her life under the Soviet regime. Its
convoluted language undoubtedly entered her consciousness, incapa-
ble of setting it free. The Soviet mentality is incompatible with living in
a democratic society the same way that the mentality of slavery could
not have outlasted Egyptian captivity. Moses knew well that people who
had once been slaves can never become free; he knew that forty years—a
generation's worth of time—had to pass before the Jews could enter the
land of their freedom. Even in a free society that Russia is trying hard to
become, Tatyana's mother—despite her possible good intentions—can
never be free. In fact, a free society is impossible with her presence, with
even a miniscule trace of her kind of thinking: her lifetime must pass
before any crucial changes can set in.

Tatyana's daughter, a child born after the fall of communism, has the
potential to be that much-needed new generation which would galva-
nize the drastic change of the Russian society, a potential to create this
society's new ethical standards and to embody its new moral consciousness. Yet she grows up at the time of confusion, the time of troubles, as
the post-1991 years became known in Russia, a period when the old
mentality would not loosen its tight grip and the new consciousness was
much too young, much too inchoate to ever win the decisive battle.

Tatyana herself is the crucial link between the past and the present;
she is an embodiment of a potential to commence the forty symbolic
years of wanderings and contemplation.

Tatyana's age—twenty-seven—is poignant; it is a Janus-faced age
with each half looking in opposite directions, seeking a reconciliation
of its disparate gazes. Tatyana was old enough to have gone through
several stages of the Soviet education that were likely to have left their
lasting imprint on her mind at the time when the Soviet Union col-
lapsed. She came of age rapidly—as all teenagers are bound to do in a
country that stops existing—at the time of rapid Westernization, hapless

Russian-style democracy, and an older generation's nostalgia for the recent past. Tatyana's vision of the present is inseparable from the experience of her past. For her, the past's tangled loyalties are to be avoided in
the present in order to have a hope of building a future one day.

What is Tatyana's present as she drives her car along the highway,
noticing such a violent poster? Is it not perhaps her daughter whom she
thinks of first? Is it not for the sake of her daughter that she is moved in
her action? Perhaps it is with the future that her daughter is capable of
embodying that Tatyana is concerned, her daughter—and the future—
who should not grow up thinking that a poster "Death to the Yids!" on
the side of the road is a normal occurrence.

Two months before the explosion on the side of a Moscow highway, I
was a lone traveler from Moscow to Petersburg, on my first return trip
to Russia since my family's emigration to the United States five years
earlier. I got up early in the morning when the train was approaching
Russia's second capital and, having asked for a glass of tea from the train
manager, having propped myself on a windowsill of a speeding train,
could not help but notice "Beat the Yids!" painted in black on a fence of
some monstrous chemical plant, next to a quiet suburban station.

My gaze clouded. I imagined many other lone travelers waking up in
the morning on a similar train, noticing the inscription and never giving
it a second thought. What is written in very visible letters is normal to
them.

It was once normal to me, too. I am six years younger than Tatyana,
yet I, too, was old enough to get my appropriate share of brainwashing
by the time my home country fell to pieces.

When I started going to school, I returned home each day to face
"It's time for the Jews to get out" written in black coal across from my
family's apartment. Not only did our neighbors never bother to erase
the sign, but my family also never dared to do so. With time, seeing
the inscription became normal: the sign never provoked any second

thoughts, it became barely noticeable despite being distinctly visible. As I—along with many other Soviet children—was growing up, many things that were terrifyingly abnormal were entering our common idea of normalcy. The most such a sign outside my door could do for me was to make me quiet at school, ready to walk away from any possible offense from my anti-Semitic classmates and even some teachers. Such passive responses embodied a kind of double-speak much akin to the Soviet language: I would have shown an abiding face to my offenders, hiding any other real feeling deep inside. Such responses became normal, too.

But how long can such "normalcy" be tolerated? How long can the likes of Gennady Zyuganov, the Communist Party chief and a self-proclaimed inheritor of all there is to inherit from the Soviet age, allow themselves to define normalcy's standard in their tongue of lies?

How long can the likes of the policeman on the side of the infamous Moscow highway pretend to "not notice" a sign that is meant to entice violence while eliciting indifference to its presence?

How can the likes of Tatyana's mother ever face up to the truth about their times if their universe in its entirety is nurtured in the culture of lies?

To view the appearance of a "Death to the Yids!" sign on the side of a Moscow highway only as an anti-Semitic occurrence would diminish a much larger problem. Russia's usual level of xenophobia is now exacerbated by a deep economic crisis when much finger-pointing is seen as normal, where, in the words of our policeman, anyone can be called a Jew these days. Similarly, it is limiting to view Tatyana's action as resistance to Russia's ever-present evil of anti-Semitism. The issue is the ethics of normalcy itself, for when a society becomes used to the quotidian presence of violence and learns to ignore it, it is forever enslaved in its own culture of lies.

Tatyana's glory, then, is precisely in this concern for the future that she is able to extract from the double-edged identity that her age—the age of her generation—allows her to have. Her heroism, indeed, is in acting as a human being should in these circumstances, yet as not many people have dared in similar circumstances in Russia. In a society that is trying hard to set itself on the path of freedom and openness, in a society where contesting ideologies of the old and the new abound, Tatyana's deed is no less than a paragon of a new ethical standard. It is a standard where something that is clearly offensive should not be ignored, a standard in which one is forever concerned with the future generations that must learn normalcy in a way that is free of doublespeak, a standard in which normalcy is free of concern to untangle itself from the layers of lies eager to embellish it.

The action of the twenty-seven-year-old Muscovite Tatyana Sapunova is singular, yet it is undoubtedly the first resonant step on the path toward the civil society.

Notes

1. *Izvestia,* May 30, 2002. Here and throughout all factual references about the events of the explosion are given from this issue. All translations from the Russian are mine.
2. Nadezhda Mandelshtam, *Vospominania* (New York: Chekhov, 1970), 25. Nadezhda Mandelshtam's memoir is also published in English as *Hope Against Hope.* Here the translation from the Russian is mine.
3. Mandelshtam, *Vospominania,* 27.
4. *Izvestia,* May 30, 2002.

Made by Us

Young Women, Sweatshops,
and the Ethics of Globalization

SARAH STILLMAN
2005
Yale University

ON THE NIGHT LI CHUNMEI died, there wasn't a single toy in sight. No Buzz Lightyear, no Pocahontas, no Minnie Mouse. The grinning stuffed characters that Li brought to life each day in China's Bainan Toy Factory weren't around to see her frail body rocking back and forth on the bathroom floor. Nor did they hear her coughing up blood. They were already on their way to Disney stores in America, waiting to be wrapped in brightly colored paper for the holiday season. It was Li's roommates who discovered her bleeding from the nose and mouth; they immediately called an ambulance, but her heart stopped before it arrived. Like me, Li was nineteen years old.

The district medical examiner in the industrial town of Songgang says he doesn't know the exact cause of Li's death. But there is talk. Friends and coworkers attribute it to *guolaosi*—an increasingly common phrase that means "overwork fatality" and generally applies to young laborers in China's booming sweatshop industry. After nearly four years of making Disney toys for shipment to America, it's as if Li's slender body finally decided to say, "No: I cannot carry another heavy box of plastic eyeballs or velvet paws; I refuse to breath another gulp of hot factory air swirling with multi-colored dust; I will not last another sixteen-hour shift for the sake of $1.92 in wages."

And so, Li Chunmei's father traveled three days and nights from the peasant village of Xiaoeshan to recover her lifeless body. He tried to follow his own advice to Li—a mantra he'd uttered half a decade ago as his daughter left their mountain hamlet for the sweatshops of Songgang: "It's bad luck to cry." Since the funeral, he has returned to tending his scattered patches of wheat and rice, all the while hoping that guolaosi won't circle back to claim his other daughter, twenty-two-year-old Li Mei, who also left home for the factories. Li Mei harbors fears of her own, but there is little time to nurse them. No, she has work to do.

Close your eyes, stick out your finger, and spin the globe. Chances are, you'll land on one of the countless nations where goods destined for the United States are being produced with the help of young women's sweatshop labor. In an era when most American manufacturers have discovered the profit-boosting miracle of low-wage offshore production, teenage girls are increasingly bearing the burdens of globalization while reaping relatively few of its tremendous rewards. Tragedies like Li Chunmei's no longer read like horror stories from a parallel universe; instead, they seem part and parcel of the ethical crisis plaguing our international corporate economy. Herein lies one of my generation's greatest dilemmas: as global trade opens up new opportunities for society's economic and social advancement, how can we ensure that its path is charted by ethical as well as financial imperatives?

If the developing world's toy industry is any indication, globalization's moral compass is in desperate need of repair. This December, as U.S. college students like me trek home for the holidays, three million toy workers in China alone—the vast majority of whom are young women like Li Chunmei—will be locked inside some 2,800 factories to produce the season's hot new toys in time for Hanukah, Christmas, and Kwanzaa.

They will work fifteen hours a day, seven days a week, thirty days a month, while earning wages as abysmal as twelve cents an hour. Many will be required to handle toxic chemicals with their bare hands; some will be physically or sexually abused in the process.

Although China scrapes the very bottom of the sweatshop barrel, exploitative factory work marks a right of passage for young women across the developing world. In Bangladesh, girls as young as thirteen stitch caps for American universities like Cornell, Columbia, and Georgetown. In Nicaragua, young women sewing garments for Sears and J. C. Penney recently lost their jobs for demanding the right to unionize. In American Samoa, teenage girls producing clothes for Wal-Mart, Target, and other U.S. retailers were held as indentured servants in the Daewoosa factory—cheated of their wages, beaten, starved, and molested until the factory owner was detained for human trafficking. The depressing inventory of abuses goes on like Satan's wish list to Santa.

Given all this, I am stunned by the mounting gulf between my daily reality and that of the average teenage girl in other corners of the world —places as distant as China and as close as Central America. Has globalization—touted as the great homogenizer—in fact rendered our lives unrecognizable to each other? Perhaps the only way to know is to ask, which is why I quickly embrace the chance to visit with Lydda Gonzalez.

When hip-hop superstar P. Diddy launched a new clothing line with the slogan "It's not just a label, it's a lifestyle," I somehow doubt he had Lydda Gonzalez in mind. Lydda, a nineteen-year-old from Honduras, once sewed shirts for P. Diddy's posh "Sean John" label for the paltry wage of fifteen cents apiece. Like Li Chunmei, she figured that sweatshop labor was her only hope of pulling her family out of poverty.

In 2002, while I was packing my bags for my freshman year of college, Lydda was starting her job with Southeast Textiles—a Honduran factory producing for Sean John, Old Navy, Polo Sport, and other popular name brands. While I was busy attending history lectures and poetry seminars, she was enduring compulsory pregnancy tests, twelve-hour shifts six days a week, and mandatory unpaid overtime. While I was catching up on sleep over summer vacation, Lydda was staring at a pink slip; she and fourteen coworkers were fired from Southeast Textiles after lobbying for better working conditions.

Now, Lydda Gonzalez and I are fighting the wind on a harsh November evening in New Haven, carrying bags of grated cheese and pinto beans to a dinner lecture at Yale's Latino Cultural Center. Lydda shouldn't be toting groceries tonight, I know; she is one of the guests of honor. But, as she jokes in Spanish, "No es nada nuevo": hard work, for her, is nothing new. Besides, there's a whole lot of food to transport; a big crowd of students and community members will soon gather to eat tostadas and listen as Lydda imparts her striking but sadly quotidian account of working in a maquiladora factory.

This blustery walk is my first moment alone with Lydda since she arrived at Yale in the afternoon with two other Honduran sweatshop workers and Charles Kernaghan, director of the National Labor Committee in Support of Human and Worker Rights, a human rights group. The team of four has been traveling the U.S. in a gray van, visiting high school and college campuses in hopes of rekindling the student anti-sweatshop movement. Last week, Lydda and her cohorts Fabia Gutierrez and Martha Iris Lorenzo spoke at a crowded press conference in front of P. Diddy's soon-to-be boutique on New York City's Fifth Avenue, denouncing the appalling working conditions in Sean John factories. Tomorrow, they will share their testimonies before the U.S. Senate. But right now, in the wind that is blowing us sideways and making us huddle close with elbows intertwined, Lydda is mine for a brief flash; the others have scurried ahead. There is so much to be asked.

What does she think of America? It is like *la luna, las películas, un sueño:* the moon, the movies, a dream. Is she scared to go home now that right-wing Honduran newspapers have labeled her a terrorist? She refuses to give in to fear; two hundred union members have promised to greet her at the Tegucigalpa airport. What do most girls our age do for fun in Honduras? See movies, go to the *discoteca*, hang out in the street. Does she have a boyfriend? Oh. Do *I* have a boyfriend? We blush.

I already know the more formal details of Lydda's biography. She recited them to a crowd of seventy attentive Yalies earlier this afternoon, and I'd read the *New York Times* and *Washington Post* profiles. I am aware that Lydda began her first job at age eleven, working in a bakery. I know that she moved to Honduras's San Miguel Free Trade Zone when she was seventeen, hoping to find employment inside the maquiladora factories surrounded by tall metal gates and armed guards.

I understand that she was quickly hired by Southeast Textiles. That she sewed 190 Sean John shirts a day. That the only drinking water inside the factory often contained fecal matter. That her supervisor urged her to work faster with shouts of "Donkey," "Bitch," and worse. And the grand finale: that when she finally spoke up and asked to be treated with dignity, she was fired and blacklisted from the Honduran maquiladora industry.

But there is so much more to be known—things that newspaper articles and public testimonies can't divulge about years of sweat and quietly preserved dreams in a world with horizons half the size of my own. I notice it when we stop by my dorm room to pick up the bags of groceries and rest for an instant between the afternoon lecture and the evening dinner event. Lydda and I begin chatting about our dream jobs, and she remarks with a sheepish smile, "I would have liked to be a writer." "Me, too!" I respond, eager for common ground, not realizing until later the vast difference between her "I would have liked to be" and my "I hope to be." I ask if she keeps a journal. "No, when I come home from work at night, my bed is my diary," she replies somewhat cryptically. I want to ask more, but I realize we're late for the dinner. We grab the groceries and run.

Charles Kernaghan has the first indignant words before the crowd at
the Latino Cultural Center. His booming voice knows how to command
attention; each sentence catapults from his lips like an exclamation
point on steroids. He emphatically waves a gray Sean John shirt in the
air as he hollers at wide-eyed Yalies: "These women started working
when they were eleven years old! . . . Lydda made fifteen cents for this
forty-dollar shirt! That's an enormous mark-up: DO THE MATH!"

Once Kernaghan has purged his fireball homily, Lydda walks slowly
to the front of the room. "Mi nombre es Lydda Eli Gonzalez, y soy de
Honduras. . . . My name is Lydda Eli Gonzalez, and I am from Honduras." The room falls silent. "I am nineteen years old."

Lydda, too, has learned the art of working a crowd. But her style
takes the audience for a spin: if Kernaghan was thunderous, she's as
hushed and concentrated as lightning; if he flung his words like boo-
merangs, she places each sentence calmly before you in all its naked,
unpretentious dreadfulness.

"My job is to attach sleeves to the shirts," she explains. "There is a
lot of dust in the air. . . . You breathe it in, and you go into the factory
with black hair and come out with hair that is white or red or whatever
the color of the shirts we are working on." She tells of being forbidden
to talk to her coworkers, of being sexually harassed by supervisors, and
of being searched by random male guards on the rare occasions when
she was allowed to use the bathroom. Like any good organizer, Lydda
finishes her testimony with an entreaty: "There is too much injustice
in the Sean John factory, and that is why I came here. . . . We sew your
clothing. Please demand that the companies treat us with respect.
Thank you."

Next, Fabia Gutierrez strides to the front of the room—an undeniably sexy forty-five-year-old union leader wearing tight embroidered
jeans and a fake leather jacket. A maquiladora worker for nineteen years
and now a seasoned labor organizer, she knows how to make the big
links. She speaks heatedly of the Free Trade Area of the Americas

(FTAA), a trade agreement being negotiated between the United States and all of Latin America (except Cuba). If passed, the mammoth FTAA might unroll a red carpet for big business, encouraging footloose industries to scour the Americas in search of cheap wages and minimal labor regulations. "Right now, the multinational corporations are waging a campaign to wipe out the Central American labor movement to pave the way for the FTAA," she concludes in animated Spanish. "We need your help to stop them."

The tale of the toiling sweatshop worker has been told before, perhaps even to the point of cliché. Companies have been condemned; apologies have been delivered; "Codes of Conduct" have been nailed to factory walls. And despite it, the misery has continued. For that reason, the National Labor Committee selected these brave women from thousands working in Honduran maquiladoras because they were ready to cry out for something bigger, something bolder. Lydda, Martha, and Fabia were ready to talk World War Three.

Most of the unsettled faces in the room tonight seem excited but overwhelmed by the prospect of their conscription. When it comes time for Q&A, hands spring up with inquiries about how students can take up arms. "First of all," Charles Kernaghan commands, "realize that there are 15.6 million college students in the U.S. today, and that you have $268 billion dollars a year of purchasing power." In other words, aim and fire with your pocketbooks. "We're not pansies," Kernaghan says, drawing a few laughs. "This is guerrilla warfare."

But Lydda soon chimes in. Her quiet words remind us that the military analogy is more than a cute rhetorical flourish. When she returns to Honduras next week, she explains, she will likely face intimidation and even death threats. Who knows what the Honduran newspapers will call her next; they've already tagged her a "terrorist of the maquila," a liar, and a traitor to her country. But Lydda won't be turning back. Next week, she'll ask to be reinstated at the Sean John factory.

It's clear that we, too, are needed on our home turf: to write letters to
Sean John and other companies, to raise consciousness, and—perhaps
most significant—to throw a wrench in the upcoming Miami negotiations of the FTAA and other trade deals negotiated without young
women like Lydda or Li Chunmei in mind. With that rally cry, their talk
is suddenly done. People rise in a standing ovation.

Some jot down notes on their hands or loose scraps of paper. The
room echoes with that strained sense of the in-between: Should we cry
or should we cheer? Maybe both? As I begin folding chairs, I find myself wondering how long Lydda's words will fill our heads and hearts.

Soon, we've reached departure time. Lydda grabs my hand. "Continue your struggle," she says, stealing the words from my mouth. I'm
not quite ready for her to go. I had promised to play her P. Diddy's latest
album; she'd mentioned that, until she came to the United States, she
had no idea whom she was sewing shirts for (that is, until Mr. Kernaghan
described P. Diddy as "the ex-boyfriend of J-Lo"). I had meant to ask
her about her family and her friends, and maybe to tell her about mine.

Instead, we hug. She descends the steps of the Latino Cultural Center into the unfamiliar cold, turning back to wave.

When I return to my dorm that evening, the women's stories weave in
and out of my mind. I sit on the couch with my roommate, and we talk
about the otherworldliness of having Lydda, Martha, and Fabia in our
room just five hours ago, drinking milk and chatting. We feel like fish in
dirty water as we use a National Labor Committee report to take an inventory of our suite:

> One Nike T-shirt: Made by company that employed
>   Martha for five cents a shirt.
> One Adidas soccer ball: Made by company notori-
>   ous for antiunionism, low wages, and abuse of
>   young women workers.

One Barbie doll, legs missing: Made in China by
Mattel, in factory much like Li Chunmei's. Average worker age = fourteen.

Two pairs New Balance sneakers: Chinese workers
there are paid eighteen cents an hour and forced
to live in crammed twelve-person dorm rooms.

At some point the list-making gets old. The message is clear. Somehow we've become submerged in a system that genuinely repulses our
ethical sensibilities. The 1990s may have been the decade of the depressing sweatshop exposé, but I finally see why the past few years have
rendered talk of sweatshops blasé. If we can't untangle ourselves from
the corporate icons we depend upon, then the only way to maintain our
sanity, too often, is to close our eyes. My roommate reminds me that
Lydda didn't come here to stir up guilt. She came with a mission and
finished her talk with a plea: "We need people in the streets." I get on-
line and book an eighty-nine-dollar JetBlue flight.

It's settled. I am going to protest the free trade negotiations in Miami.

Three police helicopters hover above our heads like giant, genetically
modified mosquitoes. Bright spotlights slice through the dark as throngs
of activists hustle in and out of the abandoned warehouse that's been
reclaimed as the "Convergence Center"—a headquarters in downtown
Miami where people from around the country can gather to plan direct
actions against tomorrow's Free Trade Area of the Americas meeting.

This is a motley crew. Some are here because they believe the FTAA
will wreak havoc on the environment—ushering in the destruction of
rain forests, the patenting of biodiversity, and the production of genetically engineered crops. Others are here because they fear the FTAA will
enshrine investors' rights at the expense of American workers, causing
massive job losses as more manufacturing plants are shipped south of
the border. Still others have come out of anger that the treaty is being

negotiated in secrecy, by undemocratic institutions that all but ignore the voices of civil society.

I am here because the moral battle over sweatshops is here. In its current incarnation, the FTAA is structured to drastically accelerate corporate globalization across the Americas—largely at the expense of young women my age. An epic free trade treaty that threatens to repeat the bloopers of past trade agreements on a larger scale, the FTAA will invite U.S. industries to set up factories in Latin America that have virtually no accountability to labor and human rights standards.

Many neoliberal economists rationalize this system of exploitation, arguing that "sweatshops are better than no shops, right?" They might even point out that Lydda Gonzalez's earnings at Southeastern Textiles surpassed Honduras's prevailing minimum wage of fifty-five cents an hour by more than ten cents.

Yet relativism doesn't erase the fact that sixty-five cents an hour is still not a salary of survival. It doesn't mitigate the degradation Lydda and many other young women confront daily: needing special permission to use the bathroom; being sexually harassed by supervisors; and facing antiunion intimidation from managers. Nor does it exonerate U.S. consumers from our duty to demand more of the multinational corporations whose products fill our closets and deck our bodies, as well as from the trade negotiators who purport to represent our will.

I have good company in which to raise my voice against the FTAA. Hundreds of activists are already funneling into the Convergence Center to meet fellow protesters and to brainstorm creative acts of civil disobedience. Thousands more are expected to fill the streets tomorrow.

As the evening goes on, the whine of the helicopters reminds us that whatever we are planning for tomorrow, the police are busy preparing for it. Clearly, the stakes are high in this fight over the future of globalization. Tomorrow, the goal of more than 2,500 riot cops will be to create the illusion, contrived as it may be, of business as usual. The goal of the direct action protesters, on the other hand, will be to create crisis—a loud, media-savvy, in-your-face state of emergency. As well-known labor activist Lisa Fithian puts it, "I create crisis, because crisis is that edge where change is possible."

After hearing Li Chunmei's chilling story and listening to Lydda Gonzalez's testimony less than one week ago, I have a slightly different take on things. My goal is not to *create* crisis—it already exists in abundance, as Lydda can attest. My hope is that the thousands of us marching together will be able to *unveil* it, to *make it visible* as a first step toward rendering global sweatshops untenable. The moment globalization enabled so many of the wealthy and powerful to detach from the realities of exploitation—shipping the abuses thousands of miles away—was also the moment that sweatshops became, to them, morally tolerable. My belief is that the reverse will also prove true: the moment that the sad fact of sweatshops explodes in the streets—half carnival, half apocalypse—could be the moment that young women like Li and Lydda are finally recognized as fully human.

The next day starts as pure circus. I can understand why the media might overlook the serious motivations driving many of the protestors; it's easy to get lost in the whirl of drums, chants, songs, and even a conga line. I begin to explore, weaving in and out of speeches, heated political conversations, and guerrilla theater performances under the hot sun.

Suddenly, the spirit of carnival disappears and everyone is frantically running, though we're not quite sure why or where. We come face-to-face with a line of riot cops in front of the massive wire fence separating protesters from trade ministers. I'm brought back to earth, back to the enormous moral issues that are on the line today. I begin to feel claustrophobic. It looks as if a few people are getting arrested thirty feet in front of me. *What am I doing here?* I find myself asking.

An answer comes zipping back almost reflexively as I hear someone shout, "Corporate greed kills!" Several years ago, such a cry might have struck me as an overzealous cliché, but today it does not. I think of how

Lydda's supervisor once screamed, "Hurry up! Do you know how many girls are lined up in China who would die for this work?" I remember Li Chunmei, who proved him right.

And, for a moment, I grasp the bigger picture. Lydda now has returned to the Southeast Textiles factory in Honduras to sew and fold as I chant and march. She has plans to start a union and believes that the other workers will join her. But she also knows that the battle for young women's rights in the sweatshops cannot be won in a single locale—especially in an age of transnational capital. She has challenged people like me who sit within the belly of the corporate beast, and I am here to answer.

This is not a movement that will be stamped "Made in the USA." The tag won't read "Made in Honduras" or "Made in China." Instead, the profound battle over the ethical future of globalization will be assembled by young women everywhere—those fighting the sexual harassment of their supervisors, those refusing to handle toxic chemicals with their bare hands, those leading the struggle for unionization, and those rallying against unfair trade deals. It's a movement that will feature girls bent over sewing machines *and* university computer screens. It will harness our sweat and sorrow for the sake of human rights and social progress. And, if we do it right, our struggle will raise the ghost of Li Chunmei and the dreams of Lydda Gonzalez into the same blue sky our daughters will inherit.

Works Cited

Garcia, Michelle, and Michael Powell. "P. Diddy Feels the Heat Over Sweatshop Charge." *Washington Post,* October 29, 2003, C03.

Interviews with Lydda Gonzalez, Charles Kernaghan, Martha Iris Lorenzo, Fabia Gutierrez, and Barbara Briggs, November 13, 2003.

Interviews with anti-FTAA activists, November 19, 20, 2003.

Pan, Philip. "Few Protections for China's New Laborers." *Washington Post,* May 13, 2003, A01.

The Mask

The Loss of Moral Conscience and Personal Responsibility

KIMLYN BENDER
1992
Jamestown College

> The mask was a thing on its own, behind
> which Jack hid, liberated from shame and self-
> consciousness.
>
> —William Golding, *Lord of the Flies*

IN WILLIAM GOLDING'S *Lord of the Flies,* proper English schoolboys in uniforms and choir robes become savages who forsake ethical principles and commit murder. What allowed this deviation from civilization to savagery? It was not the creation of weapons; it was the creation of the mask. It was a painted face of colored clay and charcoal that facilitated the abandonment of ethics by the boys.

Jack and the hunters in *Lord of the Flies* find a freedom behind the mask that allows them to commit savage acts that otherwise, ostensibly, their moral consciences would not allow. Of all of humanity's contrivances, the mask creates the greatest freedom; it enables the extension of the will into the immoral, simultaneously freeing the individual from the moral conscience and personal responsibility. The mask creates a false identity that confuses and hinders attempts to determine responsibility and administer justice.

One of the achievements of our time is the perfection of the mask, if not in a literal way, then certainly in a metaphorical sense. The masks of today are more sophisticated, and much more effective, than those of the past. They have led to a breakdown of ethics, for, while not abolishing ethical principles, they have rendered them ineffective, either by providing a haven for immoral conduct free from responsibility or by frustrating attempts to determine personal responsibility. But most detrimentally, they have not only provided a freedom from the moral conscience but deadened it as well. The challenge of ethics today is to focus not on the masks but on the individuals behind them and to reawaken within the individual a renewed sensitivity to the moral conscience, bringing every area of life and action under its guidance.

The mask we use to cover our unethical behavior has its origin in the human need to be ethical. The human need to be ethical is reflected in the pervasive need to justify our behavior. This arises from an intrinsic fear of being unethical, for we realize that betrayal of the moral conscience results in guilt. The human need to be ethical is therefore reflected in these two events of human experience: guilt and the moral conscience. The moral conscience is the internalized sense of the "ought" directed toward universal moral principles; guilt is the experience felt at failing to adhere to the moral conscience that calls us to the sense of the "ought" and the ethical. I use the term *ethical* in its widest sense to refer to that which furthers justice, honesty, integrity, and life rather than death. I see these as universal principles held by the majority of people of all time and in the Western tradition contained in the ingrained if not acknowledged Judeo-Christian ethics and the ethics of the rights of humanity recorded in the U.S. Constitution.

The ethical imperative is often in conflict with an equally strong inclination to act immorally and commit actions that violate our ethical conscience and the ethical principles we hold. It is this desire to act unethically while avoiding guilt and maintaining ethical integrity that has led to the creation of masks, separate identities from our perception of our essential character. Not only do we create separate identities, but we create separate compartments of our lives to which our personal ethics do not apply.

The identity of the mask does not eliminate the moral conscience but circumvents it, for it elides ethical principles from sectors of our lives behind the assumed identity, thereby freeing us from guilt and the moral conscience. The mask therefore fulfills our opposing desires to perceive ourselves as ethical while committing actions that compromise the moral principles we and society embrace. This is the freedom from shame that the mask can bring.

The mask is thereby created by the compartmentalization of our lives. It is the excision of our personal ethics from our public life and occupation, resulting in an ability to make occupational decisions apart from ethical guidelines. Of course, there has always been a distinction between behavior public and private, *but this has never been an ethical distinction.* Certain proprieties have always required specific behavior in distinctive areas of life, but the same ethical guidelines applied to every area. A comprehensive ethics formerly guided every aspect of one's life, every action, but we have now created distinctive ethics for distinctive areas of our lives. These distinctive ethics are in fact new principles that replace traditional ethical principles behind the mask.

For Jack in *Lord of the Flies,* his mask was the painted face of the hunter, behind which he could commit acts which his English mores and ingrained ethics would not have allowed. The masks of today's society are more subtle. Four contemporary masks that we have created are the masks of the businessperson, the politician, the scientist, and the doctor, and behind these the vacuum created by the removal of traditional ethical principles is filled with the insertion of new principles. Some of the greatest breaches of ethics have occurred under the auspices of good or neutral principles or policies, and no segment of society is exempt from this. In the business world, *profit* is a positive term, a by-product of our economic system, and yet behind the mask of the businessperson the principle of profit easily replaces all principles of ethics, with the consequence that financial gain becomes an end to which ethical means no longer apply.

Government is not immune from this misuse of policy. Actions that promote the so-called good of the nation or national security often fall outside of the jurisdiction of ethical principles; prudence, rather than principle, guides the great majority of political policy formation. Behind the mask of the politician government is allocated its own version of diplomatic immunity, as if *power* itself were a justification for its own abuse.

The mask of the scientist has allowed *progress* to be elevated in science to a status that excludes ethical imperatives. While ethicists such as Hans Jonas have realized the dangers to humanity that technology holds, ethical principles to guide scientific undertaking are often lacking or nonexistent.[1] Progress is the guiding axiom and justification for all scientific undertaking.

Medicine also seems to have changed its ethical imperative; the "preservation of life" is at times replaced behind the mask of the doctor with the amelioration of pain, and the eradication of *pain* has opened up a score of ethical dilemmas and questions that have placed the definition of life in jeopardy. "Life not worth living" was a motto often used in the Third Reich to justify its program of euthanasia, and although today such atrocities are universally condemned, the current discussions concerning euthanasia must seriously consider what is at stake by replacing preservation with pain as the primary directive of medicine. It seems that the urgency of pain has caused ethical caution to be disregarded.

We mask our worst actions with our best intentions. Although *profit, power, progress,* and the amelioration of *pain* are good or ethically neutral concepts, they, along with many others, often replace ethical guidelines behind the mask and are used to justify unethical actions, numbing the moral conscience. But the shelter provided unethical conduct by the masks is not the only reason for ethical confusion; they are aided by an increasingly complex society.

The freedom from personal responsibility that the mask can bring is aided by the unprecedented complexity of the modern world. Whether created intentionally or as a by-product of modern society, this complexity is itself a mask that provides freedom from self-consciousness and a haven for unethical behavior. It has established a new ability for the individual to submerge one's identity into that of the corporate entity, whatever that entity may be, and one's actions within that entity are lost in the shuffle. Demonstrating responsibility for unethical and often illegal actions is rendered impossible; no one can be found to fault.

The freedom from self-consciousness that Jack found behind the mask in *Lord of the Flies* was a freedom not only from the self-consciousness of shame but also from the self-consciousness of personal identity as he became a part of the collective mask of the hunters, which had the "throb and stamp of a single organism."[2] The collective mask of the corporate entity allows personal actions within that entity to be viewed not as one's own but as those of the larger entity. This provides a freedom from personal accountability, as the complexity of the mask deflects all attempts to determine personal responsibility for unethical conduct.

The combination of the personal mask providing liberation from the moral conscience and the collective mask of complex corporate institutions in which individuality and self-consciousness are lost is the most sophisticated mask of our time. It has ushered in an age of scandal as ethics seems no longer able to deal with the present magnitude of moral perplexities. The mask of today is in fact the incorporation and systemization of evil, seen in its most sinister form in Nazi Germany and its attempt to destroy European Jewry. The symbolic mask of the Nazis enabled by the dehumanization of the Jews, facilitating the elimination of the moral conscience and the loss of personal identity in the Nazi killing machine, resulted directly in the absence of guilt, shame, and personal responsibility at the Nuremberg Trials.

While the mask of our time calls us irrevocably to address systemic evil, we must do so in a way that does not neglect to address the individual. The bane of our time is focusing on the complex mask of a system while failing to confront the individuals behind it. In focusing on a system we often fall into two temptations.

The first temptation that exists in dealing with complex corporate systems and the unethical conduct that plagues them is twofold. The first step is to "dehumanize" the system, viewing it not as an aggregation of individuals and their actions but as an entity that possesses its own ontological identity. The second step is then to endow the contrived entity with moral status, positing good or evil in the system, rather than in the actions and individuals that compose or are involved in it. Concepts themselves, furthermore, may be given ontological status and viewed as inherently evil. Racism, drug addiction, and other social ills are often addressed as entities that have a real existence in which evil is intrinsic.

Of course, certain systems are better than others, and some concepts do possess inherent value. Nevertheless, this is a dangerous temptation, for it presents a problem that appears so intricate and unmanageable that it seems impossible to confront and can often lead to a pessimism that accepts unethical behavior and corruption as innate and essential traits of complex systems such as economies or government. Worse yet, to give in to this temptation is to succumb to addressing masks rather than addressing the real problems behind them; we address an intangible system and concept rather than a tangible individual and action. Racism does not exist "out there," as if it possessed its own existence. It exists only in individuals. Moral evil cannot exist outside the human heart.

The second temptation in addressing systems is to substitute legality for morality. This is a harmful substitution, for legality does not provide the internal impelling force necessary as the basis for ethics and cannot instill the sense of the "ought" that is necessary for ethical action. It imposes legal restrictions, not ethical imperatives. Legality is concerned primarily with public matters and does not provide adequate normative restraints on private conduct. Although it involves prevention and education, its primary purpose is retribution, and therefore deals with the minority, the exception, those who often willingly betray their ethical conscience. Of course, legality is necessary and often overlaps morality, but without morality, law is rendered ineffective—it is only effective if the majority of citizens desire and follow it. It is naive to think that we can fill an ethical vacuum with legal matter. We attempt, however, to utilize legality to bring about an external ethics, an ethics of coercion. But for ethics to be substantial and normative, it must be an internalized ethics of consensus.

We must avoid the temptation to address systems apart from addressing individuals and to substitute legality for morality. The need for an internalized morality rather than an external legality steers us toward an ethics based on the moral conscience. But it may be asked, "Why the individual conscience rather than the collective?" The answer lies in considering two comrades of conscience: guilt and responsibility.

One of the greatest assets for the shaping of ethical conduct, guilt has been relativized into near extinction. This has been achieved not only by the freedom from shame that the mask can bring but also by the social sciences of psychology and sociology, which often view ethical conduct as an amoral phenomenon. We have been so indoctrinated into believing guilt a negative thing that to feel guilt is often equated with a mild type of mental deficiency. We fail to realize that the voice of the moral conscience often speaks the language of guilt in order to bring a modification in thought and behavior. To eliminate guilt, the moral conscience must be numbed. Thus we find a curious lack of shame in our society. When confronted with wrongdoing, there is more of an embarrassment at being found out than a shame of being morally at fault. The greatest sin of our generation is being caught for a crime, not committing the crime itself.

It would be a mistake, however, to say that guilt has disappeared. It has only taken on a new form. Corporate guilt is in vogue in our day and age, as we acknowledge an involvement in systems of guilt. While we are involved in systemic evil, there is a danger in focusing on these abstract forms of guilt while turning a deaf ear to our own personal guilt and failing to address our own personal unethical conduct. C. S. Lewis remarks on this and rightly states that "corporate guilt perhaps cannot be, and certainly is not, felt with the same force as personal guilt."[3] Collective guilt will not bring about ethical or social reform until we deal with personal guilt and personal reform, for social guilt does not normally place a sufficiently heavy burden on the individual to entail corrective action.

Closely linked to this idea of the burden of guilt is the burden of responsibility. Decisions by groups in boardrooms are often of a nature that an individual would not make, but the ability to diffuse individual responsibility into the group often results in corporate decisions that no member of the corporation would claim for his or her own. Ironically, rather than pooling the moral conscience, it is diffused in the group setting; it seems to dissipate into the atmosphere. The group will always make more ethically suspect decisions than the individual, for the group can never bear responsibility in the same manner as the individual.

The diffusion of the moral conscience behind the mask of the collective in terms of both guilt and responsibility provides the necessity for an ethics of the individual moral conscience to supersede the collective. We must propound an ethics that begins with the objective reality of the individual moral conscience while viewing shame and guilt in context as positive modifiers and correctives of behavior. In a time in which the moral conscience is often rationalized away, it remains, though wounded, a real experience of human existence. Both religious and secular philosophers have constructed ethical theories from the objective reality of the moral conscience. Secular ethicists, such as Erich Fromm, assert that humanity is the only species endowed with a moral conscience, and from this they derive an objective ethical system.[4] Religious philosophers, such as Hastings Rashdall, have argued from the personal moral conscience to the existence of God—that is, the moral argument. Rashdall speaks of the "deliverance of conscience" to the mind that is a real object of experience.[5] Even though there is no unanimous consensus as to what is right and wrong in *all* instances, the sense of right and wrong, the sense of the "ought," is in itself an objective reality.

An ethics that is based on the consensus of the individual moral conscience will eventually lead to the questions of education and methodology. Even if the moral conscience as an objective reality is innate and therefore need not be instilled, it must be fostered. "Can ethics be taught?" is a burning question today, but rephrasing the question synonymously can be beneficial in clarifying the issue and finding an answer. Ethics is essentially associated with value judgments, and if we rephrase the question above as "Can values be taught?" we find an answer. Values can be taught. It is a fallacy to think that they cannot be, for if they are not taught, they are adopted. Values are never lost; they are replaced by others.

The great accomplishment of the mask is its ability to provide a haven for value substitution. These substitutions need not be bad values for good values, but good for better. It has been stated above that profit, power, progress, and the amelioration of pain are good or neutral concepts; they are unethical, however, if they are all that we offer posterity. What is important to a society can be recognized by what it deems important to pass on to its children. Unfortunately, it seems that we have emphasized materialism, power for its own sake, a headlong rush into the future, and a painless existence of hedonism as the greatest goods of life. We have forgotten, or forsaken, the concept of "life as an art" in which there are higher goods for which to live, a higher life governed by

ethical imperatives and such simple terms as honesty, integrity, and justice.[6] We have substituted incentives for imperatives. We cannot expect
ethical behavior from a society that is motivated purely by incentives
and expediency; ethical conduct is not always profitable or practical.
And until we realize this and act on it, our youth will only emulate our
selfish and unethical behavior.

The substitution of transitory values for supertemporal ones behind the mask has led to a striving for pleasure and painlessness at all
costs, in which the meaning of existence has been lost. For this reason,
we cannot address the ethical vacuum without addressing the existential
vacuum. The loss of a comprehensive meaning to life has made ethics a
meaningless art. It has led to a loss of a comprehensive ethics that guides
all of life and has fostered the creation of the mask. Material wealth,
power, pleasure, and painlessness are sought as the ends of life and are
sought with no ethical restrictions placed on their acquisition; they are
the goals of existence. The existential vacuum compels us to address
the moral and spiritual vacuum in society. Harvard psychiatrist Robert
Coles comments on the tragedy, "intellectually as well as morally and
spiritually," of our neglecting to address and treat moral and spiritual
questions in public education for fear of violating the Constitution.[7]
Our failure to come to terms with the spiritual void has left us unable to
deal with the impending moral nihilism. We must give people a meaning and a reason to be ethical; as Jonas asserts, "metaphysics must
underpin ethics."[8] For this reason, we must seriously reconsider the
necessity of religion for morality. Secular ethics have not met the task.

The failure to pass on worthy values and meaningful existence to
our children may be the greatest infraction of responsibility in our century. We pass on the cherished goods of our unauthentic living: we give
posterity our masks. If we are to give our children ethical guidance, we
cannot do it by our present feeble attempts of a fragmented ethics, in
which we superficially talk of a business ethics, a medical ethics, or a

legal ethics. This fragmentation of ethics in conjunction with a compartmentalized life and society does not provide the means for managing ethical predicaments faced in many areas. We must submit to our youth an ethical perspective, a Weltanschauung, which guides and directs action in every facet of life. And ethics *must* regulate every area of life. *We cannot punch ethical time-clocks—we cannot wear masks.* This ethical Weltanschauung cannot, however, be taught purely by word; it must also be taught by deed.

Gerald Fleming relates an incident of World War II Germany that illustrates this point. Dr. Bernhard Lösener, adviser on Jewish affairs in the German Reich, when learning of the mass killings of German Jews in Riga on November 30 and December 8, 1941, made an appointment with his superior, Secretary of State Dr. Wilhelm Stuckhart. Lösener protested the killings and, when told by Stuckhart that the killings were "orders from the highest level," replied, "There is a judge inside me who tells me what I have to do." Lösener was relieved of his position and because of his complaints "remained a lower-rank senior civil servant until the end of the war."[9]

While we know little else about Bernhard Lösener, this much can be said. He refused to betray his moral conscience, the "judge inside," and rationalize his actions, and he refused to lose his personal identity and responsibility in the system. *He refused to wear the mask.* And he was willing to pay the price for taking what was the only ethical course of action, recognizing that in an evil system, apathy is compliance. Our only hope for ethical reform resides in these courageous individuals of integrity, these transparent heroes who remain true to the moral conscience within. We must hold them up as examples for our youth and strive to become heroes ourselves.

This view may be criticized by those who state that Lösener's stand was insignificant in the path of the Nazi juggernaut of Jewish destruction. Yet we must ask, what would have happened if one thousand people, or one million, following the dictates of their moral conscience, had stood up against Jewish annihilation? Surely history would have been written differently.

It may be said that people such as Lösener will always be in the minority; they will never be able to resist the massive systemic evil of our time. Victor Frankl, himself a survivor of the Holocaust, agrees that such people compose a minority and that they "always will remain a minority." Nevertheless, he states, "I see therein the very challenge to join the minority. For the world is in a bad state, but everything will become still worse unless each of us does his best."[10]

Frankl, a survivor of the most hideous mask of systemic corruption and evil the world has ever experienced, sees the only hope for combating this evil in the individual. Only the individual guided by moral conscience who "does his best" can remedy the masks of complex evil that confront us in this age. Ethical renewal must be a grass-roots movement. Grass-roots movements begin at home, and home is the individual.

The existence and development of the mask demonstrate that humanity's "essential illness" is not ignorance but rebellion.[11] *The challenge of ethics today is not to instill a new ethics but to unify all of life under the dictates of the moral conscience: the challenge is to take off the mask.* Only when we take off the mask can we see unethical behavior for what it is. We must give the ethical principles of honesty, integrity, and justice jurisdiction over every area of our lives, over every sector of society. Only by doing this can business, government, science, and medicine be redeemed from the moral crisis that plagues them today.

The need to take off the mask is urgent, for the mask not only circumvents the moral conscience but eventually kills it. The mask overcomes and replaces the face of the one who wears it—Jack was overcome by his mask, we by ours. We put on the mask to become what we are not, what we are ashamed of. The tragedy of the mask is that we become what we have attempted to avoid; we become immoral and unethical, and the voice of the moral conscience is in time silenced within us. If Friedrich

Nietzsche's pronouncement that "God is dead" and "we have killed him" was the telling mark of the nineteenth century, then the death of the moral conscience is the mark of our own.[12] Only by removing the mask and listening anew to the moral conscience and following its precepts can our moral illness be cured.

Notes

Epigraph: William Golding, *Lord of the Flies* (New York: Putnam, 1954), 58.

1. Hans Jonas, *The Imperative of Responsibility* (Chicago: University of Chicago Press, 1984), x.
2. Golding, *Lord of the Flies,* 138.
3. C. S. Lewis, *The Problem of Pain* (New York: Macmillan, 1962), 60.
4. Erich Fromm, *Man for Himself* (New York: Fawcett World Alliance, 1965), 234.
5. Hastings Rashdall, *The Theory of Good and Evil,* 2nd ed., vol. 2 (London: Oxford University Press, 1924), 206.
6. Fromm, *Man for Himself,* 28.
7. Richard N. Ostling, "Youngsters Have Lots to Say About God," interview with Robert Coles, *Time,* January 21, 1991, 18.
8. Jonas, *Imperative of Responsibility,* x.
9. Gerald Fleming, *Hitler and the Final Solution* (Berkeley: University of California Press, 1984), 106–107.
10. Victor Frankl, *Man's Search for Meaning* (New York: Washington Square, 1984), 179.
11. Golding, *Lord of the Flies,* 80.
12. Friedrich Nietzsche, *The Complete Works of Friedrich Nietzsche,* vol. 10, ed. Dr. Oscar Levy (New York: Macmillan, 1924), 167–169.

Choices and Challenges

Issues of Conscience in Jewish Literature

AMY JESSICA ROSENZWEIG
1990
Northwestern University

I AM A STUDENT AT A prestigious and wealthy institution where I have been taught that there is little of higher value than prestige and wealth. I am studying at a school that has millions of dollars invested in South Africa, a school that has on its faculty a tenured professor who has published a book calling the Holocaust a hoax. I and my peers have lived our entire lives conscious of the menace of the nuclear threat. It is we who have attended substandard schools because the defense industry was deemed to be a more worthy recipient of tax dollars than our education. And it is we who have been mocked as an inert, passive generation, selfish and self-absorbed, as we stagger under an immense load of world problems, our outraged protestations registering a barely audible cry in the universe. I live in a time when millions are homeless, when one out of every four women is sexually assaulted in her lifetime, when we are becoming inured to the notions of a permanent underclass and a world that is being poisoned to death.

There are simply too many ethical dilemmas that confront me daily for me to attempt to narrow them down or prioritize them. To select one as the quintessential ethical problem to address in this essay is to make a mockery of the question. The underlying dilemma, more in keeping within the essay topic of the meaning and challenge of ethics today, is how we can function in a moral way in the face of immorality. Our first and greatest task must be to work to set alight our too-comfortable consciences. The burning question I ask is where we can look to develop a conscience, having been well educated that greedy consumption is acceptable and that ethical standards are irrelevant.

I am a student of literature. I have always searched in books for answers to questions that trouble me. It is within Jewish literature that I have found authentic ethical touchstones. Echoes of my own efforts to live a fair and just life in a world that is often unfair and unjust resonate in the writings of such authors as Bernard Malamud and Primo Levi, A. B. Yehoshua and Elie Wiesel. Modern Jewish literature provides no easy answers but offers a profoundly meaningful framework for understanding the questions. The literature not only provokes its readers to think in new ways about the many ethical dilemmas confronting our society but also provides a vehicle for grappling with them and demands that the reader develop a conscience.

Issues of conscience are vital and recurrent themes in contemporary Jewish literature. Jewish writers seem compelled to reconcile an acute sense of moral responsibility with the necessary human impulse for autonomy and self-protection. The intensity with which this problem is approached is matched only by an acute sense of failure when impossible ethical standards are confronted by human imperfection. Often this results in a dramatically different version of the hackneyed cliché of Jewish guilt. What is so fascinating about this guilt is not only the different ways in which it manifests itself in literature but the moral questions that it insistently raises and presents the reader. Invariably, the stories force the reader to confront the issues personally. Because of the complexity of the stories and their lack of simplistic solutions, the reader must often wrestle as hard as the protagonist. It is in our willingness to join hands and hearts with these protagonists in this essential struggle, to enter into dialogue with them and see them as our partners and guides, that we can find a means for discovering within ourselves an inner voice.

Bernard Malamud's stories are especially concerned with this idea of moral responsibility. "The Last Mohican" is the story of Arthur

Fidelman, a mediocre talent who has traveled to Italy to complete a book on the painter Giotto, and Shimon Susskind, a beggar he meets immediately on his arrival in Rome and who shadows him throughout his trip. The story is a study of the spirit of charity. The central conflict develops between Fidelman and his conscience. Malamud presents us with a complicated dilemma by allowing us to see Fidelman as a sensitive, not ungenerous man. We can sympathize with Fidelman's mounting aggravation with the beggar Susskind's ungracious, unlovely need. The message of the story is clear; it is necessary to give to those in need simply because they are in need and you have something to give. When Fidelman, who owns two suits, does not give one to Susskind, who has none, Fidelman suffers from loss of his "peace of mind."[1] The conflict Fidelman feels reveals itself in a mysterious loss of his inspiration, which leaves him with a feeling of "growing anxiety, almost disorientation . . . a feeling that was torture."[2] He cannot see the ultimate connection between his conscience and his creative life, his passion. Malamud draws a lifeline between our ability to fully experience ourselves and our lives, and our ethical behavior.

When Fidelman thinks, "History [is] mysterious, the remembrance of things unknown, in a way burdensome, in a way a sensuous experience. It uplifted and depressed, why he did not know," he refers not only to the Italian landscape but also, unwittingly, to his struggles with his own tradition.[3] What is so difficult about accepting this "burdensome, sensuous experience" is reflected in the following exchange between Susskind and Fidelman:

> "You know what responsibility means?"
> "I think so."
> "Then you are responsible. Because you are a man. Because you are a Jew, aren't you?"
> "Yes, goddamn it, but I'm not the only one in the whole wide world. Without prejudice, I refuse the

> obligation. I am a single individual and can't take on
> everybody's personal burden. I have the weight of
> my own to contend with."[4]

This is the difficulty with which Fidelman and the reader are confronted. What is so compelling in this story is the slowly dawning realization of Fidelman, and thus the reader, that the distinction we have made between our burdens and others is largely artificial. We gain strength and meaning in our lives when we lighten the burdens of others, and thereby acknowledge our interconnectedness. This complex problem is one of the central moral issues in this highly ethical literary tradition, and although it is largely resolved for Fidelman by the end of the story, the issues it raises are far too difficult to leave the reader complacent and untroubled.

This ideal of human interconnectedness is not to be confused with self-abnegation and sacrifice. The function of a well-developed conscience is not to place impossible ethical standards before the individual. This is one of the lessons for us in Primo Levi's *Survival in Auschwitz*. Perhaps because it relates the horror of the Holocaust, *Survival in Auschwitz* contains issues of conscience that are even less easily dismissed. The guilt and sense of moral failure in Primo Levi's book are palpable. While the book is rife with examples of moral bankruptcy, what is particularly compelling is the unreasonable guilt that Levi experiences. One would think that any person who survived the camps, particularly without collusion with the Nazis, is simply absolved of guilt over transgressions, real or imagined. No other person would hold a survivor responsible for being crushed under the impossible weight of total oppression. Levi, however, cannot forgive himself for being only human. His guilt is reflected in the preface, where he feels compelled to point out that his is not merely testimony but "a quiet study of the human mind," as though it were not enough that he simply testify.[5]

Levi describes the truly extraordinary behavior of another inmate,

Steinlauf, whose method of coping with Nazi atrocities is based on the belief that since "the Lager was a great machine to reduce us to beasts, we must not become beasts . . . we still possess one power, and we must defend it with all of our strength for it is the last—the power to refuse our consent."[6] But Levi writes that in his retelling of Steinlauf's speech he is using "my language of an incredulous man," clearly demarcating a line between this man who lives by pristine, impossible standards, and himself.[7] When he articulates the Nazi resolution to first destroy the humanity of the Jews and then kill them more slowly, Levi writes, "Who could deny [the SS] their right to watch this choreography of their creation, the dance of dead men, squad after squad, leaving the fog to enter the fog? What more concrete proof of their victory?"[8] Levi's considerable moral outrage seems directed at himself and his fellow prisoners for not somehow proving the Nazis wrong, for not overcoming that which could not be overcome. We recognize the painful irony of Levi's anger in the face of Nazi atrocities that become more unspeakable in the light of Levi's unflagging ethical self-scrutiny. Levi finally acknowledges that "survival without renunciation of any part of one's own moral world—apart from powerful and direct interventions by fortune— was conceded only to very few superior individuals, made of the stuff of martyrs and saints."[9]

Levi nevertheless writes punishingly of the oppressive shame he felt after witnessing the hanging of one of the rebellious inmates. We are silenced before Levi's insistence on holding himself morally accountable. We have no alternative but to look searchingly within ourselves with intensified expectations.

One of the great lessons which the writings of Primo Levi and Elie Wiesel have to teach us is the primary importance of cultivating a sensitive conscience. The Holocaust provides us with the ghastly result of ethical impotence. Other authors such as Thomas Mann have echoed this in their writings. Mann suggests that the rise of fascism is directly connected to the failure of a culture to develop consciences in its members, the failure to demonstrate the connection between abstract, intellectual ideas and human lives. This separation of the emotional and intellectual, apparent in Mann's *Doctor Faustus,* is the first step in deadening the conscience, eliminating a living, breathing ethical code. But as Wiesel writes, "Because Auschwitz symbolizes the culmination of violence, hatred and death, it is our duty to fight violence, hatred and death."[10]

In *Dawn,* Wiesel tells the story of Elisha, a concentration camp survivor who has been recruited by a man named Gad to fight against the British occupation of Palestine. He is charged with the execution of British officer John Dawson, whose murder is in reprisal for the execution of Jewish fighter David ben Moshe. Wiesel brings us into Elisha's conscience in the final hours of his agonized struggle with himself, before he is to kill the officer. The conflict we experience with Elisha is enormously complex: How can we not rejoice with Gad's invitation to turn Elisha's future into an outcry, "an outcry first of despair and then of hope. And finally a shout of triumph"?[11] And yet how can we not be troubled by the edict to "kill those who have made us killers" and grieve Elisha's transformation into one capable of murder?[12] The power in the story lies in the realization that "an act so absolute as that of killing involves not only the killer but, as well, those who have formed him. In murdering a man I am making them murderers."[13] The intensity of this burden for Elisha, who has lost his family and his childhood in the camps, is no less intense for the reader, for we too are survivors. Wiesel's story speaks to us of our responsibility to honor those who perished by renouncing murder and hatred. We must be vigilant in remembering because therein lies the means by which we may guide our steps in ethical behavior.

Philip Roth's story "Defender of the Faith" revolves around the relationship between Sergeant Nathan Marx and Private Sheldon Grossbart. Grossbart repeatedly uses their bond of Jewishness to manipulate privileges for himself and the other Jewish soldiers. Grossbart feigns

religious observance to avoid cleaning the barracks and to wrangle a
weekend pass from Marx. Roth's story shares common elements with
"The Last Mohican." Both are concerned with our ethical responsibility
for each other, particularly a Jew's responsibility to fellow Jews. Both
stories address the importance of using one's relative wealth, be it power
or material goods, to help others. What particularly links the stories are
the altogether unlikeable personalities of those who are in need. Malamud's story comes to terms with itself by the conclusion: Fidelman is
released from his guilt by giving his suit to Susskind, affirming the ethical ideal of charity. But Roth does not leave the reader, or his characters,
with any easy answers.

Sergeant Marx capitulates to a number of Grossbart's requests, only
to find out that the infuriating Grossbart has manipulated him and
abused his privileges. Despite Grossbart's irritating behavior, it is
through his insistent reminding of Marx to "stop closing your heart to
your own" that Marx is able to regenerate spiritually and experience
feelings of human connection and responsibility.[14] Grossbart triggers in
Marx warm memories of his Jewish childhood, and as Marx reveals, "I
indulged myself to a reverie so strong that I felt within as though a hand
had opened and was reaching down inside. It had to reach so very far to
touch me."[15] It is the exasperating Grossbart to whom Roth assigns one
of the more powerful insights in the story, in his philosophically profound description of the Messiah as a collective idea. "Together," Grossbart says, "we're the Messiah. Me a little bit, you a little bit."[16] Nevertheless, Grossbart is a shirking, manipulative liar. Is it simply the bond of
Jewishness that he shares with Marx which should compel Marx to
help him? The reader and Marx wrestle with this question throughout
the story and do not come to any comfortable resolution.

Marx avenges himself against Grossbart, with considerable cause,
by preventing Grossbart from maneuvering himself out of being sent
to fight in the Pacific. We share Marx's momentary satisfaction, and we
are equally stricken with guilt: "Behind me, Grossbart swallowed hard,

accepting his [fate]. And then, resisting with all my will an impulse to turn and see pardon for my vindictiveness, I accepted my own."[17]

Although it is left to the reader to wrestle with the uncomfortable ambiguity of the story's issues still further, to try to ascertain where responsibility truly lies, the underlying message for the reader is unambiguous. Ultimately, we must acknowledge our common bond of humanity. Regardless of judgments that might follow, we must always begin with this fundamental recognition. Our survival as moral beings is absolutely dependent on it, as it is the source of our ethical treatment of each other.

In "Facing the Forces," A. B. Yehoshua addresses this concern with respect to Israeli-Palestinian conflicts. The story revolves almost exclusively around issues of conscience and our moral responsibility for one another. Whereas Malamud, Levi, Wiesel, and Roth seek to make universal statements about ethics and collective responsibility through the narrower experience of individuals, Yehoshua does something very different. He uses the larger issue of the conflict between Jewish ethics and violence against the Palestinians to explain the personalities of the individuals. The few, tersely drawn characters in the story are almost strictly allegorical: the tongueless Arab, his victimized daughter, the guilty, immobilized Israeli, the staunchly and blindly committed head of the Afforestation Department. The forest that the nameless Israeli is required to watch for fires grows over the ruins of an Arab village. The implication is that demolishing the Palestinians in order to build a Jewish homeland, no matter how beautiful, is not congruent with Jewish ethical standards. Although the fire that destroys the forest suggests that without communication the only resolution is conflagration, the question remains whether the ethical discomfort can ever be eradicated.

This story, written in 1963, is still stunningly relevant today. The call to genuine communication is still as powerful. Yehoshua reminds us that we must accept the pain that comes with having a sensitive conscience, acknowledging when necessary the injustice we might have perpetrated, and that we must not allow "the high commanding view to make [us] dizzy."[18] It is only through dulled consciences that we can commit acts of violence against one another, a faulty vision that permits us to see others as less than fully human. In "Facing the Forests," we grapple with Yehoshua's difficult truth: that the ends do not justify the means but are formed by them.

Although the topical concerns shift and the means of articulating them alter with each author, the strong undercurrents of moral struggle and ethics unite all of these works. Issues of conscience consistently prove to be of primary concern to contemporary Jewish writers. Jewish authors provide us with invaluable antidotes to the ethos of apathy and selfishness within our society. This makes this literary tradition enormously important because we as readers must continue to be confronted with ethical concerns in order that we can seek to resolve them meaningfully in our own lives.

Notes

1. Bernard Malamud, "The Last Mohican," in *The Stories of Bernard Malamud* (New York: Plume, 1984), 59.

2. Malamud, "Last Mohican," 63.

3. Malamud, "Last Mohican," 56.

4. Malamud, "Last Mohican," 56.

5. Primo Levi, *Survival in Auschwitz*, trans. Stuart Woolf (New York: Macmillan, 1959), 5.

6. Levi, *Survival in Auschwitz*, 36.

7. Levi, *Survival in Auschwitz*, 36.

8. Levi, *Survival in Auschwitz*, 45.

9. Levi, *Survival in Auschwitz*, 84.

10. Elie Wiesel, *The Night Trilogy* (New York: Hill and Wang, 1985), 134.

11. Wiesel, *Night Trilogy*, 134.

12. Wiesel, *Night Trilogy*, 144.

13. Wiesel, *Night Trilogy*, 169.

14. Philip Roth, "Defender of the Faith," in *Jewish American Stories*, ed. Irving Howe (New York: NAL Penguin, 1977), 392–393.

15. Roth, "Defender of the Faith," 380.

16. Roth, "Defender of the Faith," 388.

17. Roth, "Defender of the Faith," 401.

18. A. B. Yehoshua, "Facing the Forests," in *Modern Hebrew Literature*, ed. Robert Alter (West Orange, NJ: Behrman House, 1975), 364.

Public Sins and Private Needs

PEGGY BROPHY
1991
Colby-Sawyer College

BIG BROTHER HAS LOOMED as one of the most-feared folkloric monsters in our society for almost half a century. According to the mythology, the ogre will arise when citizens relinquish too much of their personal freedom for the sake of the common good. The government will then invade our privacy, dictating what we think and do, in the name of public well-being. The so-called conservative wing of American politics has imagined the harbinger of this terrifying oppressor to be communism and has focused on such preventive measures as waging anticommunist campaigns at home and abroad and fighting against any governmental encroachment on private enterprise. Ironically, such actions have muted many dissident voices and have led to bigger and bigger corporations that represent fewer and fewer interests. The "liberal" wing has regarded erosion of individual freedoms as the key harbinger of Big Brother and has rallied to prevent dilution of personal rights, especially in relationship to free expression, as evidenced in campaigns against censorship and against restrictions on organized demonstrations. Yet these campaigns often have ignored the welfare of other individuals, such as those residents of Skokie, Illinois, who had survived Nazi concentration camps and then had to endure fascists marching through their neighborhoods. In truth, both political sides' attempts at staving off Big Brother have obscured the real issues involved in examining the inextricable relationship between private and public welfare. Rather than needing to fear two-way viewing screens in our bedrooms and corporate boardrooms, we need to understand that our governmental decisions about "public versus private" already reflect the interests of the powerful. Laws and fiscal policies reveal that the dominant culture's conceptions of right and wrong determine what is deemed private and what is regarded as public, and these distinctions have served to punish the politically weak and to protect the strong.

The most basic problem any society confronts in differentiating public from private centers on the fact that no actual line exists between the two domains. Nothing happens to the individual in private that does not affect, to one degree or another, his or her view of and participation in public life. Likewise, everything that occurs in public affects the private lives of individuals. Such public forces as formal education and media wield tremendous influences on the family's so-called private childrearing. Similarly, while women are raped and beaten in private, the reasons for these acts of violence are public in origin. In turn, the repercussions of men's violence against women spill back into the arena of the larger society. Regarding the tangible effects of public attitudes on personal lives, feminist author Alison Jaggar points out: "The perception of women as sexual objects restricts more than their sexuality: It also encourages sexual harassment, makes it difficult for women to be taken seriously in non-sexual contexts, and provides a covert legitimization of rape. In these ways, it limits women's freedom to travel safely alone and denies them equal opportunities in public life."[1]

A few years ago, a man in Concord, New Hampshire, explained how he beat his wife after she dropped a bottle of milk in a store. He claimed to have hit her out of personal rage. Yet the two had finished their shopping, driven all the way home, and carried their purchases into the house before he struck her.[2] This lengthy chain of events does not indicate an anger disorder on the part of the individual. Instead, the man's pattern points to his having acted to demonstrate who was in control and to maintain a position of power that society has traditionally assigned the husband. The man intelligently waited until he was home to punish the woman, because he had reason to believe that he would be protected if he performed in private.

Following the beating, though, the woman faced issues that were undeniably public in nature. First, she had to call a male, tax-supported police department that dislikes dealing with "private" domestic disturbances, even though such complaints constitute about half of the calls for assistance that police receive.[3] Then the woman had to encounter a cold court system that is dedicated to the ideal of due process rather than to helping people. Most of all, she had to endure the reality of a society that blames women for getting hit while producing men who hit. Where, for this woman, is the imaginary line between private and public? Jaggar explains:

> All relations between women and men are institu-
> tionalized relationships of power and so constitute
> appropriate subjects for political analysis. Much
> radical feminist theory consists in just such analy-
> ses. It reveals how male power is exercised and re-
> inforced through such "personal" institutions as
> child-rearing, housework, love, marriage and all kinds
> of sexual practices, from rape through prostitution to
> sexual intercourse itself. The assumption that these
> institutions and practices are "natural" or of purely
> individual concern is shown to be an ideological
> curtain that conceals the reality of women's system-
> atic oppression.[4]

To our society's credit, citizens have become increasingly aware that the historically guarded sanctity of the home often has served as a wall behind which some people could abuse others. All states now have child-abuse laws, and since 1980, several states have made it illegal for husbands to rape their wives. Nonetheless, in using a rubber yardstick to measure where the public scope begins and stops, elected officials have created some strange boundaries. For example, for the past four years, homosexuals have been officially banned from being foster parents in New Hampshire. The obvious implication is that legislators believe that a parent's sexual preference has an effect on children, which in turn produces some kind of repercussion that does not serve the public good. Yet the questionnaire used to ascertain whether foster parents are homosexual does not ask if they are child beaters. The same legislature that contends that asking people about their private sex life is justified by society's need to protect the young has not allocated one cent of funding for child-care centers. New Hampshire is not an exception: the majority of states still have laws on their books that, in one way or another, make homosexuality illegal, while few states provide any funding for child care.[5] In 1986, the U.S. Supreme Court upheld a Georgia law banning homosexual relations, but a federal child-care bill has yet to be enacted. Why is homosexuality a public issue while ensuring adequate child care is a private matter?

One possible explanation for this discrepancy is that legislation against homosexuality was passed without mention of a price tag, whereas the tax dollars needed to finance child care are always cited in discussion of such bills. Yet maintenance of vice squads in police departments does cost money, as does the arrest and prosecution of people. In other instances, money has nothing at all to do with how our institutions determine what qualifies as a private right or a public crime. In the summer of 1989, a Florida court found Jennifer Johnson guilty of drug dealing because she used crack during her pregnancy. In the same state at the same time as the sentencing, no doubt many men were smoking cigarettes in the presence of pregnant women, but they did not need to fear being tried for harming a fetus. The greatest irony of Johnson's conviction is that documentation exists that on two occasions during the early part of her pregnancy, she attempted to enter drug treatment programs that were government-funded. In both instances, she was turned away because she was pregnant.[6] So, society first refused to help her and then held her responsible for not getting help. The court decision sent the message that the public intends to punish mothers who fail to protect fetuses but acknowledges no obligation to help mothers in providing this protection.

In contrast, a quite different conclusion about who should pay for reckless actions was reached in a matter involving businesses, as opposed to a poor woman. The federal government repeatedly refrained from intervening in the affairs of a large number of savings-and-loan institutions in this country, even though government officials were aware of growing problems within the companies. The noninterference was based on the premise that corporate enterprise is "private." Yet now that the firms have failed, at least five hundred billion dollars in tax monies will be used to compensate for stockholders' losses.[7] This hands-off policy toward big business, because it is "private," until troubles explode into major problems, which are deemed "public," is repeated over and over again in such cases as Chrysler's bailout and the ratepayers' reimbursement of losses to the junk-bond buyers who helped Public Service of New Hampshire sink into incredible debt. If the stockholders of the savings-and-loan companies do not have to pay for their mistakes, why does Jennifer Johnson? The point could be made that bank losses hurt people only in their pocketbooks, whereas Johnson's baby was physically harmed. Yet manufacturers of handguns know that their products can kill people. All the same, their sales are protected by the individual's "private" right to own a weapon. Tobacco companies exist on the profits of selling a substance that kills more people than any other drug in our society, and the government even subsidizes the growing of tobacco. Individual rights advocates argue that people choose to smoke; yet children do not always have a choice about being in the presence of those who smoke—any more than Johnson's baby had a choice about absorbing crack. In terms of private motivation, Johnson was driven by her addiction, whereas the cigarette companies are driven by money. Why is harming someone because of your illness a public issue but harming people because of profits a private matter?

The answer to that question is identical to the answer why selling marijuana is a crime but selling alcohol is permitted: the dominant culture disapproves of the one action, while the other action falls within the range of society's norms. So, whether a matter is considered private or public depends on society's standards of good and bad. Any behavior will be regarded as a question of private choice as long as those in power consider the realm of choices to be morally acceptable, and any behavior will be regarded as being subject to public regulation if the possible choices include one or more that the powerful consider to be morally unacceptable.

The tremendous influence that moral judgment wields in the determination of "public versus private" can be seen clearly in the debate about abortion in this country. Pro-choice advocates say that abortion is a private matter because they do not consider abortion to be "bad." Pro-life advocates argue that abortion is a public issue because they do consider abortion to be "bad." In truth, abortion is no more private in nature than decisions about which hospitals should have CT scans and no more public in nature than gun ownership. In the case of legalized abortion, the practice of abortive medicine needs public regulation. Also, public forces greatly influence who gets an abortion and who does not. Currently, a pregnant sixteen-year-old in the suburbs of Philadelphia is far more apt to have an abortion than a pregnant sixteen-year-old in New York City's Spanish Harlem. Are pro-choice supporters willing to fund abortions for everyone? How would pro-choice proponents react if far more female than male fetuses started being aborted? What if abortion began being used as a means for genocide? These questions merit the concern of all of us, not just a woman alone. On the other hand, if abortion is illegal, women will die in private because of public decisions. Children will be born into the private hell of not being wanted, and the deprivation of their lives will affect the larger culture. Will society provide privately for the babies whom our public laws force to be born? Those in favor of individual choice need to consider genuine societal concerns. And those opposed to choice need to admit that if abortion is a public issue, then childbirth and child-rearing are public concerns, too.

In the same way that morality determines what society will legislate against, the possible violation of the dominant culture's values regarding acceptability also decides what will receive public funding. If the realm of possible consequences of money not being provided falls within what the powerful consider permissible, tax dollars are unlikely to be spent. For example, virtually no government money was allocated for AIDS research or treatment until those in power had been convinced that people besides homosexuals and drug abusers would be dying from the disease. Even now, almost all AIDS funding goes to research, whereas a drop of money is used to help those who already have been stricken, demonstrating that our society is reluctant to assuage suffering when the pain is perceived as punishment for what the powerful consider to be sins.[8]

At the present time, questions about what constitutes public business are on the front burner because a growing shortage of government funds, in collision with a growing demand for public funds, is pitting neighbor against neighbor. In an article about decisions at annual town meetings in Massachusetts, James Powers noted:

> The government we have had, particularly since the Depression, has been based on a contract between generations and an understanding that everyone benefits if his neighbor is properly educated, housed and kept healthy. So the young have paid for Medicaid, the elderly for schools, and society has prospered. But as the price has climbed, citizens have

grown reluctant to pay for services they don't use—
or don't realize that they do.[9]

In more states than Massachusetts, the outcome of basing decisions
about private and public on the largest number of voters affected by a
lack of funding has led to taxpayers chopping school budgets, whereas
such "essential" services as snowplowing and garbage collection have
been left intact. In such a climate, the disenfranchised—that is, children, the illiterate, the mentally ill, the mentally disabled, and the frail
elderly—stand little chance of being included on the government's public funding shopping list.

Nonetheless, despite their large numbers and having the vote,
women, the traditional keepers of the so-called private realm, are likely
to constitute most of the victims of the country's mounting disregard for
social welfare. Because they constitute a large portion of the poor in our
society and, even if currently above the poverty line, face better odds of
becoming poor, and because they have been oppressed historically by
distinctions between private and public, women are in great jeopardy.
Jaggar states:

> One of the interests shared by women is the avail-
> ability of quality goods and services such as food,
> clothing, housing, medical care and education. Of
> course, everyone has an interest in these, but women
> have a special interest because it is they who, accord-
> ing to the prevailing division of labor, are respon-
> sible for making these goods and services directly
> available to their families.[10]

About a fourth of the households in this country are female-headed,
and the number is climbing, yet women earn an average of only sixty
cents to every dollar men make.[11] If shelter, food, and medical care become labeled as basically private needs for women to meet alone while

education and child care grow ever more inadequate, a major portion of society will be condemned to perpetual poverty. Seventy percent of the more than fourteen thousand homeless people who received services from state-supported facilities in the small state of New Hampshire last year were women and children.[12]

Against the power of "majority rule," concerned citizens can fight the discriminatory application of "public versus private" in ensuing political debates by revealing the underpinnings of our philosophical premises. First, the arbitrariness of using the private-matter label needs to be shown for what it is—namely, intrinsically flawed. Homes do not exist outside society, and our society does not exist without homes. If children are not educated, if the sick are not treated, if the poor are not fed, and if hope is not provided for the hopeless, our entire society suffers.

Second, the time has come to loudly and repeatedly denounce the contention that rational thinking about such distinctions as "private versus private" exists separately from emotions. Morality, reasoning, and feelings are distinguished by our language but not by their source or their character. All arise from an individual's interaction with the environment and derive their only reality from the chemo-electrical interactions of neurons. No morals, no thoughts, and no emotions exist outside a brain; and if one looks inside a brain, distinctions cannot be made between the nature of the "emotional" and the "rational." People created the concept of morality to identify thoughts that originally were believed to be God-inspired, created the concept of rationality to identify feelings about what appeared sensible, and created the concept of emotionality to identify thoughts that were "rationally" regarded as having arisen from physiological reactions. We now know that no member of this mental triad is more or less cognitive in nature than the others. And none is a more valid criterion for decision-making. Yet, because our society has structured itself on the false contention that reasoned arguments contain more worth than so-called emotional reactions, the powerful feel justified in using what they define as "logic" to arrive at political decisions while deriding emotional pleas as out of bounds for determining public policy. In truth, all political decisions are necessarily emotional in nature, regardless of whose definition of "emotional" is used. Such contentions as "I don't want to pay for that," "We're not getting our money's worth," "Someone should do something about that," and "People need to learn to help themselves" are no less emotion-filled judgments than "Let's do this out of the goodness of our hearts."

We need to recognize the fallacy of deeming certain arguments as emotional and others as rational in order to stop deluding ourselves into thinking that the rightness of our decisions has an existence outside of our perspective. We need to recognize selfishness as selfishness. Then we could take the biggest step of all and come to realize that the world neither stops nor starts at our front doors. The day has long since passed when a person could live on this planet without needing to worry about what the other human creatures were doing. Toxic fumes recognize no boundaries of privacy. Deforestation has public consequences that none can escape. Lamb's blood on a door will not keep nuclear catastrophe from a house. In the same way, although the response to this example could sound a lovelier note, a baby's cry is not a request for privacy.

Because "private" and "public" exist only as mental constructs, they are social products. Thus, all changes in society's norms alter people's conceptions of private and public. Because we all evolve in and with our social environments, we should be constantly aware that our opinions about what merits the cloak of privacy and what deserves public involvement arise from prejudicial values. We cannot remove our values because they form an integral part of our worldview; and, even if we could, we should not remove them because they often serve important functions in promoting group and individual welfare. Nonetheless, we can most certainly adjust them by employing compassionate logic.

In the debates ahead, perhaps society could subdue its fear of Big Brother and the use of the imagined ogre to argue against developing a social conscience by envisioning government as a big sister. This idealized sibling would take care of us when we were young or weak but would not discourage us from being our unique selves. She would be interested in our needs and wants but would not read our diaries. And when younger or weaker members of the family needed help, we could join her in providing care. The building of such a familial relationship could begin with us.

Notes

1. Alison M. Jaggar, *Feminist Politics and Human Nature* (Totowa, NJ: Rowman and Littlefield, 1983), 179.
2. William Brophy, unpublished report on batterers' group conducted for the Central New Hampshire Community Mental Health Center Family Violence Program, 1984, 10.
3. Susan Schechter, *Women and Male Violence* (Boston: South End, 1982), 161.
4. Jaggar, *Feminist Politics and Human Nature*, 101.
5. W. B. Allan, "What Is a Minority?" *Vital Speeches of the Day* 61, no. 7 (1990): 203.
6. Derrick Z. Jackson, "Inequality and the 'Fetal Rights' Concept," *Boston Globe,* March 25, 1989, A24.
7. L. J. Davis, "Chronicle of a Debacle Foretold: How Deregulation Begat the S&L Crisis," *Harper's Magazine,* May 1990, 50.
8. Andrew Purvis, "Case of the Unexplained Deaths," *Time,* March 26, 1990, 53.
9. James Powers, "Cafeteria-Style Government," *Globe Magazine,* April 1, 1990, 19.
10. Jaggar, *Feminist Politics and Human Nature*, 335.

11. U.S. Bureau of the Census, "Characteristics of the Population," in *General Social and Economic Characteristics: U.S. Summary* (Washington, DC: Government Printing Office, 1983).

12. NH Division of Mental Health and Developmental Services, *New Hampshire Emergency Housing Commission Annual Report* (Concord: NH Division of Mental Health and Developmental Services, 1990).

Ethics Through a Cracked Windshield

MARK REEDER
1997
University of New Hampshire

> You, Reader, wherever you are, are not a
> complete beginner in this subject. You al-
> ready have some idea what "good" and "bad,"
> "right" and "wrong" mean, and you know
> some acts to be right, others wrong, some
> things to be good and some bad. Now these
> are precisely the topics with which Ethics as
> a subject of systematic study deals. Further, if
> you did not already have this knowledge, you
> could not make a start on the subject at all.
> —A. C. Ewing, Introduction to *Ethics*

I THOROUGHLY AGREED SIX weeks ago until the owner of the shop said, "All you have to do is make a crack in the windshield with a hammer," as he walked around toward the front of my car.

With some calculation, he stopped to line himself up with deformed plastic and rumpled sheet metal that had once been a hood and bumper. He squatted, baseball catcher–style, eyeballed a line toward a spot on the windshield. Walking to the passenger side of the car, he pointed out the imaginary dot, relative to the area that should receive the hammer's blow. "Matter of fact," he added as an afterthought, "hit right on the windshield wiper arm and I'll write that into the estimate, too."

I considered replacing the windshield last summer but never got around to it. Now, with the car dismantled in the body shop for two

196

weeks, I figured it was a good time, so I told the shop owner to replace the windshield while the damaged front end was under repair—"I'll pay for it out of my own pocket." Evading eye contact, while looking down at his clipboard, he said, "If you want, I'll just write it into the estimate." "But there isn't any damage from the accident," I explained, "it's just pitted with age, you know . . . diffracts the sun, makes it difficult to see." I think he tried to suppress a deceitful grin—"Oh yeah, I know, don't worry about it," he said, "we can fix it, save you the cost, and no one will know the difference." That's when he pointed out the imaginary hammer spot. Did he really believe that no one would know the difference? Potentially invisible, wearing Plato's "ring of Gyges," I had the choice to act on either an internally based ethic or an external relative ethic based on material gain. But I stood there, culpably silent, at once stunned by both his suggestion and my lack of an immediate decline.

The following day, he called with his estimate. The first question was whether I had taken care of the windshield. "It would be unethical, I can't do it." Finally some conviction! The words simply tumbled out. Weakly, he countered that I "might want to keep in mind that the insurance company is going to want to use cheap after-market parts." He was trying to justify squeezing more out of the insurance company. "Yeah, I know, but I can't compromise myself, no matter what the insurance company may do." "Well, you're honest and you have a conscience," he sighed, "there's nothing wrong with that." His last phrase—"there's nothing wrong with that"—was the most shocking. It was as if he was defending, or perhaps tolerating, my refusal to defraud the insurance company. Suggested here is that "honesty" and "a conscience" are not always understood as moral imperatives—the implication being that, relative to the circumstances, honesty and a conscience fall into a range of tolerance in which the individual picks through degrees of right or wrong.

Consequently, our cultural ethos tolerates the myriad of individual definitions of right and wrong. In contrast, to my own credit, and quite appropriately, I felt guilty; appropriately, I was ashamed at my own waffling. I had mulled over the predicament. Yet some decisions are life altering, too little too late after only seconds. How had I come to be in this place of indecision on a simple issue in which I "knew" what was right? Have right and wrong become so relative in society that making an ethical decision requires an apology?

What was it that made this decision an infusion of complexity? The prospect of getting a four-hundred-dollar windshield "for free" was a tempting proposition. I was already facing a five-hundred-dollar deductible. I called a friend and explained the situation—she gave me no easy answer, only that I would have to follow my conscience. The monetary temptation to a struggling student was powerful. After all, the windshield should be replaced for safety reasons, right? The faulty reasoning of victimhood and misplaced causality clouded my vision. I am not sure that I really made the right decision until the moment I was called on to answer the question: "Have you taken care of the windshield?"

Tzvetan Todorov is poignant in his essay "The Wrong Causes for the Wrong Reasons." He remarks that "in some ways, collective behavior resembles individual psychology."[1] After the experience with the auto-body shop, Todorov's characterization was all too apparent, as we shall see. Thus I wondered if the thread of such a notion could be traced from the personal realm into the weft of the country's ethical fabric.

Perhaps, for I encountered a similar ethos in a textbook used in an environmental issues and ethics course last semester. The author defined ethics simply as "what we believe to be right or wrong behavior."[2] Who is we? Right or wrong behavior measured by what standard? Are these beliefs constant, absolute? Using which ethical system? Are right and wrong relative or equal? Does it matter? In the current "ethical" environment, these are important questions.

Sadly, although they were raised in an environmental *ethics* and issues course, these questions rubbed against the grain of what I heard most often—mantras for the now "virtuous ideals" of diversity and tolerance—yet the radical environmentally conscious element in the class seemed the least tolerant.

There was no mention of ethical systems. Relative situations where solutions were dubbed "moral" or "ethical" based on the needs and beliefs of certain factions—the environmentalists, for instance—were discussed. It seems that regardless of the subject, "educators" plug "diversity and tolerance" whenever possible. Somewhere along the line, diversity and tolerance became virtues that are now part of the ethics discourse.

Mark Helprin points out in "Diversity Is Not a Virtue" that "almost every scholastic body in the country now considers itself a kind of Congress of Vienna with the special mission of making its students aware of race and ethnicity."[3] The 250 million people in this country are reduced to a half-dozen categories by bureaucratic reductionism. Then, students are force-fed these classifications in the name of diversity. According to Helprin, complex racial and ethnic assessments, not unlike Hitler's Aryan Decree, are now commonly made.[4] It has become a litmus test of sorts. What is happening now is as "wrong as it once was—not merely because of the effect but because of the dangerous principle that individuals do not transcend the accidents of birth."[5]

I do not suggest that we discriminate against accidents of birth, but ethnic diversity and toleration have also fostered the idea that diversity and toleration are in themselves ethical. Transcending accidents of birth requires a level ethical playing field, not merely an equal playing field.

Diversity and toleration as virtuous ends are leaking into all manner of society—mostly, I suspect, as Helprin does, through a failing education system. Last year, a classmate who was fulfilling her student-teaching requirement at a junior high school encountered this tolerance that was really relativism in disguise.

One sixth-grader stole belongings from a fellow student's desk. In confronting the guilty student, the classroom teacher insisted that "this was inappropriate behavior." "No!" blurted my friend, "chewing gum in the classroom is 'inappropriate behavior,' stealing is wrong." The classroom teacher refused to make a critical judgment concerning theft —perhaps fearful of damaging the student's self-esteem and facing irate parents? Yet is not the ability to make judgments the fruit of education? Montaigne and Alfred North Whitehead, among many others, were clear about education's responsibility to foster critical minds capable of exercising informed judgments.

Unfortunately, as evidenced by the sixth-grade classroom teacher, the author of the college textbook, and the owner of the auto-body shop, designations of right and wrong have become relative, owing to a demise in the internalization of ethics and moral imperatives. My father recently spoke of an annual corporate-required ethics seminar. Hearing his experience, I recalled the relative ethics presented in the environmental ethics and issues class. He related how frustrated he was "because all of the scenarios laid out for [them] had relative ethical answers— [relative to the potential benefit of the organization]—dictated by the instructor." He then said, "I can't believe it." He continued, "But on a related subject, one of the guys who works for me said off-handedly that he would rob a bank if he wouldn't get caught. We need more than just a seminar! Now, how do I appraise *his* performance?" And the cultural dissemination is so complete that this sense of toleration is understood as natural. Since my encounter at the auto-body shop, I have puzzled over my inability to make an immediate decision. How did I come to this?

There are two ways to view things, especially situations such as these. First, we might view them as they are, seeking to discover how they came to be and how they are related to other things, or second, we may compare them to an ideal of what ought to be. The former view may be called natural, whereas the second is critical. Ethics is ipso facto critical. It requires judgment by a set of standards, it requires an exercise in discrimination—something intolerable to toleration. The problem with contemporary society, in its anxious need for toleration, is that, inappropriately, ethics has been moved from the *critical* point of view into the sphere of the *natural.*

We lost the mindset not only to discriminate but also to make judgments. We have tied our civic hands behind our backs and must now look toward legalism and the courts to regulate individual consciousness. But, like the education system, this too is failing, as Richard E. Morgan expresses in "The Crisis of Constitutionalism." A newly graduated lawyer, he relates, was "turned on" by constitutional law, in school, "'because it had so little to do with law.'"[6] The new esquire went on trumpeting that "'Constitutional law is moral philosophy, pure and simple. All that stuff about the Framers and their intentions—well, all that the past really tells us is to try to do the right thing.'"[7] It seems that our constitutional tradition is simply viewed, like ethics, as "so multifaceted and ambiguous that all that can be extracted from it is 'try to do the right thing.'"[8] It would seem that the right thing has become opaque. From this newly graduated attorney, again keeping Todorov in mind, we can trace the thread of individual behavior reflected in the collective and into the ethical fabric of the country, into its institutions. Exemplary is the Supreme Court, reflecting yet even more relativism. Justices David Souter, Anthony Kennedy, and Sandra Day O'Connor wrote, in their opinion on the *Planned Parenthood v. Casey* decision of 1992: "At the heart of liberty is the right to define one's own concept of existence, of meaning, of the universe, and of the mystery of human life."[9] In this decision, the Supreme Court thus validated subjectivism: any definition of life, no matter what or how, is not only valid but constitutionally protected. Echoing Morgan's essay, William J. Bennett asserts, in the pages of *First Things,* that "the Supreme Court is deconstructing the text of the Constitution and is often incoherent in its reasoning." As Bennett reminds us, "If this relativism becomes the coin of the judicial realm, we are in for very bad times indeed—judicially, politically, morally." He goes on to ask: "What about the other, and in many ways more problematic, issue, namely, the moral sensibilities of the broad public?"[10]

Bennett's concern is reminiscent of a passage in F. M. Cornford's *Before and After Socrates.* The opinion of the Court expressed here, the relativistic definition of life, is comparable, in Cornford's words, to "discover[ing] a new principle of morality."[11] Proclaiming it without fear or compromise might incur the resentment of a society that lived by "the morality whose limitations are to be broken down."[12] Also, there is a "risk of being misunderstood by hearers who are already chafing at those limits, but may not be capable of grasping the new principle in its positive implications."[13]

Undoubtedly there lies a danger in saying: Do what is right in your own eyes, "because some of your hearers will run away with the notion that you mean: 'Do just as you please'; [without grasping] the all-important proviso: 'But first make sure that your eyes see with perfect clearness what is really good.'"[14] This was likely the spirit of the justices' opinion. But below the surface of the *Casey* decision was the current of *Roe v. Wade;* thus, the *Casey* decision conceded that the "Roe rule's limitation on state power could not be repudiated without serious inequity to people who, for two decades of economic and social developments, have organized intimate relationships and made choices that define their views of themselves and their places in society, in reliance on the availability of abortion in the event that contraception should fail."[15]

We could set aside the issue of abortion and simply consider the reasoning behind the judiciary's decisions; as Morgan and Bennett suggest, it is incoherent. Comparing their reasoning to Cornford's all-important and Socratic proviso, seeing with perfect clearness what is really good, we have to ask if the Supreme Court is able to conceptualize such a condition. Cornford captures the essence and implications of the condition set forth by Socrates: "If you see the truth and act upon it—as you must, when you really see it—you will find happiness in possessing your own soul; but you may find that doing what you know is right may be anything but pleasant—it may cost you poverty and suffering."[16]

What we can extract here is that one should be concerned with the condition of the inner self in the matter of ethics and morals—not the external, as mirrored by people concerned with economic and social developments—people who have organized intimate relationships and made choices that define their views of themselves and their places in society, based on the availability of abortion if contraception should fail. I felt guilty over a windshield and the thought of economic gain through insurance fraud. I can only wonder about the potential guilt and shame of, say, theft or abortion.

Though I am a male, I am still unable to even process the idea of organizing even the material aspects of my life around abortion. So, Mr. Bennett, I fear you may be too late. As I see it, the "moral sensibilities of the broad public" are already desensitized. I guess it is just natural.

Naturally the auto-body shop owner assumed I would hammer my own windshield. After all, having paid hundreds in auto insurance premiums, what have I gotten for it? I was in an accident; what if the windshield *had* cracked? The insurance company would pay then; why not now? It is a *natural* desire to save money by replacing the windshield through the insurance coverage. The shop owner *naturally* has an interest in adding what he can to his own bottom line. And *naturally*, insurance actuaries expect it and include these costs in formulating premiums. Applying the Supreme Court's *Casey* decision reasoning, one could plan their behavior accordingly. The auto insurance company has even planned on it. Paradoxically, society is outraged by rising premiums, while individuals who compose society are out "smashing windshields" in response.

There is a vicious circle of a tacitly accepted kind of vigilante justice. And both individual conscience and public opinion are salved by this incoherent line of reasoning. This line of reasoning is convincing until one asks, "Is this how it ought to be? Is it ethical?" When asked, these

questions reveal only one proper answer. It is not a question of tolerance or alternative courses of action. One should not ask "Is this the
wrong thing to do?" but "Is it the right thing to do?"

The individuals here—the cooperating teacher, the textbook author,
and the auto-body shop owner, the young attorney (not excluding myself for even the thought), and the collective members of the Supreme
Court—all exhibit the encroachment of toleration into the field of ethics. There is an overarching social penchant for toleration, but it is individuals who compose the state.

As Bennett feared, we are reaching the point where there are no longer any conscientious citizens able to give moral assent to the state that
they compose. The current ethos is suffused with either an unwilling-
ness or an inability to articulate a concept of moral imperatives. It all
seems fairly relative. While we concern ourselves with toleration, relativism, and liberality, there is a widespread social chaos.

The Court's definition of liberality, "one's own concept of existence,
of meaning, of the universe, and of the mystery of human life," synony-
mous with tolerance, is at once contributing to and ratifying "America's
widespread social chaos."[17] Its reasoning is as incoherent as the auto-
body shop owner's suggestion that there is nothing "wrong" with honesty and a conscience. Likewise, it is just as incoherent to label theft
merely inappropriate behavior. It is as faulty as the relativism of simply
reducing the definition of *ethics* to what we believe to be right or wrong
behavior. For the young attorney, it is enough to "try to do the right
thing"—but that is not good enough. Trying has varying degrees of
effort.

Following Bennett's remarks in "The End of Democracy?" Midge
Decter insists that "what we are dealing with is, in short, a cultural,
rather than primarily a judicial, problem."[18] Ms. Decter, the last I knew,
the judiciary was selected from this culture. Accordingly, recalling Todorov's suggestion that individual psychology is sometimes reflected in
the collective, "our culture is operating on the same philosophical prem-

ise, stated in the *Casey* decision, that we all have a fundamental right to create and live by our own sense of reality." In circular fashion, at the same time, people are creating their own sense of ethics. As I have been alluding to all along, this sense of reality and ethics falls into the purview of the natural sphere.

To repeat, it is a subjective and selfish sphere in which one is concerned only with viewing themselves as they believe they are, seeking to discover how they believe they came to be and how they believe they are related to other things. Following the *Casey* decision, the natural sphere and, hence, the consequential ethical perspective are encouraged to grow ever more imaginative and expressive, and it protests not only the hint of standards and ideals of what ought to be but also, as I have experienced, those who strive for them. In the wake of conflicts between clashing realities we have become entangled in legalism and a "crisis of constitutionalism."

With enough legislation we can guarantee the ever-increasing variety of rights—diverse and, hence, ethical—that are subsequent to the hair-splitting effects of multiple realities. Under the circumstances, just crack the windshield; ethics is simply the changing winds of "what we believe to be right or wrong." If you can't but tried to do the right thing ... well, at least you tried. Theft in middle-school classrooms is no more than inappropriate behavior met with subtle warnings and gentle posturing. What the child learned is not to get caught. If it were told today, Plato's "ring of Gyges" parable would be met with laughter—drive-by murders are spectacles in broad daylight, and the perpetrators who are caught express not remorse but victimhood.

The combined effect of all this is a twist on the Spartan sense of punishment: one is punished for getting caught, not for committing the crime itself. The twist? When caught, punishment results from not articulating a plausible argument that, relative to the circumstances, the behavior had justification. In response, we need to resurrect the Aristotelian ethical ideal that one should do without being commanded what others do only from fear of law. Ethics should be internalized—pure and simple.

Such an ideal should be ingrained throughout society in general, but more specifically, it should be instilled through education. To restore ethics, it "seems to me," as it did Montaigne in his essay "Of the Education of Children," "that the first lessons in which we should steep [a child's] mind must be those that regulate [his or her] behavior and . . . sense, that will teach [children] to know [themselves] and to die well and to live well."[19]

I do not want to believe we are complete beginners in this subject, that we have no idea what "good" and "bad," "right" and "wrong" mean, that we do not know some acts to be right, others wrong, some things to be good and some bad. But these are precisely the topics with which ethics as a subject of systematic study deals. Relative ethics, on the other hand, is an oxymoron. For those of us who already have this knowledge, we need to make a start on the subject with those who do not. The task may take on the appearance of Sisyphus's uphill battle, but push we must. They need to understand 'tis better a pitted windshield than a pitted soul.

Notes

Epigraph: A. C. Ewing, *Ethics* (London: English Universities Press, 1956), 1.

1. Tzvetan Todorov, "The Wrong Causes for the Wrong Reasons," *The Morals of History* (Minneapolis: University of Minnesota Press, 1995), 47.

2. G. Tyler Miller, *Sustaining the Earth: An Integrated Approach* (Belmont, CA: Wadsworth, 1996), A22.

3. Mark Helprin, "Diversity Is Not a Virtue," in *Reinventing the American People: Unity and Diversity Today,* ed. Robert Royal (Grand Rapids, MI: William B. Eerdmans, 1995), 72.

4. Helprin, "Diversity Is Not a Virtue," 72.

5. Helprin, "Diversity Is Not a Virtue," 72.
6. Richard E. Morgan, "The Crisis of Constitutionalism," in Royal, *Reinventing the American People,* 79.
7. Morgan, "Crisis of Constitutionalism," 79.
8. Morgan, "Crisis of Constitutionalism," 79.
9. U.S. Supreme Court, *Planned Parenthood of Southeastern Pennsylvania et al. v. Casey, Governor of Pennsylvania, et al.* Argued April 22, 1992. Decided June 29, 1992.
10. William J. Bennett et al., "The End of Democracy? A Discussion Continued," *First Things* (January 1997): 19.
11. F. M. Cornford, *Before and After Socrates* (London: Cambridge University Press, 1964), 49.
12. Cornford, *Before and After Socrates,* 49.
13. Cornford, *Before and After Socrates,* 49.
14. Cornford, *Before and After Socrates,* 49.
15. U.S. Supreme Court, *Planned Parenthood of Southeastern Pennsylvania et al. v. Casey, Governor of Pennsylvania, et al.* Argued April 22, 1992. Decided June 29, 1992.
16. Cornford, *Before and After Socrates,* 49.
17. Bennett, "End of Democracy?" 19.
18. Midge Decter quoted in Bennett et al., "End of Democracy?" 21.
19. Montaigne, "Of the Education of Children," in *The Complete Essays of Montaigne,* trans. Donald M. Frame (Stanford, CA: Stanford University Press, 1958), 17.

ON EDUCATION

Bridges

ALLISON HANDLER
1992
Williams College

MY ETHICS HAVE BEEN about building bridges. Given the increasing diversity of ideas and orientations in this society, it seems to me that there is a concomitantly increasing need for mutual support among different groups. It starts with discussion and with tolerance of differences, and progresses toward understanding, celebration, and pride in those differences. And it starts, like most large projects, locally.

One afternoon sometime during the middle of an unusually warm Berkshire September, I nervously prowled around the floor outside the recital room after my audition, waiting to hear whether I would be accepted into the Williams College Gospel Choir. The choir directors had asked me why I wanted to join. It was not a question I had expected. I hadn't thought it would matter to them why I wanted to sing in the group. However, it must have seemed odd to the choir's directors that a white Jew would want to sing in a black Christian tradition.

I had said something about my desire to be part of the supportive and emotionally close community that this choir represented, and I talked about the difference for me between religious belief and spirituality—the one being somewhat exclusive and the other unifying. I did not mention my other purpose in wanting to be in the group: aside from my joy in singing, I wanted to learn something about black Christians, and I wanted to show them something about Jews.

I had tried, during my freshman year of college, to set up a black-Jewish dialogue, cosponsored by the Black Student Union and the

Jewish Association at Williams. My rabbi, himself an activist who had organized similar dialogues, came to the campus to act as moderator. He spoke eloquently of the role that Jews had played in the Civil Rights Movement during the sixties, but it was not long before our small discussion group became mired in the usual concerns: several Jewish students present took umbrage with Louis Farrakhan and Jesse Jackson, and several black students voiced their displeasure about Meir Kahane and Israel's trade agreements with apartheid-stricken South Africa.

What began as dialogue between two groups dissolved within an hour's time into a cacophony of wounded cries. I could not understand how two peoples, both historically wronged in some very similar ways, with common experiences of slavery and oppression, could fail to see each other as necessary allies.

There is so much more to overcome, I thought to myself then. What could be the purpose of group unity and group pride if it precludes the formation of coalitions with others? How can we have selected our leaders and spokespeople in such a way that we have alienated those who could be potential allies? Furthermore, how can we consolidate group strength and at the same time reach out to those whose experiences are not at all like our own, to cross cultural, racial, religious, and gender gaps to build bridges rather than burn them?

Welcoming me as a new member of the Gospel Choir, its directors gently asked whether I knew that they said prayers before and after each rehearsal and concert. No, I said, I did not know. Would that make me uncomfortable, they asked. No, I replied, and I asked whether they would feel uncomfortable knowing that when I said the words "Jesus God" I would not be having the same religious experience that they were. I was tense; we were all being unbelievably polite. I had to know that their decision to include me in their group was a large one for them. Did it seem to them queer, or subversive, or insulting? I was trying to cross a line, and it was difficult to reach out past surface politeness to be honest without being disrespectful.

At first, I was uncomfortable during the moments we prayed together. While I consider myself a spiritual person, I have always struggled with my own religious beliefs, and I wondered whether I was now betraying my Jewish heritage in some way by addressing with Christian words whatever God there could be. Some of my Jewish friends were less than helpful. While they did not openly criticize my participation in a Christian choir, they talked around their opinions in such a way that it became clear that they saw me as moving away from the Jewish fold. Perhaps that threatened their own membership in our community.

I reminded myself that I was meeting people whose experiences I did not immediately understand from my perspective as a white Jew. The gospel singers were not all people of color, and those who were, were Asian, Indian, and Latino as well as black. But I was the only Jew.

I began to view Gospel Choir as a way of continuing the dialogue I had tried so unsuccessfully to start three years earlier. On a one-on-one basis, I was going to try to create links between twenty or so blacks and one Jew.

The problem with trying to connect with people of distinctly different backgrounds, for me, is that while I don't want to censor my words and even my thoughts in the interest of politeness and decorum, at the same time I don't want to be insensitive to the experiences that have shaped other people's identities. I do not expect others to meet me on my terms as a white, Jewish, urban woman. On the other hand, there is only so far past those experiences of my own that I can reach to understand someone else.

We were listening to a tape of another gospel group singing a song that our director wanted us to learn. I thought the piece was incredibly beautiful and complicated, and I was excited about it. The black woman next to me was not happy with the ending of the song. She said it wasn't "blackness"; it didn't sound like "blackness" to her.

What was "blackness," to her? What spoke to her from the voices and breaths of other songs, but not this one, that was "blackness"? I wanted to know, but I couldn't ask. Having read Toni Morrison, Audre Lorde, Richard Wright, Ralph Ellison, Langston Hughes, and Zora Neal Hurston, I could make a guess. I tried to imagine what I would say to someone who asked me to describe what was particularly Jewish about Klezmer music, or about Tillie Olsen or Bernard Malamud. This woman with whom I sang in choir could probably no more describe for me what "blackness" was about for her than I could enlighten her about what "Jewish consciousness" is for me.

To say that group consciousness is nontranslatable, however, is not to wave the white flag. An ethic of coalition building is a constant pursuit: it spans generations and progresses slowly, but it works at a number of different levels.

Joining a black Christian choir was one way that I could begin to work on my stereotypes about blacks. Having grown up in New York, it is in some important ways easy for me to relate to people of color. I have known them all of my life. I went to a public high school with an eclectic student body, and took it for granted that throughout my life I would study, work, and live with people of varied backgrounds. Yet in other ways, as a white woman raised in this city I have some very big prejudices about people of color. No one who lives in this city can ignore the realities of Howard Beach, Bensonhurst, or Crown Heights.

Listening, then, to the testimonies of my black friends in the Gospel Choir during prayer before we rehearsed together taught me a lot about their experiences. Mostly, they were personal testimonies about family issues or academic pressures, and members of the group prayed for each other's health and safety.

But one man described a recent incident at school in which some white students driving by in a car had yelled obscenities out of the window at him. It made me feel so ashamed to be white. It made me angry at those people, and I wondered what had been done to them to give them their anger toward black people. And I realized that I had a lot of thinking to do about my own anger, about my own association of blacks with violent crimes, my fears of black men that derived from watching television, reading newspapers, and being accosted in the street and subway.

It is so easy, I thought as I listened to that testimony, to hurt someone. It is so easy to know exactly where to sting. There seems to be an infinite supply of racial jokes, ethnic jokes: the one about the three gay guys in the bar, the one about the seven feminists and the sheikh, the one about the pope, the rabbi, and the black man. The litany is endless, and it attacks every possible means we have of identifying ourselves. Jokes may be at the more benign end of ways to hurt other people, but they can be as incisive as epithets.

I can usually respond to a prejudicial joke by feigning misunderstanding. Why was that funny? I'm sorry, maybe I'm just a little slow, but could you try to explain that humor to me? That kind of response is not effective, however, when you are faced, not with a friend telling you what she thinks is a really funny joke about the Arab, the Jew, and the camel, but with someone calling you a kike and telling you that Hitler didn't do enough. Or with someone driving by in a car and yelling that you are a dumb nigger who should go back home.

And how am I supposed to be building bridges to these people when their vision of me is colored by their associations with bigoted or supremacist white people, perhaps with prejudiced Jews, and when my vision of them is tainted by my associations with separatist or criminal black people? It was a good metaphor, but it seemed more and more like a pipe dream.

The first step in becoming allies with someone is to be proud of yourself. Hillel phrased it nicely: If I am not for myself, who will be for me? I do not find it difficult to be proud of being a woman, nor of being a Jew. It is always easier to be proud of your heritage if that heritage is historically the underdog.

There is, indeed, a rich and amazing legacy of artistic, literary, philosophical, and scientific achievement in the European tradition from which my family comes. And there is equally a legacy of military and cultural imperialism, invasion, enslavement, and oppression. By virtue of my being a woman and a Jew, I can lay claim to some understanding of what it means to be oppressed, in a loose sense of the word. But the fact remains that while I can hide my religion easily, I can't hide my skin, and my skin places me squarely on the side of the oppressors. And while I do not believe in group guilt or generic blame leveled generally at all white people, I am acutely aware of my privileges, my advantages, because I am white.

The difference between my background and the backgrounds of some of the other singers in the Gospel Choir is apparent in their body language with each other, and with me. It is apparent in their speech patterns with each other, and with me. I found in myself an exciting malleability that let me meet them somewhere in between our experiences. At dinner one evening after rehearsal with some of the other altos, I noticed a change in my personality. I liked the way a new self could emerge in reaction to and interaction with these people.

When I tried to describe to a friend of mine this feeling of experiencing people on a different level, he called me a racist, told me that I was play-acting. He asked whether my change of personality meant that I spoke jive in Gospel Choir and Yiddish in the Jewish Association. I thought he had missed my point entirely.

I am celebrating difference, I said. That's Racism, he said.

I had choir rehearsal that night, but how could I focus on learning songs when I was Racist? No longer racist with a lowercase "r," which to me simply meant skin-conscious, but malignantly prejudiced and bigoted. The muted tension that I felt, with some individuals more than others, because of our skins seemed more overt to me all of a sudden. I felt as if I had regressed; I had never thought that there would be a way to get around race, but I had entertained the notion that I could work *with* it.

I wondered whether the other white singers in the choir grappled with the same issues I did. I also wondered whether any of the black singers begrudged us our membership.

I know that some of the black members of the choir are separatist. I know that the choir director has, in the past, been criticized for her classical vocal training, because she sings the music of white men. I know that she loves more than anything to sing the Gospel as her way of thanking God for the gift of her voice, but she also enjoys singing classical arias and lieder, and that has raised the hackles of some of her black friends.

Knowing all of this, I find it increasingly hard to have dialogues without resorting to the politeness that society has inculcated in us. Civil society is an oxymoron. It teaches us to be genteel on the surface, to obey laws and do our civil duty, to uphold some vague moral code. Beneath that surface, there is a diseased social outlook that incites violent action and speech, and presents an arsenal for mutual denigration and destruction. We who have been societally conditioned to fear, loathe, or ignore difference would be hard-pressed to change our behavior overnight.

Change, though, is so necessary. The conflicts in New York, this city of foreign countries, run along lines of race, class, gender, sexuality, ethnicity. In so many ways, the city is a microcosm of national and global ills. We live in a frenetic and violent world, but perhaps not one that is hopelessly violent.

We start with ourselves. I must be for myself, Hillel said, and continued: But if I am for myself alone, what am I? Being for others, reaching out to others, works fine on paper. There are very real and painful obstacles, however, that the critic will be quick and sharp to point out. What do we do, for example, when it becomes clear that our advances are not wanted? How do we find in ourselves the capacity to continue to reach out when others continue to hurt—or reject—us? How can we respond to taunts, jabs, and prejudicial remarks toward us and toward our friends? How can we risk losing friends when we stiffen at prejudicial jokes and comments, and are told to "lighten up," that it was just a joke, can't we take a joke for God's sake?

Some days, I just can't take a joke. And some days, I don't feel at all like reaching out. Meir Kahane is dead, but Israel still does business with South Africa, and people like Farrakhan are still around. Those names still stick in the throats of blacks and Jews. Apparently, coalition building is not only a slow process, it is unbelievably frustrating. Still, it is the only ethics I believe in.

I don't buy into Kantian notions of categorical imperatives or universalizing action. Morality is not a metaphysically grounded option; it is a necessary addendum to the human condition, in order for that condition to sustain and better itself. For me, it is couched entirely in terms of other human beings: human beings are the source of each other's joy and suffering, and their social problems are what ramify throughout the environment to cause ecological disasters. Humans create and destroy bonds with each other, but whether by legal or social contract, we are bound together in communities. And since those communities are anything but homogeneous, all we can ethically do is try to build bridges. And if not now, when?

Forty-three Cents

Learning to Share in Ladakh

LESLIE BARNARD
2004
Pomona College

IT IS STRANGE TO THINK that Jigmet is only thirteen. Yesterday, she invited me to go on a walk. Her perfectly bald head and delicate, bird-bone face gleamed in the evening sun. As always, she wore the standard deep red robes of a Tibetan Buddhist nun. We trekked up the rocky moun-tainside toward a distant monastery. I trudged purposefully, while Jig-met skipped from stone to stone, laughing and humming the tune of a mantra in praise of the Three Jewels. I had heard it before and began to hum quietly in time. Jigmet's narrow back was bent under a gigantic basket of fresh apricots that wheezed juicily with every step she took. She wouldn't let me help with the load, though I offered again and again. As we turned upward, losing sight of the grumbling, gray river where we swam, bathed, and laundered our clothes, the young nun turned to me and asked, "Why did Osama bomb Washington? I mean," she said, "what made him sad enough to do that?" I had no answer. I had never thought of 9/11 in terms of the sorrow of terrorists.

We finally reached the foot of the ancient gompa. *Jigmet spread the oozing treasures she had lugged from miles below across the bottom stair leading up to the prayer room. As we turned to leave, the old lama who had received us at the door reached for Jigmet's sticky palm, thanking us and begging us to stay for tea.* Man, *she said in her language.* Man ju-le. *But no matter how many times she refused, he persisted, tugging gently at the edge of her robe, even searching my foreign face for a look that could mean yes.*

Located in the remote trans-Himalayan region of Kashmir, Ladakh or "Little Tibet" has been an enclave of Tibetan Mahayana Buddhism since 200 BCE. In Ladakh it is polite to decline any offer several times before accepting. Sometimes it is necessary to cover your cup or even veer away from your hostess as she approaches bearing a warm teapot and a plate stacked with homemade bread. If you do not decisively refuse, a Ladakhi host or hostess will never stop showering you with gifts of food, tea, and time. Even children know no other way.

In Ladakh, if a child whose allowance for an entire month is twenty rupees (approximately forty-three U.S. cents) spends five rupees on a small chocolate bar, he or she will instinctively share it with all the other children hovering around the candy stand, whether he or she knows them or not. It doesn't matter if adults are watching. This practice has nothing to do with rules or punishments. It comes from a deeper place. Like most Americans, I had been raised to believe that the more I earned and achieved over and against my competitors, the more I would have, the more I would be. In Ladakh, however, this is not the case.

I told one of the nuns that my bag was still tied to the Jeep. Taking a moment to calculate the grammar of her response, she asked me, in surprisingly coherent English, why I always used that word. "What word?" I asked.

"My," she said, "you always say: my this, my that, but we say our—our bags, our food, our land . . . like that." Perhaps noticing the tattling tint of my cheeks, she added, "I guess the languages are just different."

In time I realized that my pronoun use disclosed a profound distinction between my own culture and that of Ladakh. The nun's confusion at my constant division of all things into categories of mine and not mine begins to reveal her own radically relational concept of self—a concept so unlike my own that had I not seen it articulated in the language and lives of the Ladakhi people I would never have recognized it as a viable possibility.

I came to Ladakh as a volunteer and a student. I planned to live in a local Buddhist nunnery and teach English at an understaffed primary school. On my arrival, Ringzin Tsering, a young Tibetan college student whose father had been a freedom fighter during the Cultural Revolution, was recruited to show me around town. Over a couple cups of tea in a dimly lit café I asked Ringzin what religion he practiced. He quickly replied that he believed in them all and that Buddhism, especially, was very nice. He went on to tell me that Buddhists believe in emptiness or *sunyata*. This means that the distinction between *I* and *you* is simply a matter of convention. "*I* and *you* are only words, only names," he insisted. "In reality, I am constantly transforming in response to the world around me. From moment to moment I am never the same. I am dependent on the food I'm eating and the fork in my hand and you. If you are angry right now I will be sad, if you are happy then so am I. So, naming the points where I begin and you end is, in a way, meaningless, because all of this, everything"—he proclaimed, waving his mug first toward the ceiling and then the floor—"only exists in so far as it is interconnected. Right?"

Before Ringzin would allow me to excuse myself for a long-forestalled bathroom break, he took my hand, saying, "It is not that nothing exists, but only that nothing has permanent, independent existence. So, the self dissolves into an intricate network of relationships that are always in flux." I grinned, nodded effusively, and promised that I had understood it all. And to some extent I had. But as more and more children pressed dried apricots into my pockets or poured water into my cupped hands or slowed their pace so I wouldn't have to walk to school alone, I began to understand emptiness in everyday ethical terms. I discovered that even Ladakhis so small in stature that they spoke primarily to my hipbones possessed the instinct of interconnectedness. I had encountered a living view of the world, which presumed, paradoxically, that the more one *gives* to others the more one ultimately has and the more we all have in the end.

Though Ladakh has been predominantly Buddhist since long before the birth of Christ, the ethic of interconnectedness palpably present in Ladakhi society is not only a consequence of religious belief but is also grounded in the people's traditional way of life. Owing to its inaccessibility, inhospitable climate, and scarcity of resources, Ladakh was not an object of colonial designs. Until recently it stood out as one of the few subsistence economies that remained virtually intact and relatively untouched by the outside world. It is significant that in this isolated, local context the network of relationships necessary for survival were apparent and even tangible. In traditional Ladakhi villages, composed of fewer than a hundred houses, the scale of life made the ethical theory of interdependence a visible reality.

Is there much crime here?

Oh no.

But, there has to be a little, sometimes. There is a lot of crime where I come from.

I heard of a kid stealing something.

Come on, that's it?

You see, if someone did something, everyone would know. So then what would they do? Just leave? Apologize? No one would trust them after that. Then how would they get by?

As folksinger John Prine observes in a quirky number about a couple attempting to conceal an illicit affair, scale matters. He sheepishly croons, "In a town this size there's no place to hide." In traditional Ladakhi villages people could see how their actions affected the well-being of the community, and themselves as a part of that community.

Enclosed by towering peaks and vast stretches of uninhabitable desert, Ladakhis did not have the option of moving west to the next manifest destiny any time they committed an offense. The lack of anonymity this small-scale, closed system engendered, combined with the intimacy felt by families that grew up together, farmed together, and prayed together all their lives, inevitably fostered a strong sense of accountability within the community. This kind of ethical integrity, which pervades every aspect of life in Ladakh, is much more difficult to achieve in a large context where the forces of a faraway bureaucracy can only uphold a rigid list of institutionalized justices.

At first I couldn't understand it. Why did everyone call me nomo-le, nomo-le, like they'd forgotten my name? I thought it meant foreigner or white. I thought maybe they were making fun of me, of how I dressed or talked.

Today I found out that nomo-le means little sister.

Traditional Ladakhi communities were close-knit enough that corruption and crime were virtually nonexistent. Buyers and sellers inevitably had a personal connection and were therefore dissuaded from carelessness or abuse. The *goba* or village head could speak face-to-face with those over whom he presided and therefore was motivated to act in response to their interests. The goba of a Ladakhi village has probably held most of his people's children in his arms and will attend some of their parents' funerals. Relationships like these, as opposed to distantly generated, variously motivated mandates, have characterized Ladakhi governance and moral life.

As subsistence farmers, coaxing primarily barley, peas, and turnips out of the craggy terraces of the high-altitude desert, Ladakhis have had to become acquainted with the way the earth responds to their actions. Because the food they eat originates from the land they plow, they have inherited a sensitivity for nature's needs and limited capacities. In the city the water and soil on which your life depends are sometimes hundreds of miles away. In a subsistence economy, one look across the land can approximate how many mouths it will support.

As a result of this necessarily intimate connection with nature, in traditional Ladakhi society, resources were used conscientiously. Virtually all plants were gathered and used as food or medicine. Dried dung was collected to be burned as fuel in winter when temperatures sink as low as minus forty degrees Fahrenheit. If an old robe, hand-spun from yak hair, could no longer be patched back to health, it was packed with mud and used to fortify the walls of a weak area of an irrigation channel.

This pragmatic resourcefulness is echoed in Buddhist belief and derives, in part, from sunyata, which claims that if we exploit the earth to which we are undeniably bound, we are actually inadvertently exploiting ourselves. Buddhist teachings, which assume that most of us have been animals and even insects in our former lives, recognize that we do not live alone and are not set apart from the rest of the natural world.

Today one of the older nuns sat and watched as a bedbug feasted greedily on her fingertip. Its once drab fleck of a body, now a striking neon red, had swollen to twice its former size when she finally took it outside and allowed it to alight. When I asked why she waited so long she told me, "If it had been me, and it easily could have been, I'd have been grateful for that last bit, wouldn't you?" At the time this seemed part nonsense and part brilliance, but whatever it was I could not stop imagining my own face in the trunks of trees, the eyes of spiders, and the open palms of stooped panhandlers. I wondered—could it have been me?

The Ladakhi worldview invites us to wonder if it could have been us. It requires us to see ourselves in every inch of the world around us and to respect it as we might respect our own bodily selves. What if, as Ringzin claims, the branch of a tree waving at me through a frosted windowpane might as well be called I? What if everyone I met was like a sister or a brother? Or even like a blood cell, contributing to my survival even as I, in turn, enliven its being?

But what happens when someone peeks over the twenty-thousand-foot crests, that have, for centuries acted as the stoic, stony guardians of Ladakh's traditional culture? What happens when the boundaries sustaining Ladakh's small-scale community begin to erode under the weight of external political and economic pressures? Traditional Ladakhi society had the advantage of being an intimate, closed system, in which it was obvious that the Buddhist philosophy of interdependence was not only valuable but, furthermore, true. Within the past several decades Ladakh has been absorbed into the vast global community. As a result, the outward signs verifying the validity of the ethic of interconnectedness are becoming less and less visible.

Since 1974, when the Indian government opened Ladakh to tourism and initiated a comprehensive development program in the region, the small-scale, subsistence economy that historically reinforced the Buddhist ethic of sunyata has begun to disintegrate. Based on the Western model, development efforts in Ladakh have focused primarily on construction and expansion of infrastructure such as roads and energy production sources. A substandard Western-style health care system and narrowly defined educational paradigm that focuses heavily on acquisition of the English language have also been introduced.

There are no desks or blackboards in the classroom where I teach. Students must share pencil stubs and eraser crumbs. Tashi, a young nun, showed me her social studies book today. The scene depicted looked familiar enough to me, but Tashi was spellbound.

She ran her finger across the page, stroking the happy white faces. She read aloud in stilted English: Bobby, stop watching the television. Sally, clean up your toys. Was she imagining herself in the scene?

Tashi is seven. She hauls jugs of water from the three-hundred-gallon community tank down the road, refilled twice a week, to the kitchen of the nuns' hostel where she lives. She washes all of her own dishes by hand and helps cook every meal. She does her own laundry in a nearby irrigation ditch.

She sometimes catches a glimpse of the programs playing on the shopkeeper's television two streets down, but the other kids are taller so she can never see much.

In the picture she showed me, Sally, wearing a short blue skirt and shiny black loafers, couldn't seem to decide what drawer to store her dolls in. Bobby, who had his own watch, was lounging in a loveseat, absentmindedly flipping through channels.

We turned the page to find Sally's mother brushing her teeth with water that flowed freely from the faucet of a porcelain sink.

They are millionaires, Tashi said, not like me.

As a result of the booming tourism business and increasing government subsidies on imports, commerce has been growing rapidly. Increased trade has invited traffic and pollution, prompted a rural-urban influx, and given birth to a sprawling slum in the capital city of Leh. Disparities in wealth, which were virtually nonexistent in an economy where 95 percent of the population fell into what could be called a middle class, are now on the rise. In the traditional economy accumulation had natural limits. There was a point at which more yaks or more barley became a burden. Money, on the other hand, can be stored in a bank and requires no maintenance. The idea of wealth for wealth's sake has made its way across the Himalayan desert.

Lolo liked me from the start because I was a Westerner. He wanted to know everything about me. He asked me if I drank or had boyfriends. He hugged me whenever we met, which I had been warned against, as it is not a Ladakhi custom. While his traditionally dressed mother and brother weeded the flowerbeds around the hotel they owned or carried warm water to the rooms of perturbed foreign guests, Lolo stood at a street stand in a black leather jacket selling Buddhist relics to the highest bidder and practicing English idioms on attractive European girls.

On my days off from school I would come into Leh and sit in his restaurant grading papers. He asked why I was wearing Indian clothes. He warned that they would just fall apart. What happened to my nice American outfits? Why was I so dirty? Did I ever stay in hotels or was I always at the hostel with the nuns? Did they even have running water there or electricity? He asked me why I wasn't interested in clubs or shopping, why I seemed to spend no money. I wanted to ask him why he gelled his hair every day, why he never dressed traditionally, why he always rode around on that terrible motorcycle and never worked in the garden with his mother. I wanted him to be pristine, serene untouched Ladakh, a treasure chest of ancient intuitions. He wanted me to be the progressive, modern, fast-paced West that could make him a magic million.

For a while we were not on the best of terms. I secretly rejoiced when he was ticketed for riding his motorcycle without a helmet after I had warned him against it several times that day. Perhaps he derived similar enjoyment out of informing me that I had become quite fat during my two-week stay in rural Tia. In any event, eventually Lolo and I stopped talking about things we didn't agree on, like whether I needed to take a shower with running water. Now we talk about the one thing we both know is true, that things don't happen in isolation, that the West is changing Ladakh and that Ladakh is changing the West, and that for better or worse as microwaves and prayer flags cross continents, trading places, all things living are inevitably intertwined.

In contemporary Ladakh, the land one farms is rarely where one gets one's food, as most modern farmers grow cash crops for export. These days, Ladakhis are governed by district commissioners they will never meet. The cramped, dirty city of Leh now supports a burgeoning population of displaced persons looking for work at whatever cost. In spite of these changes, however, the ethic of interconnectedness somehow survives. Though city dwellers do not enjoy the intimate social network traditional villages provided, and though families are becoming increasingly scattered as men travel to the cities to sell their prayer wheels to tourists, every Ladakhi person still refers to every other person as if he or she were a blood relation. The people of Ladakh still speak and behave as if all beings are in fact inextricably bound, in spite of the fact that the complex economic and political structures that characterize the modern era have to some extent disguised this fact. Even in modern Ladakh, good and evil are not seen as separate poles. Just like *I* and *you*, good exists only in terms of evil and therefore, on some level, does not exist at all.

Lhakpa is my best friend here. A monk, and headmaster at the school where I teach, he is always late to class because he was fixing something for a cousin or a brother or a sister, which by now I knew just meant a friend. Bob is one of the other volunteers. Born in London, but of Indian descent, Bob is almost twice Lhakpa's height, and watching them argue resembled watching a perturbed pelican peck at a worm that just keeps dividing into more and more squirming segments.

Bob told Lhakpa he didn't like the American government.

Lhakpa said that he personally did.

What about the war in Iraq, you like war, Lhakpa? Bob snapped.

Yes, I do, Lhakpa said.

You like war? You like it when people die? Lhakpa, what are you saying?

He's saying—I began—but I didn't know what he was saying.

I'm just saying it's good what Bush is doing, just like what the Chinese did in Tibet was good.

That was good? Didn't your uncle die in the Cultural Revolution? I was surprised Bob brought that up.

But Lhakpa wasn't. He said—There is an old Buddhist saying. I can't remember it exactly. But it's something like, what is good without evil? How can your friend teach you to have patience when they just agree and agree? Tibet had to learn that it was vulnerable, that the outside world was changing all around it. Your enemy is actually your best friend because only your enemy can show you the parts of yourself that you cannot see in the mirror.

Lhakpa's understanding of the interpenetration of all things is so complete that he has the ability to perceive even seeming dualisms such as good and evil as inextricably intertwined phenomena. Though he has plenty of friends who adore and admire him, when a testy foreign tourist belittled Lhakpa for his lack of English proficiency, he became her shadow, following her everywhere, insisting that they spend more and more time together. I was mystified by his interest in this grotesquely sunburned woman until I recalled his appreciation for the Cultural Revolution that had killed his only uncle.

My time in Ladakh made me realize that there are other ways to see the world, other eyes that trace the threads between creatures, drawing out a luminescent vision that insists upon the inherent oneness of all life, even apparently "evil" life. However, it is one thing to take pity on a face, or a voice, or the daughter of someone you used to know, but it is a stretch of our moral muscle to extend ourselves to a smeared statistic caught under the wet print of a coffee cup on the last page of the *Times*. The same rules of give and take that applied in hundred-person Ladakhi villages are just as valid on a larger scale, but because we cannot look down from a throne of clouds on the whole earth at once while still seeing all its nooks and nostrils and peculiarities, these codes are significantly harder to comprehend within a broader scheme.

In this uniquely challenging modern era, an era in which the value of the dollar on any given day can determine who eats in Africa and who doesn't, connectedness cannot and must not be denied. Jigmet's assumption—that the September 11 attacks were not simply random acts of isolated evil but were instead a sorrowful response to a preexisting relational reality—is eerily insightful. Though I still have no answer to her question, I am beginning to understand why she might have asked it and why we must allow ourselves to listen to the complex causes of suffering, of which we are undeniably a part. Like this thirteen-year-old nun, musing on a moment that occurred half a world away from her home in Ladakh, we must learn to understand ourselves as beings that do not end at our own fingertips. Beings that, in fact, may not end or begin at all.

I have been home for four months now. I can barely remember the smell of the market in Leh—raw meat swinging from hooks, baskets of goat heads looking and not looking, the red dust of the road, incense, chimes, and laughter. . . .

Yesterday I was reminded of Ladakh.

One of my professors is dying. My other professor, his dear friend of forty years, started weeping in class today. Suddenly the room condensed into a single burning coin.

All of us, regardless of where we were sitting, were somehow in the exact same place, yearning to reach into our teacher's heart and touch it, softly, wordlessly. As other bodies in the room began to quiver with grief, I could have sworn we were a single entity, mutually heaving under the weight of a finite world.

When I think of Ladakh I think of saplings sprouting out of the soft bellies of dead trees. Sometimes, when I am walking through the woods in the evening, I cannot tell where the old lives end and new ones begin.

The Ethics of Transformation

COURTNEY MARTIN
2002
Barnard College

AN AGGRESSIVE HAND shot up on the right side of the classroom. It belonged to Vuyiseka, a slender young woman with a perfectly oval face and an almost completely shaven head. There was a fire in her eyes.

"Yes, Vuyiseka?" I asked.

"I want to read my poem today." She was adamant.

The class miraculously quieted down, shifting back into their wooden seats and putting their bags into their laps. It was the first day of the poetry workshop that I had initiated, and no one thus far had volunteered to read any of their work out loud. Vuyiseka was born brave.

She read. She read a piece about regrets, about God's forgiveness, and about hope. She read standing up at her desk, delicate hand shaking against the stiffness of the paper, lips curling around each word laboriously. She approached the last line: "I wish I had never . . . that is in the past. The new me promised never again to say 'I wish I had never.'" As she reached the end her face grew swollen and tense. She burst into tears. The class went wild with applause. Vuyiseka was yearning to express herself, to name something that had grown up inside of her.

It was not until someone asked her to put a pen to paper and purge some kind of inside epiphany, however, that she realized what she was capable of. The simple combination of a pen, a piece of paper, and the bravery to assign words to her emotions created Vuyiseka anew. She became a poet.

And I, this American exchange student with a head full of ideas and a heart full of good intentions, became a better person. I learned so much from my experience there, not only about a nation with a nascent sense of justice and that often used and rarely understood word—diversity— but about myself. I, like all of South Africa, had felt in the dark for some time when it came to understanding the complexities of difference and the ethical implications of celebrating and cultivating these differences. My months living in South Africa and the week I spent teaching a poetry workshop to high school students there illuminated a very important truth for me. It is the kind of truth that dwells in the deepest part of who you are, the kind that doesn't necessarily have a name, but if it did, it would be something like . . . hope.

You see, there is hope. There is hope all over South Africa. You can see it in the faces of the young; hope there, of course, is not surprising. The huge eyes and naked laughter of the children who lived in the same neighborhood as me—I lived for four months in the all-black township of Langa—were saturated in the kind of light that only hope can radiate. They were full of dreams.

My little sister, the long-legged and angel-voiced Nodidi, used to tell me about her future: "I will be either a doctor or a teacher, I think. The doctor thing because I would love to save lives, but the teacher . . . well, I think I could be much better than the teacher I have." Over card games of an African version of go-fish or spoons we would all collapse in fits of laughter when my Xhosa could not get me where I needed to go; a dozen five-year-olds would reach over to my hand and point at the right card to play next, deliberate and generous in their assistance.

I, too, wanted to be of assistance. Like most young Americans, especially white and middle class, who make their way to a country like South Africa, I was filled with a sense of duty. I wanted, not only to study there, but to leave having helped. I wanted to contribute something to this teeter-totter country, at once Third World and First. I wanted to come back to my Midwestern American home with stories of empowerment, with stories of transformation. These children with their hope and dirty palms reminded me of the urgency, reminded me of all there was to make right.

So when the program I studied with introduced the month of independent study option, I immediately jumped at the opportunity. I searched the dark eyes of my playmates for the perfect thing. I started making lists of injustices in my head. There was just too much to be mended in a country so torn and tattered by violence, a violence, it must be understood, that was completely inclusive. Every citizen of South Africa is a soldier in one way or another; psychologically or physically, spiritually or reluctantly, racial war makes militants of us all.

And I, in my idealist and well-intentioned American fashion, was going to bring some small moment of peace. In some small way, I was going to make things better.

I decided to teach a poetry workshop in a township high school. I had become very involved in the spoken-word poetry scene in New York City ever since I began to go to school there; the immediacy and the political backbone of the art thrilled me. I had spent years pecking away on keyboards that didn't talk back to me, and through spoken word, I found a genre and a venue that turned poetry into something very active, something very real. In my experiences in three short years I found people were always connected by the orality of words. It coaxed them into a climate of association and liberation.

I wanted the same for these students. In my time in South Africa I had quickly learned that few South African students are taught to express themselves. Instead, the rigid curriculum introduced there—with good intention—to equalize the job market, has become vocational in its focus. Students are searching for right answers most of the time, not searching for themselves.

I spent many late nights in my little bedroom on Mshumpela Road thinking of a design for my workshop. I would talk about identity, because surely if anything was plaguing the post-apartheid nation it was that. I couldn't talk about identity, I realized, unless I first talked about history. Most of these students had never read a poem before, much less one written by a South African poet. Their history, rich with protest poetry and the ancient tradition of the *imbongi*—a poet designated by the Xhosa chief who was in charge of reciting explicitly political poetry—was mostly lost to them, getting mixed up with a past that their parents would rather forget all together. Yes, I would talk about history and identity, and finally, all twisted up and shiny with hope, I would talk about future. I decided I had to show them how to be visionary.

At the last moment I convinced a young man I had met, nineteen years old and brimming with enthusiasm about spoken-word poetry and hip hop, to teach the workshop with me. Melisizwe had, in fact, grown up in Langa, and he was eager to give something back; he had just never had the organizational fortitude to do so. When we headed into town the first day, smashed together in a packed minibus, I passed over some mimeographed sheets about the structure of the workshop.

"These are great," he said, smiling at me with a surprised smirk.

"Do you think it is too much planning?" I questioned, suddenly very self-conscious of my own ambition and glowing white skin (minibuses are far too dangerous for white South Africans to ride).

"No, no. It's good. We'll just have to explain it a lot."

When we entered the classroom, a few students looked up at me, confused by my presence in the regular school day, but most were unfazed. They grouped in corners, separated by gender, laughing and shouting at one another playfully. Their English teacher, a bald-headed man with a joyous disposition . . . though perhaps simply joyous not to have to teach his class for a week, introduced Melisizwe and me. "They are going to teach you about poetry?"

The students were clearly skeptical. They reluctantly shifted in their seats, scratchy polyester school uniforms and flesh dragged across the unforgiving wood of the desks, and all of the sudden I was met with forty pairs of eyes. I was instantly terrified. "Introduction," I thought numbly, "introduce the design of the workshop." Melisizwe looked up at me as if pushing me along with his eyes.

"Molo. As Zolani said, I am Courtney, and I want to spend time with you this week, talk about poetry, and hopefully, if you feel comfortable, have you write some of your own. We are going to start out talking about poetry in terms of history, like, you know, read some South African poets that you may or may not have seen before, talk about their intention, that kind of stuff. Then we are going to talk about poetry in terms of identity . . ."

One of the brazen young men in the back, dressed in a striped tie and a perfectly pressed blazer, interrupted, "What do you mean by identity, miss?"

"Well, you don't have to call me miss at all. I'm just twenty-one and studying here for a bit of time. I'm from America . . ."

Again I was interrupted. This time by his friend, another straight-backed, long-legged teenage boy. "Are you married?"

"No, actually I'm not at all." I was trying so hard to remember the outline I had designed, the sense it had all made at the time, the logic. "But you know I really want to talk about poetry. I want to talk about identity because I think so much of South Africa's population has been silenced . . . you know, very few people have been able to write about what their lives are like." Melisizwe got out of his chair, baggy jeans unfolding, and cleared his throat. "When you wake up in the morning, the sun is so bright, yebo, because your tatomcici keeps spending the money for the drapes on beer at the shebeen. And you are so tired and then you smell your mama's cooking, yebo, and you know it is samp and beans and that's what you've been wishing for, yebo?"

Forty heads nodded in unison; eighty eyes were transfixed on Melisizwe as he swayed and spoke.

"So that's what you are. You can write about that and you will be doing something revolutionary because no one wanted you to write about that before. The government, especially, didn't want you to write about that. But now you could, yebo? You could write about your mama's samp and beans, and no one could ever take that away from you, yebo?"

And the whole world changed forever . . . for me. Certainly for the students, whose hands began to be very busy with pencils and words they didn't know they owned, the world was different after that moment, but also—quite unexpectedly—for me.

I learned that my voice was courageous and that my intention was noble but that if I did not possess the wisdom necessary to recognize my own limitations, my work would be nothing short of unethical. It was in the sudden recognition of myself in relation to the students that I stumbled on the truth about helping people. The best way to change people's lives is to trust in their ability to change their own.

Langa Township was Melisizwe's home. He knew the smell of morning in that sun-filled, dusty place as I never could. And this, I have come to respect, was profound for those students in a way that three years of a first-class college education and a big liberal bleeding heart were not. What does *postcolonial* mean when instead Melisizwe could say, "the way your tata keeps talking about slow change, yebo"? It was as if I had the terms and Melisizwe had the manifestations.

This is not to say, of course, that I learned that I didn't have a place in that classroom or that my help was futile in a country I didn't grow up in. In fact, my epiphany was the opposite. Instead I learned that the most ethical and effective kind of assistance that I could give was to act as a facilitator, an organizer. I had the vision to recognize that those kids would benefit from the liberating power of poetry and the enthusiasm of Melisizwe, so I put them in the same room on a Monday morning in April. This was my profound role; I possessed a precious foresight for transformation, an aching need to help, and a knack for organization. It is as if I was my most effective when I was not writing the script but putting the pen and the paper in deserving people's hands.

At a time when so much heated debate centers on foreign policy, I think that my ethical epiphany is painfully clear and certainly applicable on a larger scale. As Americans we will never truly know what it is like to be South African, French, or Haitian. As Melisizwe put it, we will never know what morning smells like in a childhood home in these places. But we may visit them and we may recognize needs. This is our vision. This is our power. To become part of a community, to care about it deeply, and then to encourage that it heal itself . . . that is where our capacity to change the world dwells. We are effective only as far as we are facilitators. We are ethical only as far as we are humble. The terrorism that has recently torn our country apart, in my opinion, has no simple cause.

Some have pointed to America's big bully attitude when it comes to foreign policy as the precursor to the devastation we have experienced as of late. I would never simplify what has happened so much, but I do think there is something poignant in this argument. I have often wondered, based on my own government's reaction, if people in positions of power in this country are truly resolved about what is helpful and what is harmful to our foreign brothers and sisters. I trust that they mean well, as I did. But I'm not convinced that any of them would make the same decisions they have—in Rwanda, in Yugoslavia, in Colombia—if they had spent one day in that sun-filled classroom in Langa Township.

Americans are a big-hearted, ambitious people, but I wonder if we sometimes just move too fast to see our own effect. It is in a little stillness—in that moment of silence that followed Melisizwe's speech— that we may learn something about our own choices, about our own capacities.

As Melisizwe's explanation came to a close, the nodding heads of the eager students signified the success of my project. My vision was realized only through the eyes of the local community. It was their sight, not my own, that was the sharpest. Just as it is local communities, not the big brother of policy and capital that our country has become, that can see what is best. Americans must learn to trust other people; we must learn to give but then step back, facilitate, but not teach. We must learn to learn.

And when we have, a glorious connection will be made, a glorious transformation will take place . . . as it did in that classroom that April morning in South Africa.

On the last day of our workshop, Melisizwe and I entered the classroom like old friends. I immediately sat down in a desk next to Nobuhle, Monellisa, and Busiswe. We were all bubbling over with excitement for our final celebration: an open-mike reading in which each student was encouraged to stand up in front of the class and share one of the pieces they had written that week. Monellisa began, "I believe that we, the teenagers, we are the future of this country. It can happen if we can all fall in love with this beautiful country."

Then Lindelwa:

> I wish that I could collect the street kids
> Give them a shelter
> Give them clothes
> Give them education
> I wish that I could be a helping hand finding a cure
>   for AIDS and HIV
> I'm praying for a transformation in my country.

Luvuyo had us all close to tears:

> I wish I had never seen
> the way my friend died, but
> god disagreed with me
> that he made me to see
> everything that has happened
> to my friend that made him die
> he dies on my hands.
> fortunately,

> I was not alone with him
> but to me it seemed like I was alone.

And Wendy:

> He thought as we are black
> our brains are also black
> so we won't be able to get light in our education
> I feel so painful about that
> because apartheid is still remain in our society
> although we say we are in new freedom.

And on and on, the students approached the front of the room with new courage and spoke their minds. They were loud and they were soft, they were big-headed and they were insecure, but most of all, they were expressing themselves for the first time; for some of them, it was like speaking for the first time all over again. Finally Vuyiseka, again, marched in front of the class, this tiny soldier with huge bravery, and said, "We would like to say thanks to Courtney and Melisizwe for coming here at our school. Your being here did a first for us. It awoken that part of life that no one likes to talk about. Before you came we thought poetry was nothing but words, words written by white people, but we were wrong and you helped us to realize that. Now poetry is our new best friend. We gained a first from you guys. As they say, the pen is mightier than the sword. We actually know what it means. Because of poetry we can conquer a lot."

Who Killed Superman?

JENDI B. REITER
1993
Harvard University

WOULDN'T YOU RATHER GO to a costume party as the devil than as
God?

Intellectually, most people know that one should admire and try to
emulate figures who represent goodness: the hero or heroine of a story,
the officials who maintain order and justice in society, or the characters
who personify virtue in religious legends and tracts. Nonetheless, all
too often one feels the thrills and longings of hero worship, not when
one contemplates resembling these figures, but when one imagines one's
self as a gangster, a tyrant, or a femme fatale. Of course the mad scientist who plots to rule the world must be defeated by the law-abiding citizens of Normalville, USA, but it is the doomed extraordinary character
and not the victorious commonplace one who receives one's secret adu-
lation. William Blake realized this when he created the idiosyncratic
mythology of his poems, portraying the conflict between Urizen, the
Godlike old man who represents reason and morality, and Orc, the fiery
youth who is analogous to the devil and who is the source of energy and
creativity. Blake asserted that all artists were "of the devil's party"
whether they knew it or not.[1]

Many have commented on the glamorization of evil in our culture,
but their solutions have often left untouched the dichotomy between
goodness and glamour. A mere turning away from dazzling and amoral
modernity will not suffice, for the problem's history dates from before
our era. The legend of Faust is only one example of the basic human
need to seek excitement and meaning in life by going beyond the limits

of what is socially and morally acceptable. Nor can one simply condemn this need as immoral and advise people to avert their eyes from fascinating antiheroes the way ascetics might shun the world's temptations. This would be about as effective as telling Victorian women to stop feeling lust because it was naughty. A psychological need is not satisfied or eradicated by an intellectual conviction that it is not acceptable; it is merely driven underground, to resurface later in a distorted form. As Blake suggested, when Urizen represses Orc too much, the former becomes a tyrant. Yet if they can maintain a harmonious balance, good can come out of the "devil's" qualities.

Instead of condemning villain-worship wholesale, then, it might be more fruitful to view it as a perverted expression of a hero worship that finds no suitable objects. "Sympathy for the devil" is a sign of unreconciled tension between virtue and strength, or between the ideal of the good man as upholder of social stability and the ideal described in Ralph Waldo Emerson's dictum, "Good men must not obey the laws too well."[2] The problem is to find an iconography of virtue which recognizes both that ethical action requires awareness of one's responsibility to uphold the values and interests of one's community, and that the ethical life demands a self-sufficient courage and an independent conscience that may set one above ordinary people and even necessitate rebellion against their standards.

This paradox comes about because virtue is both egalitarian and hierarchical. It is egalitarian in that every human being has the capacity for ethical action and can comprehend the difference between right and wrong. This capacity is the common denominator that obligates us to treat one another not as means but as ends, as Immanuel Kant wrote in *The Metaphysics of Morals*.[3] When the ordinary or humble characters defeat the larger-than-life forces of evil in a story, like Jack killing the Giant, we are meant to understand that goodness is open to everyone. Yet virtue is also hierarchical, in that the virtuous or admirable person is by definition better than average. It is this aristocratic aspect of virtue that has the greatest psychological appeal, so much so that we are driven to admire villains in the absence of other characters who exceed the ordinary in a more positive way. If not tempered by the egalitarian principle, therefore, the hierarchical one degenerates into a worship of strength for its own sake, a "might makes right" philosophy that treats the inferior as less than human. Such was the motivation behind Nietzscheanism and, later, Nazism. On the other hand, the democratic society's distrust of hierarchy tends to encourage a cultural understanding of virtue as the exclusive property of ordinary people and as consisting of innocence, self-restraint, and compliance with communal norms. Strength, sophistication, and unconventional style are thus reserved for villains.

Any discussion of how adults and children in our society can be educated to take ethics seriously must therefore begin with the natural human desire to be exceptional, exciting, and strong (or powerful), and how this desire can be channeled to serve as an impetus for a love of virtue. In *The Uses of Enchantment,* Bruno Bettelheim noted that "a child identifies with the good hero [of a story] . . . because the hero's condition makes a deep positive appeal to him. The question . . . is not 'Do I want to be good?' but 'Who do I want to be like?'"[4] Images and stories affect the formation of character more than precepts do, for the former provide an emotionally and psychologically convincing answer to the question "Why should I care about right and wrong?" by presenting virtuous characters in such a way that one actually wants to emulate them. Cultural images of heroism thus help people see how they can be both self-controlled and cooperative members of a community and exceptional and independent individuals.

In our culture today, however, various belief systems and stereotypes combine to militate against a closing of the gap between goodness and glamour. The result is a Nietzschean vision of morality as a system of restraints accepted by the common people but transcended by a special few.

This vision prevails whether or not the intent is to side with the villains: the battle lines are still drawn between quotidian virtue and flamboyant vice. The beliefs responsible for this unhealthy dichotomy are frequently extreme versions of, or side effects of, cultural traditions that have formed our society's character: democracy, the nineteenth-century association of goodness with domesticity and passivity, a Rousseauian identification of innocence and unsophistication with moral purity, and the exaltation of weakness in one tradition of Christian thought. While some of these beliefs have made great contributions to our culture, with simplistic forms of them in popular images of virtue, there is no appropriate role model for strong and exceptional individuals or those who have matured beyond the age of innocence. When qualities that have little psychological appeal, or that cannot be maintained past childhood, are the culture's objective correlatives of "goodness," then it is easy to see why being good seems phony, preachy, oppressive, or boring. The ways in which this problem manifests itself in popular culture, and the consequences for our society, are discussed below.

Children are especially sensitive to the tension between respectable goodness and admirable rebellion, for they are subject to restraints at a time when they are least able to understand why their self-development should not be completely unfettered. Because of this, books and television shows that are designed with a "message" for children need to strike a balance between gratifying a child's wish for vicarious independence and exciting action and making sure that that action occurs within the context of acceptable moral norms.

Superhero and superheroine cartoons are often criticized nowadays by activists and child psychologists who claim that it glorifies violence to depict a good character as using force. DC Comics recently followed this trend when the company decided to make Superman into a vulnerable, sensitive man of the 1990s by killing him. This is a fundamentally misguided philosophy. Heroes like Superman do not glorify violence; on the contrary, violence is always potentially glorified already, because violence involves danger and danger is an opportunity for courage. Superheroes are an indispensable part of a child's ethical development because the image of the superhero turns the appeal of violence into the appeal of strength in the service of righteousness, turning brute courage into moral courage. If one does not allow the possibility of a legitimate admiration for the superhero's power, daring, and style, one forces the admirers of courage to side with the brutes. Kill Clark Kent's Superman, and Nietzsche's superman will take his place.

Unfortunately, many of the books being written with the specific aim of teaching young children ethical lessons present goodness as inoffensiveness rather than as excellence. If their generic protagonist had a name, it would not be Superman but Niceman or Sorryman, a character whose virtue consists of unconditional tolerance of the faults and peculiarities of every culture or lifestyle except his own. Fairness, lack of prejudice, and unselfish and responsible behavior toward natural resources are indispensable ethical lessons, but the books that propose to teach children these lessons are generally informed by antihuman or antiachievement sentiments.

Books on the environment, for instance, portray a conflict between evil humanity and innocent nature: *Just a Dream,* whose young protagonist learns to sort his trash after dreaming that his environmental irresponsibility destroyed the planet;[5] *Little Pig,* in which a girl who won't be a vegetarian is turned into a pig and almost eaten;[6] or various books on the rain forest that depict cute animals cowering in terror before the onslaught of Progress. Books on social issues aim at leveling moral distinctions or tearing down traditional heroes, as in revisionist history books for children or in *Leonora O'Grady,* which portrays homeless people as more creative, closer to nature, and more interesting than regular adults.[7] Some of these books are no doubt well-intentioned, but they send the discouraging message that goodness is a matter of restricting one's actions and achievements whenever possible. They perpetuate the "noble savage" myth that maturity and the opportunities of adult life represent a step away from virtue.

Children whose role models are bag ladies, guilty garbage-sorters, and superheroes who get in touch with their inner child are more likely than other children to reject virtue as "wimpy" and "uncool" once they outgrow the restricted and subordinate status of early childhood. As they mature, they feel the stirrings of ambition, courage, a need for adventure, a desire to prove themselves—in short, a longing for heroism. Since goodness has already been defined for them as a state of self-doubting passivity they have outgrown or rejected, they imagine that maturity requires leaving behind the constraints of ethics as one would discard an outgrown cradle. Magazines and television news crews who have interviewed gang members have found that one of the reasons adolescents join gangs is their desire for adventure and for hard-won status, combined with the assumption that they would only be emasculated and frustrated if they recognized ethical limitations on their actions.

In adult popular culture, the situation is somewhat better. More movies and television programs are beginning to portray sophisticated and strong-willed women as heroines, whereas in the past they always suffered by comparison with the soft-spoken girl next door. Some films, like *Top Gun,* still depict the military as a place where one can mature and become strong while remaining in the service of justice and of the community.

Fantasy films and television serial dramas, however, persistently convey the idea that amorality is the most enticing lifestyle and that goodness is dull. *Dracula,* for instance, was originally a horror story the moral of which was the struggle and triumph of good people against a monster. In the latest film version of the story, the vampire is now the tall, dark stranger of whom every girl dreams, and the "virtuous" men are the typical weak and effeminate "good" young men of Victorian novels. *Batman Returns,* one of last year's most popular movies for children and adults, centers almost entirely on the exciting villains and makes the ostensible hero a brooding, barely active, self-doubting figure who in the end is unsure of the difference between himself and his adversary.

As for television shows, the guiding principle of long-running dramas is that commitment is boring. The only way a male lead can develop new dimensions or be involved in interesting action is for him to commit adultery or to maintain his relationships in a permanent state of limbo (for example, *Moonlighting*). The villains, moreover, get all the best lines and are usually the initiators of the action, while the good characters are the ones to whom things are done. These trends in popular culture teach viewers that meaningful action and personality growth are not compatible with goodness or loyalty.

Popular music suffers from a similar dichotomy between style and content. Songs with constructive messages about compassion, honesty, or courage have sugary-sweet tunes that are about as inspirational as shopping mall background music, while songs with an energetic, emotionally powerful beat have lyrics that promote promiscuity, bestiality, and cruelty. Fans of rock music thus come to associate these latter ideas with pleasing or stimulating emotional reactions caused by the music. It is especially telling that the word *bad* in rock music slang means its exact opposite, as in Michael Jackson's album *Bad*. Calling someone "bad" or "wicked" denotes one's admiration for his "cool," stylish demeanor.

In addition to these influences from books and the entertainment industry, the media's treatment of political figures has contributed to our culture's lack of role models who combine strength, charisma, and goodness. Again, the democratic leveling principle has been taken to extremes. In the name of "the people's right to know" or "checks on government power," the dignity of a political figure is demolished by sophomoric satires, questions about his third cousin's sex life, and photo-ops of him in the bathtub with his rubber ducky. It is also fashionable in intellectual circles to deride the police and the army as merely instruments of imperialism and authoritarian repression.

Of course, it is essential for citizens of a democracy to know that their superiors have feet of clay, yet we seem to think we have been naive or apathetic citizens unless we think of our superiors as clay from head to toe. The ultimate result is that we have no positive image of authority in the service of justice—in a word, no one to look up to—and we grow to imagine that an antisocial stance is more authentic and praiseworthy than admiration for those above us. Politically and aesthetically, this is the age of the antihero.

Changing the culture's image of goodness can never entirely eliminate the natural lure of the forbidden; according to the Bible, it is apparently as old as humanity itself. The presence of images of heroism, however, would go a long way toward providing respectable and constructive outlets for some of the passions and needs that currently drive us to admire villains. Biblical heroes and heroines such as David, Deborah, and the Maccabees, and legends of the age of chivalry, might constitute a good starting point for refurnishing our store of images of virtuous strength.

To make the idea of heroism even more effective, we also need images that show us what Hannah Arendt called "the banality of evil."[8] Arendt's phrase sums up a principle that is vital to an understanding of life's ethical choices. Evil is a moral dead end, the absence of good, and destroys the self by consuming it with base sentiments and by deadening the moral sense that makes one human. It is thus hardly a means of self-actualization. Far from being an escape from numbing respectability, evil blots one out in a way that conformity by itself could not. Madeleine L'Engle captures this truth in *A Swiftly Tilting Planet* with the powerful image of the Ecthroi, the forces of evil in the Universe, whose mission is to "X" things—to make them cease to be.[9]

In the end, the culture's prevailing belief that "nice guys finish last," that virtue is incompatible with charisma and efficacy, betokens a lack of faith in the power and importance of goodness. We cease to believe that right will triumph or that truth will make us free, and so the mere mention of ethics seems irrelevant or hypocritical because everyone knows—or thinks he or she knows—that goodness is self-destructive and impossible in the real world. Tragically, this becomes a self-fulfilling prophecy. Encourage cynicism, and suitable recipients of our faith and trust become more uncommon and harder to perceive. Once we lose the habit of hero worship, we lose the habit of thinking of ethical heroism as an ideal to which we can aspire. Kill Superman, and we kill the best within ourselves.

Notes

1. William Blake, *The Marriage of Heaven and Hell* (London: Oxford University Press, 1975), pl. 6.

2. Ralph Waldo Emerson, "Politics," in *The Portable Emerson*, ed. Mark Van Doren (New York: Viking, 1946), 195.

3. Immanuel Kant, *Fundamental Principles of the Metaphysics of Morals*, trans. Thomas K. Abbot (Indianapolis, IN: Bobbs-Merrill, 1949), 45–46.

4. Bruno Bettelheim, *The Uses of Enchantment: The Meaning and Importance of Fairy Tales* (New York: Knopf, 1976), 9–10.

5. Chris Van Allsburg, *Just a Dream* (Boston: Houghton Mifflin, 1990).

6. Akumal Ramachander, *Little Pig* (New York: Penguin, 1992).

7. Leah Komaiko, *Leonora O'Grady* (New York: HarperCollins, 1992).

8. Hannah Arendt, *Eichmann in Jerusalem: A Report on the Banality of Evil* (New York: Viking, 1963).

9. Madeline L'Engle, *A Swiftly Tilting Planet* (New York: Dell, 1981).

Ethics Education Toward a More
Moral Society

KAREN HO
1992
Washington University

IN THE TOUCH-AND-GO bustle of modern-day life, in a world grappling with chaos and the uncertainty of an unknown and unpredictable future, in a fragile society struggling with conflicts between technical know-how and long-established values and beliefs, ethics is a key at the crux of the problem of forging a new and more harmonized future for humankind. The nature of ethics, and the education of the general populace in ethical principles, addresses a question at the heart of the human endeavor: "How best may I live, endure, and achieve, in the presence of and in conjunction with my fellow human beings?" By acknowledging that human beings have the ability to inflict egregious acts of cruelty and hatred against one another, as well as the potential to unleash the richness of human existence on behalf of each other, ethics education may serve to bring about self-awareness as well as foster better understanding among peoples and cultures. To exert positive change on the world and to harness human potential to achieve shared aims represent two of the most important challenges and goals faced by any society, and consequently constitute the core of the question of ethics education.

Before grappling with the question of ethics education, one must first address the nature of ethics itself, by addressing its societal basis and by examining ethical dilemmas and their underlying causes. Inherent in this discussion are the additional aspects of human nature as they relate to ethics and the nature of education in our society today. Ethics education can then be examined, as can the question of how best to design the education of ethics to meet present-day needs.

Ethics and Choice

A brief perusal of current newspapers, magazines, the news on television, or even works of literature and art will reveal that today's society is deeply troubled. Human misery comes in all shapes and sizes, from skid row to inner-city ghettos, from poverty and homelessness to street gangs, from serial killers to drug abusers. The perpetrators of crimes against humanity range from individuals to large corporations and even nations. Why do these heinous acts occur? For the most part not because of random chance or bad luck but because of *conscious human choice*. For this very reason, ethical decision-making can indeed play a role in alleviating this suffering, for the manifestations of misery are largely the results of choices on the part of both the individual and society.

Ethics, therefore, emerges from free choice. In contrast to the absolute concept of ethics as virtue extolled by Plato, modern ethics concerns the striving of all people to make better decisions to achieve beneficial and meritorious ends. Ethics asks the question of how to arrive at, and act on, decisions that are "appreciated as good by all singular persons who take part in it, [for whom] . . . the realization of the good . . . is a good shared by all."[1] Ethics constitutes a firm basis upon which a more moral society may be built.

The American philosopher and educator John Dewey asserts that the first step toward a more moral society comes in the realization that both society and the individual should shoulder the responsibility of making moral decisions.[2] This is a statement that grows more profound with each examination, especially if one interprets much of society's apathy and callousness, aversion to long-term planning, lust for instantaneous pleasure, erosion of values, and the loss of a sense of concertedness as functions of the loss of a sense of social responsibility and an accompanying loss of hope: the lack of faith in the belief that people, working either as individuals or in concert, can make a real and decisive difference for the better. To recapture that hope, society must first recognize that human beings have a deep and common need to be appreciated and that this need must be addressed in order to allow productive, supportive, and moral relationships to occur. When this need is not met, when people are made to feel powerless and alienated, the whole basis of morality, and society itself, begins to crumble. The manifestations of human misery we see in society today are reflections of deep feelings of frustration on the part of peoples whose need to be recognized as human beings with rich potential, integrity, and worth are not being met. The central need to be recognized and understood as a person embraces other needs to simply be seen by society as useful, precious, and important, not because of the amount of labor this person can produce, but because of who one is and all the unique perspectives and wealth of insight this individuality entails. Ethical theory must address these underlying needs in order to cure societal ills, not merely treat symptoms of the disease. Hence the role of ethics education: to boost citizens' self-esteem, to instill a sense of responsibility for one's actions and their future consequences, and to empower people to be able to draw on all the available resources and the wealth of knowledge that will aid in moral decision-making.

Ethics and Education: Can Ethics Be Taught?

The question of teaching ethics thus becomes one of how to teach people to be aware of their choices and to make productive decisions, the consequences of which will result in more "inclusive and enduring" outcomes and ends.[3] Is it possible to teach this process, to instill a sense of the "good"? Can ethics, indeed, be taught?

Throughout history, and across different societies, ethics has changed, evolved, donned different guises, represented different concepts. Ethics is a function of values, beliefs, culture. Because of its variety, its amorphous quality of evading definition, and its myriad meanings to different peoples, ethics does indeed seem too volatile and controversial a subject to capture and teach in schools. Nevertheless, although ethics is not formally taught in all cultures, all cultures do have a code of ethics common to the members of that society. Even the Ik, an African mountain people of northern Uganda studied by anthropologist Colin Turnbull and known as the "Loveless People" for their inhumane treatment of one another, operate on a set of beliefs based on their unique idea of good.[4] Good, to them, is food in the belly; and the Ik word for a well-fed man is the same term they would use to say "a good man."[5] Thus, to grab food from the mouth of a starving relative, to cheat, trick, steal in order to gain food, to stuff oneself to the point of physical discomfort so as to not have to share with one's kinfolk, is "good." Thankfully, other cultures and societies maintain very different philosophies and various other definitions of good; some are based on complete sharing of material goods, such as the communes in Israel known as kibbutzim. In contrast, others are based on the concept of individualism as a good, from which theories on capitalism and the free market may follow. "Good" in still other cultures and communities has run the gamut from asceticism to epicureanism, absolutism to pragmatism. Ethics and beliefs have also changed in response to emerging technologies or other societal stresses, as they must in order to remain relevant and applicable to the times. Some of the morals that emerge from different concepts of "good" have withstood the test of time; others have not, as if in accordance with a Darwinian law of natural selection applied to the various philosophies. A case in point: because of their denigrating and uncooperative behavior, the Ik are dying. Their inability to act in concert to genuinely cooperate, and to bond with one another, is catalyzing their societal demise. There is much to be learned about the nature of ethics in their society, for their sad example opens the possibility that just as the Ik's social environment and cultural definition of "good" demolished their society, a different, more encompassing definition of "good" may encourage personal growth and understanding among its members, allowing the prospering of a society on a humanitarian level. Morton Hunt notes, "A single, pervasive, easily overlooked fact proves that although we often behave abominably to our fellow human beings, we are also routinely and spontaneously caring and benevolent to them. That proof: *We endure*."[6] The statement illustrates the vital importance of the nature of the philosophy of ethics developed and embraced by a society, for it plays an active role in the health—and even survival—of a culture and community. The attitudes and code of ethics relayed from member to member, taught by action and deed, reverberate through all of society, through all time, and can maim or sustain it, wound or nourish it, depending on what is taught.

Through the examination of the changing nature of ethics, one concludes that ethics can indeed be taught successfully, since ethics *are* taught, all the time. A culture or society remains a cohesive unit for the very reason that each new generation *is* taught, directly or indirectly, consistent concepts of "good," which results in a common code of ethics for that society. Even the absence of ethical instruction, as in the case of the Ik, is in itself a type of ethical instruction. Therefore society faces a choice: we may either plunge, unguided, into the future, allowing ethics to vacillate before our eyes and evade our inquiries because we either ignore or deny it, or we may shape our lives and future consciously—conscientiously—by acknowledging ethics and its import in our lives and by sharing our discoveries and thoughts concerning ethics with one another so that an improving, evolving body of knowledge and beliefs may guide us through uncertainty. Advocates of the latter option would answer an emphatic "Yes!" to the question "Should ethics be learned and taught?" and so the question "Can ethics be taught?" becomes instead a question of what kind of ethics to teach and how to teach it.

The Teaching of Ethics

Because new technologies, as well as the challenges involved in the myriad social interactions that take place, promise to pose a continuing stream of moral dilemmas for society, ethics awareness should be addressed throughout all societies and embrace all institutions: political, social, and personal. Moreover, morality should be emphasized not as a hard-and-fast set of rules to follow but rather as general guidelines that are based on past successful solutions, experiences, and the increasing knowledge of human interactions and methods of conflict resolution. By completely dismissing ethical behavior in daily life, one generates the sorry society of the Ik; yet on the other hand, by preaching moral dogmas, by promulgating fixed "rules to live by," a society embroils itself in yet another ethical debate, that of infringing on values, of imposing beliefs on people, of violating the individual freedom to acquire one's own moral principles and beliefs. Instead, I would advocate the raising of ethical awareness in all facets of society on a more generalized yet meaningful level: by enhancing means of communication so that differing opinions may be heard and debated, by addressing feelings of apathy and alienation by giving the populace real power, on a societal level, to make ethical decisions, by emphasizing the union and reconciliation of differences that occurs in effective problem solving, by developing and promoting problem-solving skills and encouraging creative solutions, and by impressing upon people the importance of considering the consequences of an action before the execution of that action takes place.

Although a higher level of ethical awareness must occur throughout all facets of society, one of the most promising institutions of society at which we may begin reform is the school. Children play an incredibly important role in change, for they excel in adaptation, flexibility, and free, imaginative thought. One outstanding program developed on these beliefs involves student participation in skits and stories that involve opportunities for ethical behavior. Students confront issues pertinent to their lives, such as the hypothetical situation of being witness to, or participating in, an act of cheating. The children are encouraged to examine the moral question at hand in the form of short stories and skits that require consideration of all sides of the issue and the imaginative visualization of possible actions they could take and the consequences that would result. The nonprofit organization that provides the teaching materials for this program, the American Institute for Character Education, recently assessed the efficacy of its program by distributing a questionnaire to those schools participating in the teaching of ethics. The results of the survey were overwhelmingly in favor of the character education program: "Ninety-three percent of the teachers who replied said that students' self-concept had improved, 85 percent that behavior in the classroom had improved. . . . Majorities of the principals said the same thing, and 64 percent reported a decrease in vandalism."[7] Morton Hunt, who documented this report, adds, "[This] . . . sounds almost too good to be true. But comparable results have been reported by many other sources."[8] Perhaps the only reason that this "too-good-to-be-true" solution is not used more widely is that communities harbor an unjustified fear of "teaching ethics" in schools, a philosophy that in itself reflects on societal values. To include exercises in ethical thought and analysis, beginning in the primary grades, will enhance the resources and interpretation of experiences upon which children will draw when faced with a similar situation in "real life." The evidence of decreased antagonism among children as well as decreased vandalism indicates that open-ended, flexible communication, as well as discussion of ethical problem-solving strategies, can result in a more giving and sharing environment. Extrapolated to society, these results indicate that encouraging communication of ethical dilemmas, sincere endeavors on everyone's part to understand the position of the other party, and debates that reveal both sides of an issue and not merely a public relations position can lead to a more moral society.

In addition to more emphasis on "character education," there are a number of other changes that schools could make. First, schools could emphasize creative problem-solving in all academic subjects, from history lessons to mathematics. Instead of assigning and executing exercises in rote memorization, teachers and students can work together, searching for plausible solutions to problems that either have no defined "right" or "wrong" answer (such as tackling a historical situation by asking, for example, "What would you do, if you were this nation's leader?") or by trying to think up new, different methods of solving the same problem (for example, a simple multiplication problem can be solved by turning it into a question concerning area, addition, division, grouping, number lines, and so on). These activities strengthen skills for creative problem-solving and encourage bold, imaginative thought, instead of shunning the problem whose answers are not "in the back of the book," because it is too big to tackle and therefore frightening and hopeless. Education can give new meaning to matters that the child encounters; it can even facilitate the children's learning to pick their own battles, to distinguish the mere inconsistencies of everyday life from the moral injustices worth fighting against, and to combine compassion with knowledge to lead to wise decision-making by giving them a broader perspective of the world and their role in it.

The restructuring of education in general can also lead to a more ethical society. Too often teachers are forced to race against time to pack as much of the curriculum into their students' heads as can fit for fifty-five-minute sessions at a time, resulting in tests that ask students to merely regurgitate principles, formulas, rules, dates, and numbers or to apply a strict and standard protocol in order to get the right answers. The problem of education in this manner has at least three negative effects: first, students are numbed into believing there is only one "right" way of accomplishing a task, an attitude that is deleterious when applied to ethical problem-solving and the resolution of moral dilemmas, for which there is no set protocol; second, students learn to measure their worth by grades, by mere letters and numbers (a tendency that develops into adulthood, in which success later in life may be measured by salary and material wealth) and not by appreciating themselves and one another for their individuality, creativity, and uniqueness; third, education or, rather, this "training," emphasizes a "hidden curriculum," in which students are molded into docile followers, not independent thinkers. The educator John Holt identifies the "hidden curriculum," as a manifestation of the "idea that children won't learn without outside rewards and penalties . . . [which] usually becomes a self-fulfilling prophecy."[9] He continues: "So many people have said to me, 'If we didn't make children do things, they wouldn't do anything.' Even worse, they say, 'If *I* weren't made to do things, *I* wouldn't do anything.' *It is the creed of a slave.*"[10]

A. S. Neill emphatically agrees that such attitudes about children, and about ourselves, must be dispensed with. The founder of a private school in Suffolk, England, in the 1960s that was based on the principle that one can "teach a child without the use of force by appealing to his curiosity and spontaneous needs," Neill asserts that a sense of right and wrong, an understanding of morality and ethics, is a natural development in the course of a child's growth.[11] "Altruism," he writes, "comes naturally, if the child is not [forced] to be unselfish."[12] In other words, ethics, as any other subject of human thought, must be taught for its own sake, devoid of both materialistic reward and physical or psychological punishment. In summary, moral education can be supported by making certain changes in the theory and practice of education in general, by improving standards of education, and by utilizing flexible, creative problem-solving strategies with attitudes free of fear as means for promoting the moral development of children in schools.

An additional facet of education that can promote ethical thought and behavior is the acquisition and sharing of knowledge in order to facilitate understanding between people and cultures. In accordance with this view, Dewey advocates the pursuit of social and psychological research using scientific methodology, in order to increase the body of knowledge concerning human thought, motivation, choices, and action. A valid question that may be made in challenge of this view, however, is the following: Is knowledge a necessary and sufficient prerequisite to the kind of wisdom that constitutes moral decisions? If not, how do we teach that crucial step leading from knowledge to wisdom?[13] Dewey answers by stating that knowledge must be combined with that sympathetic impulse which allows us, as Harper Lee phrased it, to "stand inside someone else's shoes and walk around in them."[14] Such a process of knowledge leading to wisdom is touched upon by the science-fiction (but nevertheless realistically characterized) story *Ender's Game,* in which the twelve-year-old protagonist is enlisted in a military training school in which students are taught war tactics through playing "games." He immediately distinguishes himself by excelling in all the games and is hailed as the most promising student in the academy. At the height of his career as a student, however, he pauses to question what he is doing and becoming. In a telling scene, he reveals to his best friend and sister why he cannot continue to play the "games": "'In the moment when I truly understand my enemy, understand him well enough to defeat him, then in that very moment I also love him. I think it's impossible to really understand somebody, what they want, what they believe, and not love them the way they love themselves.'"[15] Knowledge, promulgated freely and without bias in schools, tempered by compassion that is both innate and taught, and encouraged by both the family and community, leads to wisdom and a more moral society.

Ethics education should take place not only within schools but within society as well. Reeducation and ethics awareness should embrace all institutions of a society in order to effect positive and lasting change. In his book *The Compassionate Beast,* Morton Hunt puts forth several suggestions that would support ethics and enforce prosocial behavior in society. He recommends the passing of bystander laws that would make it a crime to witness an illegal act without reporting it, a kind of insurance against the repetition of the Kitty Genovese tragedy. He writes that organizations and professions can encourage volunteer work as part of membership requirements or even professional duties, such as having doctors volunteer in free public clinics. Neighborhoods could institute "citizen crime-reporting programs," such as WhistleStop and Radio Watch, in which "citizens with two-way radios and members of CB clubs report crimes, fires, accidents and other emergencies."[16] These recommendations reinforce and support the natural urge of people to assume responsibility for one another and "hang together" to act in more ethical ways.

In the teaching of ethics, either in the classroom or within society at large, it must be remembered that ethics must be *lived* to be learned and that ethics exemplified by fellow citizens are assimilated far better than those that are taught, read about, or extolled in didactic lectures. Ethics must have reality and must be applied to everyday life. In accordance with this idea, society can also support ethics education of the general populace by stressing ethical behavior and by rewarding such behavior, not necessarily with material awards, but with public approval and the accolades of acceptance and honor. We as a society must determine whom we hold up as heroes. So much of youth today are caught up emulating film stars like Sylvester Stallone, singers Madonna or Michael Jackson, or sports heroes. Our current heroes represent a value system that admires the materially wealthy and the glamorous, and that emphasizes the wild and crazy, the extravagance of living for the moment. Unfortunately, such heroes do not emphasize the importance of planning ahead, of working and sacrificing toward a specific goal, of the importance of knowledge and the power to change that knowledge affords. We as a society must realize that the heroes a society chooses are the kinds of people children aspire to become. Why not give all people more exposure to the Albert Schweitzers and Mother Theresas of the world? From the altruistic rescuers of Jewish families during the Holocaust to the American citizens making new lives for unwanted Romanian children, there are those survivors and heroes from whom society has much to learn and in whom society has much to rejoice . . . those heroes who live their lessons of life.

Thus far the discussion has centered on the kind of ethics education that can provide the initial impetus in creating a more moral society. It provides a framework of philosophy that guides the teaching of the kind of skills needed in order to make ethical decisions but does not provide the answers to the ethical dilemmas themselves. The remaining challenges, then, are those very dilemmas: what to do about poverty and homelessness in this country, how to handle economic crises such as the one we are presently experiencing, how to diminish and eventually obliterate the drug problem, how to reduce teen pregnancies and suicides, and how to provide better health care for all citizens, just to name a few. In a world of limited time and resources, these are the ethical questions of the day. These are our challenges, our tests of morality, our society's crying need for problem solving and decision making. Why are these issues not confronted in a more encompassing, comprehensive ethical context? Why is it that the nightly news seems more like a morbid parade, a series of pictures of human suffering on a screen, about which we can do nothing? Yet we cry when we read a mother's story of her son who was killed as an innocent bystander of a gang shoot-out; we wince to see the writhing bodies in the pyres of the streets of South America on *Sixty Minutes;* we are shocked to find that three men can repeatedly assault students on a quiet campus while other students watch in horror. The acts outrage, depress, anger, and terrify us. Or at least they should. But so much of what it means to survive today is to take the nightly news as a personal warning: Don't do this, or Don't go there. Not to ask the questions: What can we do about this situation? How do we alleviate the misery? It's too easy to change the channel and deny responsibility, to make an excuse by saying, "There are cops out there for that; there's nothing I can do." Ethics education can change this. It can promote the idea that *we are who we choose to be* and that choosing to deny carries as much ethical import for ourselves, and our society, as choosing to act.

The study of Dewey's writings confirms the idea my brother once wrote: that we build our own prisons. A prison doesn't have to consist of cement and metal bars; it need only be an attitude, a fixed way of life, an unimaginative mode of problem solving (for example, "This is the way we've always done it, so let's do it this way again"). Dewey himself expressed the idea: "What makes a habit bad is enslavement into old ruts."[17] Our prisons consist of compartmentalizing and dividing the self when we should be reconciling and uniting: we have such limited understanding of one another and other cultures that we find it difficult to imagine a world without war, to envision human interactions based largely on love and respect. We build these prisons out of fear: fear rising from ignorance, fear of the unknown and not entirely understood, fear of trying new things, fear of failure, fear that if we reach out with love and get slapped in return it will be too painful to bear. So we build our psychological and philosophical prisons, not to keep the criminals, the "bad guys," in, but rather to keep everybody else out.

In response, ethics education can release us from our prisons, from our fear of one another and the rest of the world. The heart of this theory, in fact, is the overcoming of fear. What is probably scary to most is how much the model of ethical education I have presented asks us to trust one another, to believe in the next person's moral decision-making ability, in the next person's impulses of sympathy and kindness. If we start through education, in the many senses of that word, including our educating ourselves about ourselves, about one another, and about the nature of our interactions, there will emerge a deeper understanding of our roles and selves, as well as more knowledge of our options and potentialities with regard to who we, both individually and collectively, want to become. Such a future-oriented, potential-focused theory encourages human excellence over mediocrity, for it gives opportunity for the self to play a significant role, to assume the reins of this journey into the future, to find, not *a* solution, but *the* best solution to dilemmas, and act on one's decisions to the best of one's ability. It encourages people to make an investment of time and energy and sacrifice into their life. Moreover, it challenges them to live intensely, to lead life through the flights of wild ecstasy and the moments of darkest despair, because it dares people to be significant, worthy, infinitely precious, to themselves and society, and then it dares them to become even better with the next dilemma or crisis by building on past experiences. This is a vision of evolution that I share with Dewey, an evolution of humankind on a psychological and social level. Ethics education embodies the premise that because the human intellect is so capable of assimilating and applying knowledge in novel ways, because the human spirit is so resilient and flexible, that through challenge and dilemma we may emerge changed, and better than before. The implementation of ethics education marks the beginning of the odyssey toward a more moral society.

Notes

1. John Dewey, *The Public and Its Problems* (Chicago: Swallow, 1954), 149.
2. John Dewey, *Human Nature and Conduct,* ed. Jo Ann Boydston (Edwardsville: Southern Illinois University Press, 1988), 35.
3. John Dewey, *Ethics, Part II: Theory of the Moral Life,* ed. Jo Ann Boydston (Edwardsville: Southern Illinois University Press, 1989), 187.
4. Colin Turnbull, *The Mountain People* (New York: Simon and Schuster, 1972), 234–264.
5. Turnbull, *Mountain People,* 135.
6. Morton Hunt, *The Compassionate Beast: The Scientific Inquiry into Human Altruism* (New York: Doubleday, 1990), 16.
7. Hunt, *Compassionate Beast,* 218.
8. Hunt, *Compassionate Beast,* 218.
9. John Holt, *How Children Fail* (New York: Dell, 1982), 113.
10. Holt, *How Children Fail,* 113.

11. Erich Fromm, "Foreword," in A. S. Neill, *Summerhill: A Radical Approach to Child Rearing* (New York: Hart, 1960), ix.
12. Neill, *Summerhill,* 250.
13. Dewey, *Ethics, Part II,* 270.
14. Harper Lee, *To Kill a Mockingbird* (New York: J. B. Lippincott, 1960), 294.
15. Orson Scott Card, *Ender's Game* (New York: Tom Doherty Associates, 1985), 261.
16. Hunt, *Compassionate Beast,* 219–224.
17. Dewey, *Human Nature and Conduct,* 48.

ON ILLNESS

Tearing Down the Lazaretto

WIN TRAVOSSOS
1994
Harvard University

"ILLNESS," SUSAN SONTAG writes, "is the night-side of life, a more onerous citizenship."[1] Sontag uses the word *citizenship* with reason; we consider those afflicted with a malady to be citizens of another realm, another culture. We romanticize some conditions, at different times having linked mental illness, tuberculosis, and neurosyphilis to bursts of creative genius. Or we pull illness out of the world of biology and credit it to spiritual injury, as did D. H. Lawrence in saying: "I am ill because of wounds to the soul, to the deep emotional self."[2] To the ill are ascribed qualities, characteristics, abilities that we as the healthy do not possess. These conditions bestowed upon the afflicted by illness are ones we, the healthy, may experience temporarily but do not hold on to for any longer. When we characterize illness as such, we place the ill firmly outside our experience and world of reference; we make their "onerous citizenship" in another community a reality. Those who are afflicted suffer not only from physical malady but also from a social one; they do not fit the conventions of society, they are not what we know to be "normal," and they are therefore redefined as ill. Lines of separation are drawn between the worlds of the sick and the well, pushing them apart from each other.

With the advent of AIDS we can see this phenomenon, the separation of the community, appearing as it has with the great plagues of the past. With any epidemic, a trend appears: as the disease spreads, mainstream society splits off from and turns on minorities of any kind, the

267

poor, immigrants, and other smaller groups. These smaller groups are cited as isolated pools of people in which disease festers and incubates, and they then absorb the blame for introducing sickness to the general population. For societies living with an epidemic, the issue of how to fight it is intimately bound up with what groups it strikes, for reasons not always disease-related. Mainstream society takes on the role of "the healthy" and, by extension, "the well" and "the normal." Those afflicted, often minority communities or groups at the fringes of mainstream society, are pushed into Sontag's "night-side of life," becoming "the ill," the denizens of another realm.[3]

Consider, then, the lazaretto, the medieval quarantine hospital where the diseased were kept and isolated during an epidemic. The word *lazaretto* comes from *lazar,* or leper, and Nazareto, the name of a medieval hospital run by the Church of Saint Maria di Nazaret.[4] A lazaretto was a quarantine mechanism motivated as much by the desire to sequester the sick as the need to seal away those who had been spiritually or morally tainted by disease. For a society, a lazaretto becomes, with time, something more than a physical building; it becomes a name for that realm, both physical and spiritual, that the diseased occupy. The ill are contained in a lazaretto, locked into their own world, placed beyond the concerns and cares of the world outside. The quarantine element of the original word remains while the hospital part is discarded, for those who enter the realm of the ill never truly leave; they have been tainted by sickness forever. The lazaretto, as such, becomes the boundary beyond which neither side passes during an epidemic. The well seek to isolate the ill, and the ill struggle to survive within their own self-contained world. Such is the inevitable division that occurs if the separation of the community is allowed to proceed.

This much is clear; when a society deals with an epidemic, here AIDS, it never does so with only disease-related concepts in mind. Polarization inevitably occurs, with the ill and the healthy occupying separate realms, valuing different concepts, clinging to different concerns. As Sontag points out with AIDS, "from the beginning the construction of the illness had depended on notions that separated one group of people from another—the sick from the well . . . them and us."[5] This separation of the larger community into two spheres fragments it, rends it apart, sequesters individual groups. No smaller group is ably equipped to fight the disease by itself, and in the absence of links between groups, each group festers with resentment, fear, and hostility toward "the Other."[6] Separation of the community in the face of an epidemic inevitably leads to one thing: the construction of the lazaretto, isolating and dividing all in the face of suffering.

Moral individuals in communities are then confronted with one question: what can they do to counter the separation of the community, knowing what suffering results from it?

"Literature," writes Cynthia Ozick, "is for the sake of humanity." In her essay "Metaphor and Memory" she advances the notion that literature, correctly manipulated, can bind individuals together. Key to this manipulation of language is the use of metaphor, a term she takes from standard literary criticism and extends further into a way to peer into the experience of others. Conventionally, metaphor is a figure of speech that plays on the resemblance between a literal subject and an implied subject, as with Homer's "wine-dark sea." The familiar image of wine allows all to know the color of the sea, moving us into the world of the sailor, extending our perceptions into his world. Ozick points out that "metaphor relies on what has been experienced before; it transforms the strange into the familiar . . . metaphor uses what we already possess and reduces strangeness."[7]

Metaphor, at its simplest level, allows us to conjure up images from others' lives and make them our own. We cull images from our everyday lives and store them in memory; they become a base upon which we draw when trying to understand others' metaphors. Our stores of memory in turn help define who we are and what our views of the world are, for we draw on these images, interpreting them, analyzing them for lessons and information. We can turn around and use metaphor for our own ends, drawing on these images we possess, of the most basic kind cited above, which constitute our memories. When we use metaphor to communicate with others, we try to find common cultural threads that allow them to peer into our minds, to see from our point of view, to feel what we have experienced. We place an image recognizable to all side by side with an image drawn from our experience; in so doing, we try to make our memories approachable to all. We realize that when we use metaphor for our own ends, we base it on our past experiences, pulling images from memory as we see fit; metaphor holds them together and copies for others the lessons and information found in our past and history. Metaphor calls on language common to all as a way to bring different experiences together, moving an image particular to a single group into the world of general discourse. Ozick tells us: "Without the metaphor of memory and history, we cannot imagine the life of the other . . . what it is to be someone else. Metaphor is the reciprocal agent, the universalizing force . . . the power to envision the stranger's heart."[8]

Metaphor, then, is the tool of choice for the writer who communicates experience, who brings the memory and history of a single group to the cultural mainstream. Memory teaches us, shapes us, forces us to constantly reexamine how we approach life, and metaphor, through language, allows us to turn these lessons over to other minds, to other groups, to other individuals. We learn about those aspects of living that are common to all; we learn how knowledge and wisdom can be passed on continuously from group to group until all are aware and enriched. Metaphor can serve "as a means to understand what it is to be an outcast, a foreigner, an alien of any kind."[9] No longer can we engage in abstract speculation about others; we have the ability to crawl inside their experiences through an elegant tool of language. In short, the knowledge of one group can spread out to the whole community, for "through metaphor . . . those who have no pain can imagine those who suffer . . . we strangers can imagine the familiar hearts of strangers."[10]

In 1989 Larry Kramer wrote, "Over the past seven years, I have lost some five hundred acquaintances and friends to AIDS. . . . There's no time for grief or mourning, certainly not for contemplation."[11] Kramer's writing shouts, rages, tears into all who read it; his emotion is real, torn from his personal experience. He writes, as he puts it, "with death so palpable and continuously close."[12] Yet in looking at his writing, we can see that it has changed and developed as he has witnessed the growth of the AIDS epidemic in America. He has lost none of the fierce anger that characterized much of his early work; instead, we can see that the way he has chosen to fight the epidemic has shifted with time.

"I wrote for one reason: the world must know," says Kramer of his early writing. "I had an obligation: because fate had placed me on the front line of the epidemic from the very beginning, I was a witness to much history that others were not."[13] Kramer, in his own words, played the role of angry historian and prophet. He railed against institutional policies he saw as unfair, openly criticized government officials who he felt did little to fight the epidemic, wrote letters to newspaper editors, did whatever he could to spur action against AIDS. Essays in the *New York Times,* the *Village Voice,* the *Advocate,* the *New York Native,* countless speeches, two plays, and the founding of two AIDS-related activist groups followed. Driven by the death that surrounded him on all sides, he pushed furiously on all fronts to try and do what he could.

Years of bitterness followed, bitterness that came as few listened to his message and even fewer cared enough to respond and join his fight. And by 1988, "instead of persevering and hoping . . . I absorbed my rejection and frustration . . . and went home."[14] He found himself numb, confronting the blind reality that "so many deaths have not turned very many of us into fighters," that "the loss of five hundred no longer works, as it once did, as the more-than-sufficient inspiration."[15] More alone than ever, he despaired. Kramer felt that he had done all he could, that what he had done had not been enough, that he should move on to other things where he might be able to effect some change. A year of searching followed, a year during which he threw himself into other, non-AIDS-related writing.

In looking for other things to replace his crusade against AIDS, Kramer came upon a shockingly painful realization; "there's nothing else to do. There's nothing else important enough to write about."[16] In the midst of his despair, he discovered that his fight against the epidemic had changed his world forever; as he points out, "if writers everywhere were to write about these horrors, then perhaps there would be no AIDS and I would be free, we would all be free to think about something else."[17] But Kramer realized that writers everywhere were not writing about these horrors, that he was not free to think about anything else. Kramer once again confronted an American community divided against itself, ill against well, with the construction of the lazaretto well under way. In the face of the epidemic, America was rapidly polarizing, with the majority of Americans blaming Haitians and gays, among others, for having incubated the disease before its introduction into "mainstream" America. Politicians talked of quarantining or tattooing those with AIDS; few were willing to confront the disease head-on at the time with reasonable policies. Society was rapidly separating into categories of "them" and "us," to use Sontag's terms.

And so Kramer reentered the fray, battered, tired, and weary. "I have no choice. I've tried, in the past few years, to write about other things . . . about non-AIDS matters. But I can't seem to. They seem unimportant."[18] He quotes Primo Levi's *Survival in Auschwitz* to explain further the role of the writer during an epidemic: "The need to tell our story to 'the rest,' to make 'the rest' participate in it had taken on for us . . . the character of an immediate violent impulse, to the point of competing with other elementary needs."[19]

What has characterized Kramer's writing ever since is an idea implied by Levi, a metaphor that appears in his (Kramer's) earlier work but grows to fruition in his recent writing. Kramer's need to tell his story to the world, and in turn to communities both inside and outside the lazaretto, spurs him to choose metaphor as a way to link both groups. His metaphor is simple and obvious, but effective: "Each and every minute of my life, I must act as if I already have AIDS and am fighting for my life."[20] The phrase forces the well to constantly look into the lives of the ill to see what it means to have AIDS and be fighting for one's life; it forces the ill to share these experiences with the healthy, opening up the experiences common to individuals from both communities. The two experiences are placed side by side in Kramer's metaphor, joining them and promoting understanding between them. With these words, Kramer seeks to tear down the walls of the lazaretto, walls that divide and separate the experiences of both groups. Speaking for the afflicted, he says: "I don't want to die. . . . I want to live and I want to love and I want in the universal as well as the specific sense, all . . . to try to understand why this epidemic is here . . . and with your understanding, to help us, for we, and I, desperately need help."[21] In this way, Kramer attacks the lazaretto in the way he best sees fit, striking at the point of division. In asking the healthy to imagine that they are ill and to act accordingly, he pulls both groups back under one proverbial roof, forcing them to share their experiences, reducing the distance between them that occurs with the establishment of the lazaretto. With his manipulation of metaphor, he urges us to imagine the "familiar hearts of strangers," to use Ozick's words.[22] Kramer elegantly sums up his task with the words: "I don't consider myself an artist. I consider myself a very opinionated man who uses words as fighting tools. . . . Somehow I hope that if I string my words together with enough skill, people will hear them and respond. . . . I seem to have no choice but to try."[23]

What Kramer's writing does is this: it seeks to preserve the unity of the human experience and spirit in the face of a rampant plague, a black shroud of death. Whether consciously done or not, Kramer's choice of metaphor places the struggle against the epidemic at the center of the human experience, relying on something common to both the afflicted and the healthy. His need to tell his story is a response to the way his world has twisted in light of the epidemic; his response and return to writing show us that the moral individual has no other option but to confront suffering head-on when it appears. Though the fight may be wearying and unrewarding, Kramer points out again and again that the moral individual has no choice but to face it. Kramer's weapons are words, and his battlefield is the written page. His words echo those of W. H. Auden; he, as did Auden, claims that "all I have is a voice" with which to "show an affirming flame."[24] He strives to destroy the world of the lazaretto, a world of separated communities and individuals; a world where, as Ozick says, "each heart is meant to rave on in its uniqueness," where "there is no means for the grief of one heart to implicate the understanding of another heart."[25] What he strives for is a way to heal the divisions in society brought about by AIDS, a way to bridge the gap between ill and well.

"Writers," Ozick tells us, "contain our experience, and they alter both our being and our becoming."[26] Kramer, as a writer responding to the epidemic, has one final lesson for us as inhabitants of a world where an epidemic rages. "I can only go on writing what I write, if not as an artist, then perhaps as an historian. We simply must not allow whatever future world there might be to forget."[27] Kramer makes the point that what drives him is as much what has happened in the past as what can and could happen in the present and future. He implies that all actions driven by the desire to unify a split community must take place with the idea that the future be a better one for its inhabitants. Else there is nothing to strive for, to push for, to hope for. Kramer's manipulation of metaphor seeks to "transform memory into a principle of continuity."[28] By continuity, we mean the way the human experience is reaffirmed as something larger than any one group, without separation or division, a chain of being extending from the past through the present into the future.

Kramer's overall message might be restated as this: mourn the dead at the proper time and place. Respect them and honor them, but bury them. Time spent on the dead helps no one; you do them more respect by halting the spread of the epidemic that killed them. Then go out and tear down the lazaretto; bring communities split apart by the epidemic back together. Make it clear that no one, healthy or ill, can ignore any individual, writing him or her off as the proverbial "Other."[29] A whole community, unbroken, can fight an epidemic more effectively than any individual group within it. You establish the continuity of the human experience in doing so.

Then, and only then, you see, can you do something for the living.

> Remember that some day, the AIDS crisis will be over. And when that day has come and gone there will be people alive on this earth—gay people and straight people, black people and white people, men and women—who will hear the story that once there was a terrible disease, and that a brave group of people stood up and fought and in some cases died so that others might live and be free. I'm proud to be out here today with the people I love, and see the faces of those heroes who are fighting the war, and to be a part of that fight.[30]

Notes

1. Susan Sontag, *Illness as Metaphor* (New York: Anchor Books, 1978), 3.
2. Frank Ryan, *The Forgotten Plague: How the Battle Against Tuberculosis Was Won and Lost* (Boston: Little, Brown, 1992), 3.
3. Guenter Risse, "Epidemics and History: Ecological Perspectives and

Social Responses," in *AIDS: The Burdens of History*, ed. Elizabeth Fee and Daniel M. Fox (Berkeley: University of California Press, 1988), 33–66.

4. Francis Canty, personal communication.
5. Susan Sontag, *AIDS and Its Metaphors* (New York: Anchor Books, 1989), 119.
6. Cynthia Ozick, *Metaphor and Memory* (New York: Alfred A. Knopf, 1989), 266.
7. Ozick, *Metaphor and Memory*, 280.
8. Ozick, *Metaphor and Memory*, 279.
9. Ozick, *Metaphor and Memory*, 278.
10. Ozick, *Metaphor and Memory*, 283.
11. Larry Kramer, *Reports from the Holocaust* (New York: St. Martin's, 1989), 218, 222.
12. Kramer, *Reports from the Holocaust*, 146.
13. Kramer, *Reports from the Holocaust*, 145.
14. Kramer, *Reports from the Holocaust*, 223–224, 224.
15. Kramer, *Reports from the Holocaust*, 224.
16. Kramer, *Reports from the Holocaust*, 224.
17. Kramer, *Reports from the Holocaust*, 146.
18. Kramer, *Reports from the Holocaust*, 146.
19. Kramer, *Reports from the Holocaust*, 227.
20. Kramer, *Reports from the Holocaust*, 82.
21. Kramer, *Reports from the Holocaust*, 228.
22. Ozick, *Metaphor and Memory*, 283.
23. Kramer, *Reports from the Holocaust*, 145.
24. W. H. Auden, "September 1, 1939" (1939).
25. Ozick, *Metaphor and Memory*, 282.
26. Ozick, *Metaphor and Memory*, 282.
27. Kramer, *Reports from the Holocaust*, 148.
28. Ozick, *Metaphor and Memory*, 282.
29. Ozick, *Metaphor and Memory*, 266.
30. Vito Russo, as quoted in Kramer, *Reports from the Holocaust*, 277.

Identifiable Lives

AIDS and the Response to Dehumanization

RACHEL MADDOW

1994

Stanford University

I've been dropped into all this from another
world and I can't speak your language any
longer. See the signs I try to make with my
hands and fingers. See the vague movements
of my lips among the sheets. I'm a blank spot
in a hectic civilization. I'm a dark smudge in
the air that dissipates without notice. I feel
like a window, maybe a broken window. I am
a glass human. I am a glass human disappearing in rain. I am standing among all of you
waving my invisible arms and hands. I am
shouting my invisible words. I am getting so
weary. I am growing tired. I am waving to you
from here. I am crawling around looking for
the aperture of complete and final emptiness.
I am vibrating in isolation among you. I am
screaming but it comes out like pieces of clear
ice. I am signaling that the volume of all this is
too high. I am waving. I am waving my hands.
I am disappearing. I am disappearing but not
fast enough.

—David Wojnarowicz, *Memories That Smell
Like Gasoline*

Statistical and Identified Lives

Charles Fried, Guido Calabresi, Thomas Schelling, and other legal and ethical theorists have elucidated the conceptual distinction between "identified" and "statistical" lives. Although the authors differ on their exact definitions of these concepts, it can be generalized that identified lives belong to individuals whose suffering or flourishing exists and is recognizable. An identified life is saved when we respond to a specific person in need. We need not know individualized facts about this person, only that he or she is a specific, knowable person.

A statistical life, on the other hand, is not attachable to any one individual; policy makers act to save statistical lives when they take preventive measures. Three hundred statistical lives, for example, might be saved by investing in a highway safety program. The lives saved by such a measure are not attached to known individuals, but they are nonetheless real. It is not sufficient that the person or persons in question are not known to the decision makers; statistical lives are *unknowable* because they are statistically determined based on experience, prediction, or some other calculation.[1]

Much of the literature on this subject has interrogated our usual response to these conceptual categories: "It is well known that we are prepared to devote vast resources to saving identified victims. At the same time, we are much less willing to use the money more effectively to save statistical victims, for example, by investing in coal mine safety (or preventive prenatal care)."[2] In other words, we are more willing as a society (and as policy makers) to respond to known lives in danger than we are to preventing the same danger to unknowable—statistical—lives. Our reliance on technology-intensive neonatal care rather than cheaper "low-tech" prenatal care is one example of this preference. Other examples are the highly publicized and very expensive rescue of a Texas girl who was trapped in a well several years ago and the devotion of massive resources to responding to the Legionnaires' disease outbreak in the early 1980s.

Fried argues that one explanation for favoring identified lives over statistical lives is our "personalist" connection with people whom we recognize as the objects or possible objects of love and friendship. Although Fried says that the personalist argument does not justify the preference, it still stands as a plausible explanation of why we behave this way: "Relations of love and friendship . . . bring us into concrete, individualized, and emotional contact with another person. And . . . it is in recognition of the greater urgency of these relations, and of the importance for human beings of being able to realize these relations in significant ways, that [we] devote relatively more resources to saving the lives of persons in known peril."[3] In other words, we are more compelled to respond to individuals with whom we have, or can imagine ourselves having, a personal connection. But Fried also intends for the personalist argument to extend beyond people we love or feel friendship toward to all people whom we recognize as "particular persons."[4] In recognizing the individuality of a person, the argument goes, we recognize his or her humanity and therein the person's potential for being the object of love and friendship. Love and friendship motivate us in two ways: first, when they bond us personally to a particular person; and second, when we recognize a person's capacity for being connected by the same sort of bond. Although it is clear that our preference for identified lives is strongest when we have direct ties to the person in peril, the extension of the argument beyond personal ties may explain why we support policy decisions that prefer identified lives, even when we do not know the identified individuals in peril.[5]

Identifiable Lives: AIDS

One case that does not apparently fit the statistical/identified preference is the AIDS epidemic in America. Although increasing numbers of individuals were dying from the disease as early as 1981, significant attention and resources were not devoted to fighting AIDS until several years later. The mainstream media did not pay meaningful attention to the disease until it became apparent that it might spread beyond the subgroups that were already affected.[6] In November 1987—six years into the epidemic, when 25,644 people were known to have died of AIDS—then-President Reagan made his first public statement about the disease: "I have asked the Department of Health and Human Services to determine as soon as possible the extent to which the AIDS virus has penetrated our society."[7] The disease attracted resources and attention only when its threat spread beyond the groups who were already affected to the "general population."

Why did AIDS not receive attention until people recognized that it was not only a "gay disease"? Why did the people who had died from AIDS or those living with the disease not elicit major resource devotion and attention? This seems to violate the statistical/identified preference in two ways. First, the amount of resources devoted was small: the rising number of inexplicable deaths that occurred early in the AIDS crisis commanded much less attention than other similar public health crises, such as the Extra Strength Tylenol scare and the Legionnaires' disease outbreak. These other crises show that the response to AIDS cannot be attributed to the fact that the individuals who died of it were not personally known to policy makers and members of the media. The people affected by the other outbreaks were of similar status, yet they evoked much greater attention.

Second, Reagan's statement makes it clear that the public spending that eventually was devoted to AIDS was intended to stem the "penetration" of the disease into "our society"—not to stop the ravages of AIDS where they already existed. It appears, then, that statistical lives received more attention than identified lives. Is AIDS an exception to the statistical/identified rule?

I propose that the early years of the AIDS epidemic in the United States do not violate the statistical/identified rule-of-thumb because the lives of the individuals who were most recognizably afflicted with

AIDS—gay men—were *not identified* in the popular and policy-making consciousness. Because there were no identified lives at stake, the social response to AIDS was spurred only by the peril of statistical lives.[8]

A third conceptual category must be created to explain this response: *identifiable* lives. Identifiable lives fit the technical description of identified lives in the sense that they belong to known individuals whose suffering or flourishing exists and is recognizable. They differ in the crucial respect that they are not *identified with* by policy makers and "the general public"—the perceived audience to which mainstream media is directed. Because identifiable lives do not resonate personally for policy makers (Fried's "personalist connection" is not made), their peril does not command the same sympathy and resource devotion as the peril of identified lives. In the case of AIDS, significant resources were not allocated to ending the epidemic because gay men—the people with whom the disease was most closely associated—were not considered to be identifiable lives. Personalist connections were not made with gay men because their individuality and individual identity were obscured. This obfuscation can therefore be called *dehumanization.*

Dehumanization

Because the statistical/identified lives rule is descriptive, not normative, the identifiable lives category is also descriptive. In other words, I do not wish to argue that it is wrong or unjust to treat people as identifiable lives. However, I do propose that dehumanization, the mechanism that makes identifiable lives possible, also makes possible a wide category of actions that are inconsistent with common notions of justice. In other words, dehumanization has two significant implications: one, it causes some people to be recognized as identifiable lives instead of identified lives; and two, it allows us to justify things that we would otherwise recognize as injustices. Although dehumanization of people for different reasons (that is, race, sexual orientation, nationality) has different historical roots and contemporary implications, I propose that it shares these common functional elements.

Evidence for the perception of certain groups as less than human is found in the language of racism and other forms of prejudice today. In *The Report of the Independent Commission on the Los Angeles Police Department*, Los Angeles police officers are quoted referring to African Americans and members of other ethnic minority groups during their on-duty correspondence:

> "I would love to drive down Slauson with a flame thrower . . . we would have a barbeque."
> "Sounds like monkey-slapping time."
> "We're hunting wabbits. Actually, muslim wabbits. . . . Be careful one of those rabbits don't bite you."
> "Ya stop cars with blk interior. 'Bees they naugahyde. Negrohide. Self-tanning no doubt."[9]

Older examples are the Nazi propaganda films that juxtaposed images and descriptions of Jewish people with shots of scurrying rats and the bioevolutionist depiction of black people located between white people and apes on the scale of evolutionary development.

These examples are evidence of the perception of certain groups of people as less than human. This perception, which can be fostered by dehumanizing forms of representation such as the Nazi propaganda, creates the disidentification among people that is necessary for the category of identifiable lives. Although they often do have unjust consequences, the conceptualization of identifiable lives and the resulting policy decisions are not *necessarily* unjust. But dehumanization can also lead to the false justification of treating some people unjustly.

The crimes of racist states and the Nazi regime need not be enumerated here to make the argument that their beliefs about groups of people led them to engage in inhumane treatment toward those people. The racist brutality of the Los Angeles Police Department is also well documented and does not need to be elaborated here. The question at hand is whether there is a link between these actions and dehumanization.

My proposal that dehumanization enables us to justify inhumane treatment rests on an important and perhaps controversial assumption about people's moral beliefs. In order to account both for the reasons why acts of bigotry take place and why we should hope to end them, we must assume that *people do not believe it is just to treat others inhumanely.* This is fundamentally a psychological claim, not a moral claim.[10]

In "Disobedience as a Psychological and Moral Problem," Erich Fromm argues for this assumption of moral psychology by claiming that every person possesses a "humanistic conscience": "This is the voice present in every human being and independent from external sanctions and rewards. Humanistic conscience is based on the fact that as human beings we have an intuitive knowledge of what is human and inhuman, what is conducive of life and what is destructive of life."[11] It seems clear that brutal or humiliating treatment is inhumane and therefore would violate this conscience.

A similar psychological claim is made by Martin Luther King, Jr., in "Letter From Birmingham City Jail." He asserts that all people have a conscience—a knowledge of the "moral law"—that can be appealed to. This conscience tells people that things which "degrade human personality" are unjust and things which "uplift human personality" are just.[12] On this basis, King argues that segregation is unjust. He describes the mistreatment and abuses that African Americans were subjected to in the segregated South and then cites philosopher Martin Buber to show that segregation laws violate our moral conscience by "substituting an 'I-it' relationship for the 'I-thou' relationship . . . and relegating persons to the status of things."[13] But if all people recognize the injustice of such treatment, why does it take place? How did the Nazis come to power? Why was segregation the law? Why do hate crimes statistics continue to rise?

If the moral assumption is true—if all people believe that all human beings deserve humane treatment—and if segregationists, bigots, and Nazis still believe that their views and actions are just, *it must be true that they do not recognize the objects of their inhumane treatment as human beings.* Dehumanization, then, is the common link between the move from identified to identifiable lives and the false justification of inhumane treatment. Just as understanding the creation of the category of identifiable lives reveals the best strategy for subverting it, the recognition of how inhumane treatment is falsely justified opens a window of opportunity for ending it. Disabling the mechanism of dehumanization creates a crisis of conscience in which perpetrators of bigotry are forced to recognize that their actions are unjust.[14]

This assumption that all people have a moral conscience that precludes the justification of inhumane treatment (or that people have this conscience in varying degrees over time and space), coupled with knowledge of the tactics of prejudicial representation, shows the interconnectedness of bigotry and dehumanization. In the same way that prejudice allows the peril of some lives not to command the same attention as others, prejudice allows us to conceive of some groups of people as outside our acknowledged responsibility to other human beings. Dehumanizing prejudice allows us to justify inhumane treatment because we cease to recognize the objects of our prejudice as fellow persons. In the case of gay people[15] and AIDS, activists recognize that one way to improve AIDS policies (and the other negative implications of living in a heterosexist society) is to fight dehumanization. I call these tactics *rehumanization* strategies.

Rehumanization, Liberal Claims

Rehumanization strategies fall into two main categories: appeals for personalist connection and direct action. Both tactics use the symbolic power of individuals to appeal for the equal treatment of people without regard to sexual orientation. By giving evidence for the individuality and individual humanity of gay people, these strategies undermine the idea that sexual identity can negate individual identity, that a person's membership in the group "gay people" makes him or her somehow less than human and justifies treating him or her inhumanely.

Pleas for personalist connection. Pleas for personalist connection are the tactics that most clearly articulate the agenda of rehumanization. They are generally emotion-based appeals for "the general public" or specific viewers to identify with people who have died from AIDS or who are living with the disease. By stressing their individuality and connections with other people—their status as "particular persons"—these strategies attempt to undermine the dehumanization of people with AIDS and thereby move them from the category of identifiable to identified lives. During a candlelight vigil in New York City in 1983, Bob Cecchi, a man living with AIDS, said: "Like our first President, you are the father of this country. Do you hear me when I say your children are dying? This problem transcends politics. I ask for more than a simple release of funds; I am asking for an act of love. If you are my father Mr. President I am your son. Please help me save my life."[16] This plea exemplifies the emotional appeal of pleas for personalist connection.

The best-known example of this appeal is the Names Project Quilt. The project was started in the mid-1980s in San Francisco as a way of mourning those who had died of AIDS. While it still helps people grieve for those lost, it also rehumanizes people with AIDS generally by individually naming the people who have died and by giving evidence of the uniqueness of each life lost. Because panels are usually made by the friends, family, or loved ones of an individual who has died, the quilt gives evidence that every person with HIV/AIDS, even if they are not individually known to us, has connections of love or friendship: "A brilliant work of community art, the Names Project Quilt vividly testifies to individual diversity. . . . It is profoundly touching to see someone kneeling and crying at a lover's—or child's—quilt-square. But then your own tears might flow, quite independent of the specific thing being seen."[17] The quilt creates an emotionally overwhelming case for the individual humanity of each person lost to the disease, and, therefore, for their status as identified lives.

Direct action. Direct action, on the other hand, does not rely on sympathetic emotional appeals to establish people as identified lives. More often, direct action is confrontational and angry, and alienates its audiences. Nevertheless, it succeeds in many of the same ways and for many of the same reasons as its tamer strategic cousins.

I define direct action as tactics that directly involve members of the groups most affected by the problem that is being protested. Most commonly, this refers to rallies, marches, and other demonstrations that depend on the actual bodily presence of activists.[18] The best-known group associated with AIDS direct action is ACT UP, the AIDS Coalition to Unleash Power. Founded in New York in 1987, it has spawned chapters in every major city in the United States, some nonurban regions, and several cities in other countries. Although it has never claimed to be exclusively gay, ACT UP is still commonly thought of as a gay organization. For example, in the *Chicago Sun-Times* in December 1993, columnist Robert Novak used ACT UP as his example of the "militant homosexual movement," discussing their reputation and strategies at length without once mentioning AIDS.[19]

This conflation is at least partially attributable to the lasting perception of AIDS as a gay disease—hence the assumption that anyone doing anything about AIDS must be gay. Despite ACT UP's well-known media manipulation and expert spin tactics, the media and the "general public" have not absorbed their often complex anti-AIDS message. ACT UP has been vocal about the fact that AIDS is tied up in many issues other than homophobia and has explicitly disqualified itself as an exclusively "gay group." But it is apparent that the efficacy of direct action is inextricably tied to perceived identity of its participants.

Because its participants are perceived as gay people, direct action is an effective tactic for attracting more attention and resources to problems that are perceived as gay issues. This is true because direct action makes a strong case for the rehumanization of its participants. By being perceived as representative of gay people, then, the rehumanization of direct action participants moves gay people as a group from identifiable lives toward identified lives and helps reduce the apparent justifiability of treating them inhumanely.

Direct action rehumanizes its participants because demonstrated political agency is evidence for the humanity of the agent: "Once (s)he has entered the realm of polity, the political actor assumes a certain persona. We attribute certain qualities to political action which sharply contrast to the qualities we associate with social deviation. . . . Political action is viewed as prima facie evidence of rational goal-directed, voluntaristic and change-oriented behavior. Political agitation . . . demonstrates, in word and deed, that [the participants] are capable of purposive political action."[20] Because it shows that participants possess the uniquely human traits of rationality and the capacity for political agency, direct action can contradict the perception of them as less than human. By giving evidence of their humanity, the participants in direct action use their bodies to appeal to moral conscience. In "Letter From Birmingham City Jail," King gives his explanation of the decision to use civil disobedience: "We had no alternative except that of preparing for direct action, whereby we would present our very bodies as a means of laying our case before the conscience of the local and national community."[21]

In order to ensure the effectiveness of such appeals to conscience, King thought it was crucial that "one who breaks an unjust law must do it *openly, lovingly.*"[22] He commends civil rights demonstrators in Birmingham for their "willingness to suffer and their amazing discipline in the midst of the most inhuman provocation."[23] This sentiment is echoed by many other writers on civil disobedience and protest. Gandhi extolled the necessity of "courtesy and gentleness" on the part of protestors.[24] John Rawls advised that protests should not be conducted in a way that could "provoke the harsh retaliation of the majority," saying, "It is important that the action be properly designed to make an effective appeal to the wider community."[25]

Have AIDS activists followed this advice? Disrupting services at Saint Patrick's Cathedral in New York? Same-sex "kiss-ins" in public venues? Drowning out the speech of Secretary of Health and Human Services Louis Sullivan at the International AIDS Conference, and of Governor Pete Wilson at Stanford? Many of the tactics chosen by AIDS activists clearly do not meet the criteria of civility and politeness: "A basic feature of [AIDS] demonstrations is that they are meant to intrude, to provoke, to irritate, and to offend."[26] But, nevertheless, angry activists are credited with bringing about major changes in AIDS policies, such as "expediting clinical trials and access to promising new drugs, and the rapid development . . . of community-based trials."[27] Although it may be true that the anger of AIDS direct action dilutes some of its superficial persuasiveness, that anger is also crucial to the success of direct action as a rehumanization strategy because of the particular ways in which gay people are dehumanized.

In the context of AIDS, tactics that stress anger and militancy address the specific ways in which gay men generally and gay men with AIDS specifically are prejudicially represented. The common stereotypes of gay people are that they are effeminate and weak; people with AIDS are often called "victims"; and even some of the best-intentioned AIDS educators represent the transmission of HIV as the delivery of an immediate death sentence. The anger and militancy of ACT UP is evidence to the contrary. "Since [gay men] have already been identified as marginal and expendable, to be effective such political actions almost surely must rise to the level of intrusion and provocation. This is proper, fair, and rational."[28] ACT UP tactics are not civil or polite because they are not intended to evoke sympathy from or persuade their audience. They are easily confused with gay rights demonstrations because they often involve demonstrations of pride in being gay. In this way, the

anger, militancy, and sexual frankness of AIDS direct action is intended
to move gay men from the category of identifiable lives to identified lives
by establishing their status as whole persons. By contradicting essen-
tialist conceptualizations of gay people, AIDS activists create space for
gay people to be recognized as individuals—to put their individual
identity before their sexual identity. As in the case of the pleas for personalist connection, this space for individuality is crucial to the recognition of gay people's lives as *identified*. In this sense, then, AIDS direct
action has been successful because of its anger, not despite it.

As the AIDS epidemic pushes on into its thirteenth year, the demo-
graphic statistics of the disease stray further and further from the initial
misconception of AIDS as a "gay disease." I have chosen to write specifically about issues affecting gay people because the AIDS-gay conflation is fundamental to the framework of ethical and political discourse
about the epidemic during its early years. It is clear, however, that these
arguments about dehumanization and its consequences are relevant not
just for gay people of all colors but for straight people of color, immigrants, Africans, intravenous drug users, and other groups commonly
conceived of as the "hardest hit" by AIDS. Although rehumanization
strategies are still appropriate responses to these other forms of dehumanization, the conflation of AIDS and gay activism is a barrier to their
direct application to other identity groups. Rehumanization strategies
to benefit marginalized groups other than the gay community will have
to take account of this conflation and the specific ways in which these
other groups are dehumanized if they are to be successful.

Because rehumanization strategies depend on the moral conscience
of their audiences, their successes are occasions for hope for the potential for human beings to move toward more equal, just societies. Ex-
panding our knowledge of dehumanization and the ways it manifests
itself in policy and in private acts must be the first step on the road to
dismantling it.

Notes

Epigraph: David Wojnarowicz, *Memories That Smell Like Gasoline* (San Francisco: Artspace Books, 1992).

1. The statistical/identified distinction is often substituted for the distinction between lives that are in present peril and those in future peril. While these two sets of categories often map onto one another, this is not always true. For the purposes of this argument, I am concerned only with statistical and identified lives, not with the future/present distinction. I will also make the related assumption that there is no difference in the probability of success between acting to save identified and statistical lives.

2. Norman Daniels, *Just Health Care* (New York: Cambridge University Press, 1985), 223.

3. Charles Fried, *An Anatomy of Values: Problems of Personal and Social Choice* (Cambridge, MA: Harvard University Press, 1970), 223.

4. Fried, *Anatomy of Values*, 223.

5. A great deal of the literature on this subject deals with the normativity of this preference. These explorations involve complex issues of moral psychology, ethics, and decision analysis. For this argument, however, it is sufficient to know that the preference exists and that it is at least partially motivated by our psychological relationship to those who will be affected by our decisions.

6. Dennis Altman, *AIDS in the Mind of America* (New York: Doubleday, 1986), 16.

7. Quoted in Douglas Crimp, "Introduction," *October* 43 (Winter 1987): 11.

8. It could be argued that there was no major social response to AIDS because the heterosexual majority of policy makers and the "general public" did not see themselves at risk for a "gay disease." Although this factor may also be at work, the statistical/identified lives preference cannot be explained away by theories of self-interest. For example, self-interest cannot explain our greater willingness as a society to devote resources to aiding flood victims rather than to building levees and other preventive measures, even when the majority of society is clearly not at risk from floods.

9. Quoted in *Report of the Independent Commission on the Los Angeles Police Department* (Los Angeles: The Commission, 1991), 72.

10. In *A Theory of Justice,* John Rawls makes a similar argument but instead assumes a "commonly shared conception of justice" among citizens. Rawls, *A Theory of* Justice (Cambridge, MA: Harvard University Press, 1971), 365. His is a political instead of psychological assumption of commonality. As Peter Singer notes in "Disobedience as a Plea for Reconsideration," this political assumption is problematic because it leaves no room for challenges to conceptions of justice: "if disobedience is an appeal to the community, why can it only be an appeal which invokes principles which the community already accepts? Why could one not be justified in disobeying in order to ask the majority to alter or extend the shared conception of justice?. . . We surely cannot rule out the possibility that in time [a particular society's conception of justice] may appear defective." Singer, "Disobedience as a Plea for Reconsideration," in *Civil Disobedience in Focus,* ed. Hugo Adam Bedau (London: Routledge, 1991), 125–126. I propose that the standard by which a system of justice is found "defective" is moral belief, or conscience. Conscience is the ultimate location of appeal.

11. Erich Fromm, "Disobedience as a Psychological and Moral Problem," in Fromm, *On Disobedience and Other Essays* (London: Routledge, 1984), 4.

12. Martin Luther King, Jr., "Letter from Birmingham City Jail," in *A Testament of Hope: The Essential Writings and Speeches of Martin Luther King, Jr.,* ed. James M. Washington (San Francisco: HarperCollins, 1991), 293.

13. King, "Letter from Birmingham City Jail," 292–293.

14. Of course there are alternatives to the assumption that makes this argument possible, the most compelling of which is the claim that people's consciences do not share common fixed principles, but rather they are different among different groups of people and they change through experience, education, and the passage of time. Although this alternative seems entirely plausible, it is ineffective as an objection to the argument because it does not demand significant changes to the strategies suggested by the original assumption. Its main implication is

that appeals to conscience will succeed differently across time and space. This prospect seems tenable, but does not require reexamination of the argument.

15. I use the term *people* here rather than *men* because, although lesbians and bisexual men and women have not been afflicted with HIV to the same degree as gay men, all gay, lesbian, and bisexual people have borne the burden of the increased homophobia that has resulted from the conception of AIDS as a "gay disease." Altman, *AIDS in the Mind of America,* 94.

16. Cecchi quoted in Altman, *AIDS in the Mind of America,* 28–29.

17. Robert Atkins and Thomas W. Sokolowski, *From Media to Metaphor: Art About AIDS* (New York: Independent Curators, 1991), 28.

18. This definition includes both civil disobedience and other actions which do not violate state laws.

19. Robert Novak, "Whatever Happened to Clinic Access Bill? Gay Lobby Kills It Over Change," *Chicago Sun-Times,* December 9, 1993, 43.

20. Renee R. Anspach, "From Stigma to Identity Politics: Political Activism Among the Physically Disabled and Former Mental Patients," *Social Science and Medicine, Part A: Medical Psychology and Medical Sociology* 13 (1979): 766. Although Anspach's argument specifically considers the stigma of disability, her argument that disablement constitutes "social deviance" is also relevant to other means of disenfranchisement, including homophobia.

21. King, "Letter from Birmingham City Jail," 291.

22. King, "Letter from Birmingham City Jail," 294, emphasis in original.

23. King, "Letter from Birmingham City Jail," 301.

24. Quoted in Courtney B. Campbell, "Ethics and Militant AIDS Activism," in *AIDS and Ethics* (New York: Columbia University Press, 1991), 171.

25. Rawls, *Theory of Justice,* 376.

26. Alvin Novick, "Civil Disobedience in Time of AIDS," *Hastings Center Report* 19 (1989): 35–36.

27. Novick, "Civil Disobedience in Time of AIDS," 36.

28. Novick, "Civil Disobedience in Time of AIDS," 36.

Their Lives in Our Hands

Fulfilling Our Ethical Obligations to the Terminally Ill Enrolling in Research Studies

LAURA OVERLAND
1998
University of Missouri–Kansas City

ANNE HAS BEEN DIAGNOSED with stage IV metastatic breast cancer: her cancer has spread, uncontrollably, beyond the original tumor site to her lymph nodes and several other organs in her body. At this point, she is no longer in remission, and standard therapies have been unsuccessful in treating her condition. Anne has a prognosis of approximately twenty-four months to live. She has a thirteen-year-old son and financial problems, and the recurrence of the cancer has placed a considerable amount of strain on Anne's marital relationship. Anne's oncologist, Dr. Norman, has overseen her case for several months. Dr. Norman is also the principal investigator in a study on a new chemotherapy agent that has prompted antitumor responses in some women with breast cancer in preliminary studies. He approaches Anne about becoming involved in his study. When asked if she is interested, Anne says, "Yes, I'm willing to do anything that might help me."[1]

During their next visit, Dr. Norman explains that two medications are going to be used in the study, along with a placebo; medications and placebo are assigned randomly. The trial is double blind; neither Anne nor Dr. Norman will know if Anne is receiving the placebo or the new agent. The trial requires a forty-five-day "wash-out" period during which Anne must be kept drug-free before the clinical trial. Dr. Norman explains that this "wash-out" period is a typical procedure for these types of clinical trials.

Last, he tells Anne that the study will pay for the drugs and costs associated with administration for the duration of the study. Anne listens to the explanation, then reads and signs a form to indicate she consents to participate in the study.

The consent form Anne signs meets the criteria for "informed consent" required by Federal Register Rules and Regulations for the protection of human subjects.[2] According to this set of regulations, researchers must provide the following information to obtain "informed consent": (1) a thorough, yet easily understandable explanation of the research study, including its purposes, procedures, and duration; (2) description of foreseeable risks and benefits; (3) a disclosure of appropriate alternative treatments or procedures; (4) a statement of how confidentiality will be maintained; (5) information about options available if injury should occur at any point during the study; (6) whom to contact for more information or in case of injury; and (7) assurance that participation is voluntary and may be discontinued at any time without penalty.

Although these guidelines seem clear and comprehensive, they are, in reality, very difficult to achieve. In fact, the current guidelines do not sufficiently address many of the special considerations that exist in the case of terminally ill patients. Investigators may feel they have satisfied the requirement of explaining the nature and purposes of the research to participants, but several empirical studies indicate that such explanations have not sufficiently helped participants make a distinction between medical research and medical treatment.[3] Being able to make such a distinction is crucial in the process of giving valid and informed consent to participate in a research study.

A typical scenario: Anne is handed the informed consent form the same day the clinical trial is scheduled to begin, *after* elaborate preparations for the procedure have been completed, not in advance.[4] By signing the consent form, Anne indicates to her physician and the Institutional Review Board that she "knowingly agrees to the goal of the research study and makes it [her] own, becoming an active participant in the research so that it cannot then be said that the patient is being used as a means to an end."[5] Yet the possibility of being randomly assigned to a placebo condition and a "wash-out" period are not exactly in Anne's best interest, so how can it be concluded that Anne is not being used as a means to an end? Furthermore, when asked why she decided to participate, Anne states she believes that "every aspect of the research project to which [she] has consented was designed to benefit her directly."[6] Such a response indicates that even though Anne is capable of understanding the language of the informed consent form, she has not fully grasped the impact of what it is saying.

Anne has interpreted from the information she has received from the physician and the consent form and, more important, distorted that information to maintain the view that this research will directly help her.

Anne's reaction is typical among people facing the diagnosis of a terminal illness who are recruited for research participation. "I sign a release form for [the treatment] swearing that I understand that I am participating in a research project with a new drug and that I do not expect to benefit from the treatment. Lies, lies. I sign with a clear conscience."[7] Patients often cling to the belief that they will not be the ones assigned to the placebo condition, despite warnings to the contrary, a sort of "it-can't-happen-to-me" syndrome. Such a response indicates the existence of several "myths" about research that terminally ill patients may share, each one affecting the quality of the consent they are able to give to participate.

The Myth of Therapeutic Benefit

Even though conventional treatment has been unsuccessful in treating Anne's condition, she is willing to believe, wholeheartedly, that the experimental treatment will help her. She begins treatment with the experimental chemotherapy agent. After her first day, she is racked with severe nausea and exhaustion. She takes a drug to help with the nausea and sleeping pills so she can sleep through the aftermath of symptoms from the treatment. The next morning, however, she notices that she cannot move her toes or the last three fingers on her right hand, and every noise above a whisper is deafening. Very concerned, Anne telephones Dr. Norman. "Hmm," he pauses, "it's not unusual for some patients to experience these kinds of neuropathies after several treatments. However, I am a little concerned that you are experiencing them so early on." During Anne's next appointment she receives some devastating news: it is likely that if she continues in the study the neuropathies could spread, but Dr. Norman assures her this would not affect the treatment's ability to fight the cancer. Aware that her options in standard treatment have already been exhausted, Anne realizes, "If I continue with the treatment, I might beat the cancer, but I could be paralyzed, handicapped. If I don't, I could die."[8]

The truth is that, "unlike most drugs that provide a high possibility of benefit with a possibility of harm, anti-cancer drugs provide the certainty of harm with only a possibility of benefit."[9] All informed consent forms are required to reveal both foreseeable and unforeseeable risks for participation. In fact, the form Anne signed contained specific information about the side effects she is suffering from. When her physician questions her about this, she admits she remembers reading that part of the form, but she never would have participated if she had not been convinced it would benefit her directly. Anne is not alone in the "therapeutic misconception." A recent survey of participants in research at four Veterans' Administration hospitals showed that 75 percent decided to participate because they expected the research to benefit their health.[10] Another study conducted by the Advisory Committee on Human Radiation Experiments (ACHRE), interviewing 1,900 patient-subjects, revealed that an overwhelming majority of patients, despite showing a clear understanding of research goals, still expressed that they "would not have joined if they had not believed that some personal benefit might result as well."[11]

Why do our guidelines and efforts to obtain informed consent seem to be inadequate in this respect? Because terminally ill patients are often not well informed about the differences between experimental treatment and conventional treatment. By emphasizing the ways research differed from treatment in a "pre-consent discussion" with sixteen patients, two social scientists were able to double the number of patients who communicated a full understanding of the goals of the research study and how that affected them as participants.[12] If Anne had been offered a pre-consent discussion, and if Dr. Norman had told her, "Because this is a research project, we will be doing some things differently than we would if we were simply treating you for your condition. Not all the things we do are designed to tell us the best way to treat you, but they should help us to understand how people with your condition, *in general,* can best be treated," Anne might have had more realistic expectations about the amount of risk in the study.[13] Perhaps Anne would have decided to wait and review her alternatives more carefully if she had fully understood the risks.

The Myth of "Doctor Knows Best"

At the time of her diagnosis, Anne felt understandably shattered. She had begun to believe she had beat the cancer, only to find herself in a more dangerous position now than she was during her first battle with the disease. Feeling overwhelmed, she begins to form a dependent relationship with Dr. Norman. He is, after all, the man who is taking on the task of saving her life. He is the expert about her condition: he knows what to do and she feels helpless. If Anne is painfully honest with herself, she might even admit that a motivating factor for joining Dr. Norman's study was the hope that, as his subject, he would take a special interest in her and her case.[14]

The physician-patient relationship is especially crucial to someone who has been diagnosed with a terminal illness. This relationship can be a particularly strong influence on a patient's decision to enroll in experimental treatment. Often, patients perceive their primary care provider as their personal advocate and assume that their physician has much more control over the treatment course in a clinical trial than he or she actually has. "Thus, even though the doctor has explained that treatment in the research trials is randomized and [carried out] according to a strict protocol, patients often still believe that the doctor will only act in their best interests."[15] Like Anne, patients are particularly vulnerable after having received a diagnosis of terminal illness and frequently depend more heavily on their physician for decisions about treatment than patients diagnosed with nonterminal conditions.[16] Many of them abdicate their autonomy in the decision-making progress in favor of what their physician may recommend without seriously reviewing any other alternatives.[17]

The physician may be unaware of the extent to which a patient in this position relies on his or her recommendations. A comment like "It probably wouldn't be a bad idea to enroll in this study" made by the physician may be translated by the patient into "I recommend this study as a source of medical treatment for your condition." Particularly if the researcher is also the primary care provider, patients may fear abandonment or loss of care if they refuse to participate in the study.[18]

The Myth That Participants and Researchers Share the Same Goals

While she is struggling to decide whether to remain in Dr. Norman's study or go without treatment, Anne comes across an article on the

Internet about a new chemotherapy agent being tested in Europe. The new drug apparently is able to treat stage IV cancer without any of the side effects of Dr. Norman's drug. However, the new drug is still several years away from Food and Drug Administration (FDA) approval and cannot be tested yet in clinical trials within the United States. Undaunted, Anne contacts the research team for the new drug to see what she can do to get enrolled in the European study. New hope begins to surge as she waits for their response. Days later, the European oncologist contacts her. Anne's husband and son watch as her expression becomes increasingly bleak during the conversation. "What is it?" Anne's husband asks as she terminates the conversation. "I am not going to be accepted on any clinical trial," she tells him. "The single treatment that I've already received has made me unacceptable to researchers. If I survive the cancer, they will not be able to prove that only the new drug was responsible. I will ruin the data. And of course the trials are for research, not treatment. They are meant to benefit science, not people with cancer—not until years later, at any rate."[19]

Several subjects enrolled in biomedical research studies expressed a conviction that the investigator(s) would be acting in the subjects' best interest.[20] One such subject commented, "I don't believe they would offer me anything that isn't beneficial to me, in my condition."[21] It is obvious from Anne's experience that such a statement shows a serious lack of understanding of the nature of experimental procedures. This blind trust that some patients have for research impairs their ability to assess, seriously, what the risks and benefits of the research are to them.

That blind trust grows from ignorance about research agendas. Again, patients often have a difficult time distinguishing medical research from medical treatment. In medical treatment, the priority is the patient. In medical research, the priority is the knowledge that can be gained: "Researchers might be more interested in the process than in the treatment."[22] In most cases, research agendas have no effect on participant satisfaction with the outcome, but in the case of terminally ill patients the stakes are so much higher. As in Anne's situation, not understanding how research goals differ from the participants' goals can be extremely harmful to these people.

The first requirement of federal regulations on informed consent is "a thorough, yet easily understandable explanation of the research study, including its purposes, procedures, and duration."[23] However, there are both unintentional and intentional rationales behind the insufficient fulfillment of this regulation. Unintentionally, researchers often overlook how certain basic principles in data analysis will affect participants' hopes and expectations. For instance, when participants ask about the success rate of the trials, researchers give them a statistical percentage. What they neglect to mention is that "there is no explanation of what, exactly, a 'success rate' is [in the context of chemotherapy], or how it supposedly correlates with actual increased survival."[24] The percentage they have probably offered is commonly the number of participants that survived up to thirty days after the trial.[25]

Perhaps Dr. Norman neglected to explain how enrolling in his study would affect Anne's eligibility for subsequent studies because he never considered the possibility that other studies might be available to her. Perhaps he assumed that an explanation of the importance of data integrity would be over Anne's head and he did not want to burden her with such complicated details. Perhaps he did not want to have to take what might be considerable time to explain such concepts in lay terms. However, researchers also have substantial motivation to keep silent about anything that might deter potential participants from enrolling in their studies: "If patients quit the study or decline to participate, the reputation or validity of the study itself may suffer, and the investigator may find it difficult to garner support for subsequent work."[26]

Someone Has Already Scrutinized the Risks

Many patients, like Anne, underplay the importance of the consent form and process because they believe that no one would try to recruit them if the procedure were truly dangerous. A recent survey of patients enrolling in biomedical research reported "a widespread belief that checks and balances were in place, and oversight ensured that no harms could be done."[27] Some patients claimed they felt it wasn't necessary to pay attention to the consent form or whether they could understand it because they had already made up their minds to participate in the research. For example, one patient reported, "To me, they are the doctors, and once I had gotten those doctors and I trusted them . . . it was pretty much up to them. I wanted to know what I was going to be going through as far as what to expect . . . but a lot of the little nitty-gritty detail, I did not even want to know."[28]

Since the Nuremberg Code, the Declaration of Helsinki, the establishment of Institutional Review Boards, and a host of federal guidelines, it is tempting to believe nothing like the infamous Tuskegee syphilis study could happen in research today. However, it is still not safe to trust, blindly, that research protocols will live up to ethical standards. In fact, as recently as 1995, Dr. Bernard Fisher was removed from the directorship of the National Surgical Adjuvant Breast and Bowel Project for allowing data to be collected on thirty-six women who had refused to consent to participation, while informed consent forms could not be found on hundreds of other patients. He also waited eight months before reporting fraudulent data that was collected at eleven research sites. Dr. Fisher's parting comments were anything but comforting: "I challenge those in authority to audit other clinical trial databases and see how well they fare."[29]

Not even FDA approval is worthy of blind trust. The recent controversy over Tamoxifen, a cancer-fighting drug, reminds us that results can be devastating when we invest too much confidence and not enough caution in a new "cure."[30] As soon as the FDA approved Tamoxifen for treatment of advanced-stage breast cancer, many physicians, convinced of the drug's usefulness as a preventative treatment for high-risk groups, began prescribing it outside of clinical trials. Unfortunately, it was later discovered that Tamoxifen, in the ongoing clinical trials, caused a large percentage of women, all under the age of forty-five, to develop a particularly aggressive type of uterine cancer. In the meantime, several thousands of women who were only at risk for cancer were exposed to this now cancer-causing drug that their own physician had unwittingly prescribed.

The "Nothing to Lose" Myth

Anne has gone through several stages of hope and defeat by this time in her treatment process.

She chooses to leave Dr. Norman's study and search for alternatives. A little wiser, now, she begins to research the alternatives herself. She finds she has two choices: she can either find an oncologist who can prescribe the new European drug for Anne's use outside of a clinical trial, or she can look into palliative care—care focused not on prolonging life but on easing the course of the disease.

Taking the drug outside of a clinical trial is a risk. She will not be observed as closely, and there is so little known about the drug's long-term effect. Palliative care seems like admitting failure and letting the disease take her. Anne chooses what she believes to be her only chance at life: she decides to search for an oncologist who has access to the European drug. "After all," she concludes, "what have I got to lose?"

"The terminally-ill have become our favorite research subjects. . . . The reason most often cited by doctors is that the patients have nothing to lose."[31] If their choice lies between experimental treatment and no treatment, they will not hesitate to choose the treatment. A study that compared a group of terminally ill patients and patients with nonterminal prognoses reported significantly more willingness among the terminally ill group to enroll in risky experimental therapies.[32] Such findings seem to confirm that there may be a tendency among these patients also to believe that they have little to lose. However, they do have something to lose. The possibility of a quicker, more painful death is often a risk in experimental treatments, such as chemotherapy. For example, reports from a 1994 study on a chemotherapy agent for metastatic cancers, Interleukin-2, showed that "more than 80% of patients did not do any better than they usually did, in fact they did worse. They died harder."[33]

Among the more serious side effects reported from experimental treatment of cancer are permanent paralysis, infertility, and the need to wear a colostomy bag. Like Anne, patients also risk not being eligible for other studies that may have been able to benefit them more. This myth should be the first one we endeavor to dispel.

Another special consideration among terminally ill patients that is not addressed by current guidelines is the severe limitation or absence of treatment alternatives to the experimental study they may face. It is highly arguable whether any consent given under such circumstances is truly voluntary. As one ethicist points out, "Few patients would find death a realistic option."[34] Here, an important ethical dilemma arises: On the one hand, it seems unethical to solicit their enrollment in high-risk studies, in which they might be unduly influenced by the desperation of their circumstances to participate, if healthy subjects would not consent to such risks. On the other hand, it seems inhumane to deny them one of the few or only opportunities they may have for a chance at extended life.

If they are recruited to participate in such studies, patients need to be aware that they risk more than death. They risk pain, possible disability, frequently humiliating side effects, and overall reduced quality of life. Serious consideration should be given to the ethics of whether patients should be allowed to enroll in studies in which there is evidence that participation could decrease the quality of remaining life. Important knowledge is gained from such research to further biomedical science, but at what cost? Is the knowledge gained for the future worth the cost of current lives? Decisions to participate under these conditions are extremely difficult to make.

Several studies show some very important differences in conditions under which terminally ill patients make their decisions to participate in an experimental treatment compared to patients diagnosed with a non-life-threatening illness. First, patients diagnosed with a terminal illness are under considerably more stress while trying to arrive at a decision to participate in experimental therapy. At the same time, seldom do they ask for more time to think over their decisions, nor do they typically seek information from other sources about the experimental treatment or its alternatives.[35]

Often, when approached about experimental therapy, these patients may perceive it as their only lifesaving option. In a survey conducted by the ACHRE, one patient confided, "When you reach that stage . . . and somebody offered that something that could probably save you, you sort of make a grab for it."[36] According to Irving Janis and Leon Mann, anxiety and pressure may impair decision-making ability and force patients into more basic coping patterns for emergency situations. In this "state of stress, confusion and fear of conflict," terminally ill patients often find themselves in a kind of "mental and emotional paralysis."[37] They often avoid discussing their decision, often are depressed, and typically "forget or suppress information given to them by the physician during the early stages of the decision-making process, especially information on risks or hazards."[38] Although it is certain no one sets out deliberately to deceive these patients, it is clear they are not well informed or equipped to give valid consent under the current safeguards in place for them.

Perhaps because the terminally ill are generally intelligent and not otherwise handicapped people, their ability to make decisions autonomously is taken for granted. Physicians and researchers are often blind to the internal struggles and misconceptions these patients experience. Like Dr. Norman, they assume Anne's consent is informed and valid if she reads and signs the form. Several studies of consent make an obvious point that these patients are in need of more protection in the research enterprise. It is necessary for us to ask ourselves if we have done our part as researchers, ethics committee members, and a society to make sure this special population of people have all the support possible to make the decision whether or not to participate in research. Without ensuring that valid informed consent is given, we unwittingly deny these people the principle of "respect for persons"—the primary ethical justification for using human subjects in research.[39]

Notes

1. P. Appelbaum et al., "False Hopes and Best Data: Consent to Research and the Theraputic Misconception," *Hastings Center Report* (April 1987): 20–24.

2. H. Stadler, L. Hezel, and B.A. Schreier, *Social Sciences Institutional Review Board Guide Book,* ed. H. W. Uffleman and N. M. Biersmith (Kansas City: University of Missouri–Kansas City, 1992), 120–121.

3. Appelbaum et al., "False Hopes and Best Data," 20–24. Sarah Hewlett, "Consent to Clinical Research: Adequately Voluntary or Substantially Influenced?" *Journal of Medical Ethics* 22 (1996): 232–237. Gina Kolata, "When the Dying Enroll in Studies: A Debate over False Hopes," *New York Times,* January 29, 1994, A7. Pam McGrath, "It's O.K. to Say NO! A Discussion of Ethical Issues Arising from Informed Consent to Chemotherapy," *Cancer Nursing* 18, no. 2 (1995): 97–103.

4. Ralph W. Moss, *Questioning Chemotherapy* (Brooklyn, NY: Equinox, 1995).

5. Hewlett, "Consent to Clinical Research," 232–237.

6. Appelbaum et al., "False Hopes and Best Data."

7. Beverly Zakarian, *The Activist Cancer Patient* (New York: John Wiley and Sons, 1996).

8. Zakarian, *Activist Cancer Patient.*

9. Nancy Evans, "FDA and Senate Cancer Coalition Respond to Activists," in Community Breast Health Project Home Page [online database]. S.i. December 12, 1996. Available at http://www.med.stanford.edu/bca/FDA_meeting.html.

10. Hewlett, "Consent to Clinical Research."

11. N. Kass, J. Sugarman, R. Faden, and M. Schoch-Spana, "Trust: The Fragile Foundation of Contemporary Biomedical Research," *Hastings Center Report* (September–October 1996): 25–28.

12. Hewlett, "Consent to Clinical Research."

13. Hewlett, "Consent to Clinical Research."

14. Zakarian, *Activist Cancer Patient.*

15. Kolata, "When the Dying Enroll in Studies."

16. Hewlett, "Consent to Clinical Research."

17. McGrath, "It's O.K. to Say NO!"

18. McGrath, "It's O.K. to Say NO!"

19. Evans, "FDA and Senate Cancer Coalition Respond."

20. Hewlett, "Consent to Clinical Research." Kass, Sugarman, Faden, and Schoch-Spana, "Trust."

21. Hewlett, "Consent to Clinical Research."

22. Moss, *Questioning Chemotherapy.*

23. Stadler, Hezel, and Schreier, *Social Sciences Institutional Review Board Guide Book.*

24. Moss, *Questioning Chemotherapy.*

25. Moss, *Questioning Chemotherapy.*

26. Moss, *Questioning Chemotherapy.*

27. Hewlett, "Consent to Clinical Research."

28. Hewlett, "Consent to Clinical Research."

29. Moss, *Questioning Chemotherapy.*

30. Nancy Evans, "Tamoxifen Update: Debunking a Wonder Drug," in Community Breast Health Project Home Page [online database online], S.1. November 25, 1996. Available at http://www.med.stanford .edu/bca/Debunking_Tamoxifen.html.

31. Kolata, "When the Dying Enroll in Studies."

32. Nili Tabak, "Decision Making in Consenting to Experimental Cancer Therapy," *Cancer Nursing* 18, no. 2 (1995): 89–96.

33. Moss, *Questioning Chemotherapy.*

34. Hewlett, "Consent to Clinical Research."

35. McGrath, "It's O.K. to Say NO!"

36. Kass, Sugarman, Faden, and Schoch-Spana, "Trust."

37. Irving L. Janis and Leon Mann, *Decision Making: A Psychological Analysis of Conflict, Choice, and Commitment* (New York: Free Press, 1977). Kass, Sugarman, Faden, and Schoch-Spana, "Trust."

38. Kass, Sugarman, Faden, and Schoch-Spana, "Trust."

39. Stadler, Hezel, and Schreier, *Social Sciences Institutional Review Board Guide Book.*

Suicide and Public Speaking

KELLY A. DALEY
2001
Mount Saint Mary College

WHEN I WAS EIGHTEEN years old, I decided to leave this world. When I awakened to the same realm that I had tried to depart, I was underneath a haze of drugs, angry, disappointed, and despondent. Killing myself wasn't a spur-of-the-moment decision. In fact, I'd been grappling with it since about the time when I reached the age of reason—or maybe puberty. I started keeping a journal seriously when I was sixteen. Now I am almost twenty-two years old. I have about six full diaries now, and I consider them to be works of art. If that sounds pompous, please let me explain. I have beautiful handwriting, I write in different colors of ink according to my mood, and the bound books are decorated by pieces of artwork (Van Gogh's *Starry Night* is my favorite) and inspiring words from the world's great thinkers (for example, George Eliot's famous quotation, "It is never too late to be what you might have been," and song lyrics my friends and I stick in, like the one by Guns N' Roses about finding one's way in the darkness. And another from a little-known group called Over the Rhine that poignantly states, "There are those who know sorrow, and those who must borrow, and those whose lot in life is sweet. While I'm drunk on self-pity, scorned all that's been given me, I would drink from the bottle labeled Sure Defeat"). Some of my journals are bound in Asian wallpaper designs, and others have gold-edged pages. But behind all the decoration, these books contain agonized pleas for help and understanding. They document the bruising and breakdown of my body and, in turn, my spirit. In five and a half years of writing, I have amassed six suicide notes. And those are just the formal statements of my intentions. That number does not include the many pages that just say, "Help!" or "I can't do this anymore!" or "I'm suffocating!" or "Please, if there is a God. Take me home!" or simply, "WHY?" Why was I born with Epidermolysis Bullosa?

It took me years to emerge from my depression after my suicide attempt. Though I resisted the idea, I began taking antidepressants, and after several failed tries with drugs that deadened me or made me even crazier, I hit on a good chemical balance. I still struggle with my demons.

They haven't gone away; I just learned better coping techniques. Being busy and keeping my mind challenged helps me focus on things besides my physical reality. I can leap mental obstacles, though their physical counterparts thwart me. That isn't a bad trade-off. Two years ago, I took a contemporary literature class. Though everything we read changed my perceptions in some way, and was therefore valuable to my growth as a person, I was most affected by Elie Wiesel's *Night*. The story, the memory, in itself was quite necessarily moving, but the imagery, the strength of character, the depth of emotion behind the painfully told words, and the courage it took to let them out were what really affected me.

Although the circumstances arc entirely different, I have survived my own personal ongoing, never-ending holocaust since I was born, because of the chronic illness that I was born with. I do not use the term *holocaust* lightly. When Wiesel coined the term "The Holocaust," I'm sure he knew what he was saying. According to the *American Heritage College Dictionary, holocaust* means, "Great or total destruction, especially by fire." I live with a disease that has been compared to that of burn victims, except my body does this to itself, every day. I have constant wounds of different stages covering a great percentage of my body. I am always in a state of healing and breaking down at the same time. My body starves itself, trying to take in enough nutrition to heal the wounds. I could eat all day and not gain weight. If it weren't for a gastrostemy tube in my stomach, which gives me nutritional supplements, I would still be the skeleton of a girl that I was before I had the operation (I was thirteen years old and weighed fifty-six pounds). I know what it's like to be in constant pain but to grit your teeth and keep going. The blows that I suffer come from an invisible hand, but they are no less tangibly tortuous for their nebulous nature.

I never know when to expect them, and though I should be used to my various injuries, each new one catches me unaware and hurts me (my hope, my spirit, as well as my flesh) until it seems I will break. I empathize all too well with Wiesel's descriptions, yet I cling to his example of courage, of perseverance. I must add here another twist to my life story, because to leave it out would be a glaring omission: I was also born with a twin sister, who also has EB. I have a built-in best friend, a person who truly understands my suffering, but with our mutual understanding comes double the pain. Sometimes I feel as though I undergo all the ordeals of my disease twice.

It has always been difficult for me to talk of the horrors that plague me, partly because I worry that I don't have the words to explain it, that it is beyond comprehension for people who don't live it.

Mostly I don't talk of it because it's too painful for me mentally—I feel ashamed, as though my physical defects are a personal failing. Atrocities, by their very nature, whether inflicted by man or God, are not, or should not be, easily understandable. Wiesel showed me that it is possible, for cautionary purposes as well as edifying purposes, to let go of the story. I know what he feels when he looks in the mirror and feels hollowed out, but I see how he has built himself back up by the telling of his tale. It helps him help others. That is what I strive for.

So now I write and I talk. In the past year, I have spoken at a fundraiser in Westchester, New York, to raise money and awareness about EB. I have spoken before Congress and raised three million dollars for research funding. I also sing. I sang at a concert this summer with

Natalie Merchant and then presented a speech, which raised $17,200. I have brought rich Westchesterite golfers and stern congressmen to tears.

I do not enjoy putting the most intimate and horrific details of my life on stage. I do not do it for fame or recognition (I would much prefer to be known for something other than my disease).

Actually, I am drained and depressed, sometimes for weeks, after a speaking engagement. In order to draw an accurate picture for a public who has never heard an inkling about my subject, I am forced to contemplate and condense and give form to my worst memories—I create word landscapes, with a palette of blood and bodily fluids and a variety of gore. It is not bad enough that I already share these hideous moments with a barrage of nurses and doctors and home health aides, as well as selected friends and family, moments when most decent and modest people would seek privacy—but then to portray these ghastly details to large groups of strangers . . . this is, ironically, unspeakable. But I do it. I speak because I am good at it. I speak because these opportunities have been presented to me, and I feel it is my purpose to do what I can to educate the public. Having a purpose pardons me for awhile. I have a reason to keep on living. I have some sense of a Plan, and a God. I have a shaky faith that my existence is not arbitrary.

Essentially, my two great ethical dilemmas are tangled up together. The first question is, Do I want to stay in this world or, rather, Do I have the fortitude to keep on living? I have been told that despair is the greatest sin against God, because that means that I am negating my belief in him. I am human. I suffer, more than many, less than others. I despair an awful lot. In my heart, I desperately want to believe in a loving God, an all-knowing Creator that has a Plan for me, but trying to make sense out of my suffering leaves great room for doubt where a loving God is concerned. I feel as though I've learned my lessons from dealing with this illness for twenty-one years. After that, what is the point? I feel I've gotten all that I can out of this experience, yet it doesn't end. And could educating little me be the point to this?

I have to note: a friend of mine objected to my earlier depiction of God as One who inflicts atrocities. I myself had considered defining the unexplainable horrors of life as random. But I have to believe that everything happens for a reason. I do believe that God is good. I believe in a loving deity.

I am a moderate believer in an omnipotent God—an all-powerful, all-knowing, all-seeing, and all-caring being, tempered by man's free will to do with his lot as he chooses. I believe that our sufferings are tests of character. It has taken me over twenty years to come to some reconciliation with God over my sufferings. S/he and I were estranged for some time.

I do have a handle on life, even in my few years. I do not share the sense of entitlement with my peers that all good things should come to me, just because. I know that life isn't fair or easy. As simple as that sounds, it really is a revelation. I know that most people have to wade through a lot of hardship to get through to the good stuff, the kernel of truth, the heart. Simply put, we all have responsibilities and circumstances that we have to take care of. We may not like them, but that doesn't excuse us from their bind. Sometimes I think life is an ocean of asperity. But there are islands of peace that we bang into every once in awhile, and then we hang on as tightly as possible, because we'll soon be adrift again. Sometimes the islands are quite large and inhabitable, and it is possible to nest in them for some time.

The second question is, Do I want to put my most personal experiences on display, where they lie vulnerable and assailable, open to disgust, ridicule, and prejudice, as well as understanding and compassion? I obviously hope for the latter feelings, but I fear the former. But the second question negates the first. I can't leave this world if I'm in the middle of my destiny.

It is my job to maintain this vessel that houses me. I need a lot of help: my nurses, my coworkers, are also on the upkeep committee. It is not shameful or pathetic to need help (I remind myself). This is a big job. The body is the conduit for the spirit. I need to keep it in good working condition so that the spirit can fulfill its mission. I try to look at it as if I were the CEO of a company, and I have to keep things running smoothly, delegating authority, devising a strategy for my care, so that the objective can be achieved. I just happen to do most of the planning and delegating in the bathtub, while I soak off my dressings and clean my wounds. I am a naked Chief Executive Officer. And I retain my dignity and authority, even without clothes.

I've been assigned to take care of this body and perhaps learn some things along the way. I have been given gifts along with my burdens, and my responsibility is to exercise and sharpen those talents for the betterment of society as a whole. It would be selfish to keep the lessons and coping strategies I've learned to myself. I am not so arrogant and presupposing as to assume that my truths are everyone's truths or that my solutions will work for everybody. I do not believe in universal truth or in any totalizing system, but I do think that life is not all about getting. The world does not end at the tip of my nose. If what I have learned from my trials can help someone else, then that validates my experience.

You may detect a struggle in the course of this essay. You may see me wavering, even here, between purpose and dejection, faith and despair. You may hear me whine, or rail at Fate, or you may find the voice of serenity. I am not always consistent in my views, but then I don't know anyone whose heart has not been penetrated slightly by the seed of doubt—and certainly by discontent.

In some secret corner of my heart, I have held out the hope that one day I will be healed. On the rational level, I expected that this phenomenon would occur under the umbrella of medical science.

But, and I hate to admit this for fear of sounding naive or silly, the childlike optimist in me yearned for a true miracle, a total healing, that would erase my scars and make my mittened arthritic hands useful again, that would undo the corrosion of chronic wounding. A distant and buried part of me expected (well, wanted) God to come down in one of his great magic shows—but clearly that is the wrong track to be thinking on. In looking for some huge mystical event, it's easy to overlook the smaller (but not less important) details. Maybe we're all being conserved, shored up, one detail at a time. Probably our human limitations could not withstand one of those fantastic miracles that we've read about in the Bible. Probably we'd go insane, blow a gasket, if we witnessed a true miracle. The biblical stories are larger-than-life examples, parables. But they raise expectations. On some level, even if it is subconscious, it is a huge letdown to wake up every day with a chronic illness, with chronic pain, when you're asking, hoping, waiting, praying every night for a cure. Maybe the smart recourse is to lower my standards. Hence the rationality of the world of medicine. I tell you all of this not to sound preachy but to illustrate my struggle.

Several weeks ago, I went on a spiritual retreat. It was an activity totally out of the realm of my normal experience. I was skeptical, worried about dogmatics and pushy religious fanaticism. My faith was tenuous at the time. I was mired in melancholy, fed up with the trials of my life. I was thinking of committing myself to a mental institution, as the sole refuge open to me aside from absolute termination of life. My weekend with the Women Bearing Gifts group saved me. Not just for those few days was I spared, but in the ensuing days, out in the real world, I have kept my feeling of inner contentment. I am strong. I am filled up. I wrote copiously in my journal that weekend, so I would not lose my revelations, so the feelings would not be fleeting.

On the wraparound porch of a Victorian house tucked in a hidden valley surrounded by mountains, twenty minutes and many deep breaths away from the monotony and oppression of my daily life, I threw myself into the embrace of a group of kindred women (most more than double my age—my peers in terms of wisdom and life experience). I let go of my pains. The ache in my chest eased. As we studied the wisdom of the early Christian mystic Julian of Norwich, I was shaken by new theories behind suffering and new ways of viewing God.

In the same vein as life not being fair, I took that concept a little farther: God never promised that life would be easy. He did say that he would be with us along the way, but then I think, well, where is he? I need a tangible source to look to. Julian said, God is love. That brings an entirely new perspective into the mix. Love I know, love I am good at. My disability lies not in my capacity to give or receive love. I used to think I lacked a touchable, seeable, hearable deity, but really, he is all of those things. I have many people to love and be loved by. I thought I didn't know God, but if God is love, then I've been allied with him from my beginning.

Another of my great revelations is that suffering comes from craving (for health, for knowledge), and craving stems from ignorance of my own connectedness. When I realized that I do know God in knowing love, I became moored.

There are more important things in life than health, though for most people that is their benchmark, their bottom line ("At least I have my health . . ."). Having health in body does not guarantee a good life, though it can make it easier to get through. But love, love is what we're here for, what we're built for. Love can't always heal, but it can suffuse us with enough strength to deal with our trials.

I don't look at the big picture. I can't imagine living twenty more years under the regime of my illness. So I've learned to live second to second. I heartily appreciate the details of life: a great belly laugh, a poetic sentence, friends who hold my hands, a really deep breath that finds its way down to nourish the most inner reaches of me, sunlight warming me, a piece of music that makes my hips swing, a sentiment that makes me cry, a sweet and steamy cup of coffee on a frosty day, my father's voice on any day. . . . Julian said, "All shall be well, and all shall be well, and all manner of things shall be well." I believe her. The retreat helped me find it in myself to trust in the rightness of my path. In my journal I wrote, "I have hope that all shall be well in the future, but I also feel that even now, in these very seconds that are passing, I am well. I can't ask for more than that." If I am not so busy fighting to make things the way I want them to be or I think they should be, I can live the way I'm meant to. Just because something isn't perfect doesn't mean it isn't sacred.

I bear my burdens by sharing them. I cry them out on the shoulders of my dearests. I sing them out in a manner of civilized screaming. I write them out, which gives them form, sometimes a lovely form, and occasionally turns them into art. I make my ugly and painful sentiments into something beautiful on paper.

My wounds are constant and ever multiplying—but they are also always healing. I have the unique opportunity literally to be able to watch the body's capacity for healing itself and to know that my spirit can probably do the same thing.

I choose to live responsibly and consciously. I choose to live. I choose to live fully. I choose not to drop into the abyss of despair and depression, and hibernate under my covers and retreat into unconsciousness (even as much as I love sleep). I choose to take risks and to put myself out there, on the line, over the line.

So now I have told you how I came to keep living my life and how I learned to enjoy the graces in it. I have managed to reconcile extreme suffering with a workable faith in a loving God. The great paradox of my life is that I love it. I have a marvelous life: I just wish I didn't have to live it through my body.

ON GOD

The Duty of Cock-Eyed Angels

ZOHAR ATKINS
2009
Brown University

There is a painting by Klee called *Angelus Novus*. It shows an angel who seems about to move away from something he stares at. His eyes are wide, his mouth is open, his wings are spread. This is how the angel of history must look. His face is turned toward the past.

Where a chain of events appears before us, he sees one single catastrophe, which keeps piling wreckage upon wreckage and hurls it at his feet. The angel would like to stay, awaken the dead, and make whole what has been smashed. But a storm is blowing from Paradise and has got caught in his wings; it is so strong that the angel can no longer close them. This storm drives him irresistibly into the future to which his back is turned, while the pile of debris before him grows toward the sky. What we call progress is this storm.

—Walter Benjamin, Thesis IX, "On the Concept of History"

THREE AND A HALF YEARS ago, in the Israel Museum in Jerusalem, an expressionist, earth-toned watercolor of an astigmatic birdman called out to me. It was Paul Klee's *Angelus Novus,* acquired by the German Jewish critic Walter Benjamin in 1921, a year after its composition, and a focal point of his philosophy of history. After his tragic suicide on the Spanish-French border in 1940, Benjamin left the painting to his beloved friend Gershom Scholem, the historian of the Kaballah. Upon his own death in 1983, Scholem bequeathed the piece to his neighborhood museum, where I came upon it twenty-two years later. At the time, I was unaware of the painting's history, its birth in Weimar Germany, its survival from European catastrophe, its flight to Jerusalem. But the strange figure in the painting has stayed with me ever since. I have come to see it as the very symbol of our deepest challenges, as well as a guide to an ethical way.

If Klee's painting depicts—as Benjamin tells us—"the angel of history," a meek divine messenger blown by an aboriginal storm, back twisted toward the future, it is particularly significant that the creature is cock-eyed.[1] Indeed, this ocular asymmetry marks his essential nature. For the cock-eyed angel does not gaze nostalgically toward yesteryear but rather trains just one eye on the past, with the other fixed on the present. Surely if the angel can observe anything at all, he does so precisely because he sees both the past and the present at once, always regarding one in relief against the other. The angel's desire to "awaken the dead" and "make whole what has been smashed" represents an expression of deep anxiety governing the now, constantly moved by the "one single catastrophe, which keeps piling wreckage upon wreckage and hurls it at his feet."

Though the angel's wings are paralyzed, trapped in the storm "we call progress," the discrepancy in vision between the two eyes permits him to bear witness to this very problem. By acclimating himself to the disorientation, he gains knowledge of himself and his world. He has the power, in philosophical terms, to hold simultaneously a vision both of what is and what ought to be. Torn between the real and the ideal, despair and hope, struggle and submission, he does not resemble other angels—neither shining, faithful Gabriel, nor cunning, evil Satan.

Rather what Klee calls the *new* angel, what Benjamin identifies as the angel of history, we recognize as the shape of the human. Angelwise, he is deficient, even aside from his ophthalmological aberration. That is, his feet stand apart,[2] he bears a pronounced philtral dimple,[3] and he lacks his heavenly peers' supernatural power. His situation is ours. For we are angels of history, caught between an "always already" and a "not yet." We embody all that is in both the divine image (*tzelem*) and the divine shadow (*tzilum*).[4]

I have come to believe that we have a twofold responsibility as *angeli novi*, hitherto divided into two distinct responsibilities, set at odds with each other in a debilitating rhetoric of *either/or* that would force us to choose between being and becoming. In this essay, I aim to identify how we are responsible *both* for being who we are *and* becoming who we ought to be.

Our challenge takes many forms: to recognize that each of us is the being for whom the whole world was created, *and* simultaneously to see that we are nothing but dust of the earth;[5] to look up in wonder at the heavens, *and* at the same time to look down at our feet; to philosophize, question, and critique, *and* to act, answer, and take a stand; to be compassionate and submissive before the infinite call of the Other, *and* to be aware of all the others whose calls are just as infinite; to be tolerant, pluralistic, open, and humble, *and* to judge, create moral boundaries, be firm, and exhibit bravery; to be happy, optimistic, and hopeful, *and* to be sensitive that there are others who are unfortunate, unhappy, pessimistic, without hope; to delight in art, poetry, and nature, *and* to remember the netherside of the world, still awaiting improvement.

But how can we do all this? How can we ensure that we behold and thereby inhabit two realities at once? Furthermore, what are we to do when concrete, immediate action is required?

After all, even as we adopt a mindset of the double responsibility, in our daily existence we face ethical choices often requiring sacrifices. Abraham had to choose between love of family and fealty to God.[6] Antigone had to choose between commitment to the gods and loyalty to the state.[7] Neither had the philosopher's luxury to synthesize and embrace two opposing obligations. Americans cherish three ideals of "life, liberty, and the pursuit of happiness" but make countless decisions in which they privilege one over another.[8] In this moment of decision, the detached syntax of "one can" or "one might" retreats, overtaken by the definitive declaration "I will" or "I must." The matter is no longer a question of one's belief in the right to life or the right to choose, for example, but of "what will I do in the moment?" Will I abort the fetus, raise the child, give the baby up for adoption? Will I march on the state capitol, write a check to a charity, vote for a candidate, mount the soapbox? In this realm, where all "I"s are deracinated from the safe, universal home of "one," tremendous violence begins. In enlightened dialogue, "one" embraces the view of another; at the threshold of action, "I" can no longer stand by, and neither can "you."

The ancient rabbis grappled with this very problem, as it is told in a well-known passage of the Talmud:

> For three years there was a dispute between Beit Hillel [the "house" or followers of Rabbi Hillel] and Beit Shammai [the "house" or followers of Rabbi Shammai], the former asserting, "The law is in agreement with our views," and the latter contending, "The law is in agreement with our views." Then came a *bat kol* (heavenly voice), which announced: *"Eilu v'eilu divrei Elohim Chayim.* (These and these are the words of the living God.) But the law is in agreement with Hillel."
>
> Since, however, both "are the words of the living

God," what was it that entitled Beit Hillel to have
the law fixed according to their rulings? Because
[its rabbis] were kindly and modest, they studied
their own rulings and [the rulings] of Shammai, and
[they] were even so humble as to mention the teachings of Shammai before their own.[9]

The passage illuminates the virtues of humility and openness, but
what do we do in a situation or world without a "heavenly voice" to resolve our predicament? We begin by accepting the *potential* of any
moral position—be it dominant or minority, whole or partial, preliminary or fully developed—to make an equally valid claim. When we go
forth with a willingness to examine the claims of others with modesty,
we speak to our fellow citizens with a "heavenly voice," and we challenge them to do the same. Our greatest task is not merely to weigh differing viewpoints *in order* to choose the best course but to weigh them
even *after* we have chosen.

Grounded in well-worn values and placed into the world far along
certain specific roads, do we really have the capacity to imagine as true
the very things which we have rejected, ignored, or missed? Can I serve
on a jury and vote to sentence a serial-killing rapist to death while still
believing that the death sentence is inhumane? Can I enthusiastically
scribble romantic poetry while remaining aware of the poverty beneath
my apartment window? Can I do my utmost to stop the genocide in
southern Sudan while providing for the children in my home? There is
a saying among pragmatic religionists that one should pray as if the
world depends on God and act as if it depends on oneself. But is there
any way that we can make our action itself a prayer and our prayer itself
an action?

These questions seem to provoke an unsatisfactory answer. For they
seem to lead us into professing that we must choose between seeing the
world with an open and impractically contradictory mind on the one

hand, and acting in it with a resolute and narrow mind on the other, as if we cannot be creators and dreamers at once. I wish I could proffer a unified field theory of ethical behavior, a universal imperative, a perfect compass. To be ever conflicted in pursuit of the good is taxing, depressing, potentially paralyzing. Franz Kafka expresses our difficulty in the following existential terms:

> [Man] is a free and secure citizen of the world, for he is fettered to a chain which is long enough to give him the freedom of all earthly space, and only so long that nothing can drag him past the frontiers of the world. But simultaneously he is a free and secure citizen of Heaven as well, for he is also fettered by a similarly designed heavenly chain. So that if he heads, say, for the earth, his heavenly collar throttles him, and if he heads for Heaven, his earthly one does the same.[10]

In failing to provide a definitive solution, I do not mean that we can't resolve our conflict. I simply argue that a solution exists only where and insofar as we seek it. Instead of an answer, let me propose a way to an answer. That way is the ceaseless striving for justice, even after securing some measure of it. The biblical injunction *"Justice, justice shall you pursue . . ."* suggests the importance of pursuit, perhaps, over and above attainment; and by repeating the word *justice,* emphasizes its twofold nature.[11] For *justice* is repeated, according to various commentaries, so as to make clear that one must pursue justice in one's means as well as in one's ends. Our answer, then, can be found precisely in the tension between means and ends, in the disparity between our cocked eyes, in the war that is a source of world pain but also of growth, in the gray zones, whose undetermined statuses teach us most about who we are, and in the sacrifices that we make.

The simple answer as to how one can be what one ought to be, the cock-eyed angel, participating and reflecting at once, is to strive. It is true that according to Benjamin, the angel is unable "to awaken the dead and make whole what has been smashed." Yet this does not keep the angel from desiring and laboring. And who knows, perhaps if the angel didn't will, with all his being, to overturn the destructive storm blowing from Paradise, it would be even more catastrophic. But how can we cultivate the energy to strive? How, if the wreckage continues to pile up, can we prevent ourselves from capitulating and joining the growing heap of destruction?

Where does the will to wrestle with the angel that is ourselves come from, the will to be and become, rejoice and despair, tolerate and forbid, forgive and judge, believe and doubt?

The answer is love. We *fall* into love, without choice, seized by external forces, but we also stand firmly upon love, with commitment and freedom, driven by an inner voice. Here is the ultimate expression of striving, for to love is to say: "I am *not* the master of the world. I am incomplete, in need of another." Yet, to speak the simple words "I love you" is also to own one's incompleteness.

There exists no better exemplar of cock-eyed love than Moses. The greatest leader of the ancient Israelite tribe was also its humblest servant. He delivered words of wisdom, but they issued forth from his mouth slowly and with great difficulty.[12] Arguably his shining moment comes when, atop Mount Sinai, receiving the divine message, he learns that his people down below are bowing to the golden calf:

> The LORD said to Moses, "I have seen this people,
> how stiff-necked they are. Now let me alone, so that
> my wrath may burn hot against them and I may con-
> sume them; and of you I will make a great nation."
> But Moses implored the LORD, his God, and said,

"O LORD, why does your wrath burn hot against
your people, whom you brought out of the land of
Egypt with great power and with a mighty hand?
Why should the Egyptians say, 'It was with evil
intent that he brought them out to kill them in the
mountains, and to consume them from the face of
the earth'? Turn from your fierce wrath; change your
mind and do not bring disaster on your people. . . ."
And the LORD changed his mind about the disaster
that he planned to bring on his people. Then Moses
turned and went down from the mountain. . . . [But]
as soon as he came near the camp and saw the calf
and the dancing, Moses' anger burned hot and he
threw the tablets from his hands and broke them at
the foot of the mountain. He took the calf that they
had made, burned it with fire, ground it to powder,
and scattered it, and made them consume it.[13]

Here Moses calms God's anger, while using his own to propel himself toward action. Moses pleads on behalf of the Israelites, instruct-
ing God in the virtues of restraint, while moving urgently himself to
stop their idol worship. Moses rejects God's offer to reboot the nation,
knowing that such would instigate a vicious cycle of divine promise,
mortal failure, divine wrath, communal unhinging, and divine promise-
breaking. Understanding human flaws, but still valuing free will as the
engine of true partnership, Moses assuages God's ire and yet immediately holds the Israelites accountable for their actions. God's first tablets
were kept in the Ark of the Covenant along with the second set at least
in part as a striking testament to Moses' leadership.

Moses' dialogic encounter with God uncovers the meaning of the
first commandment, especially when we look at it through our cocked
eyes. The first commandment, which is not a clear commandment—

"I am the Lord *your* God, who brought *you* out of the land of Egypt, out of the house of slavery"—teaches us that God is only God insofar as he is *our* God.[14] Moses makes God *his* God through spirited, two-way engagement.

While the tradition teaches that "Torah was given to Moses at Mount Sinai,"[15] Exodus describes God giving *two* Torahs—one which Moses first *rejects* and then one which he *receives.*

By divine hand, God himself literally engraves the first set of commandments, which Moses—in turn—smashes; the second time, God dictates and Moses wields the chisel. Rabbi Yitzchak Hutner—a leading Torah scholar who audited philosophy classes at the University of Berlin in the early 1930s and fled to New York just before the Shoah— offered a profound interpretation of Moses' role as an active partner in this encounter. Hutner pointed out that, according to the Talmud, God *congratulates* Moses for his act of tablet-shattering![16]

Hutner then tunneled through a series of additional Talmudic passages to excavate the meaning of the divine gesture. If Moses' breaking and refashioning the Torah opened *aporia* in scripture and if textual ambiguity led rabbis to battle over the truth and meaning of the law, and if this divisiveness at the heart of the community ultimately culminated in the destruction of the Temple and the exile of the Jewish people for two millennia, then *why* did God applaud Moses' deed? Hutner argued that for the very reason that Moses destabilizes the truth and obfuscates our sight of the master of the universe does God commend him. For only in disagreement, ambiguity, and exile are people free, and only in freedom can they truly strive, love, and struggle for redemption. Our earlier Talmudic passage—"These and these are the words of the living God"—translates for Hutner as "These and these are the words *which keep alive* the living God." In other words, only through dialogue, argument, and multiplicity can the heavenly voice make itself heard.[17]

According to the *Zohar,* God gave six hundred thousand different Torahs at Mount Sinai because each person there heard according to his or her capacity. In this mystical conception, Torah is not a single, definitive narrative and legal code but a symphonic convergence of a world of many voices.

Can we tune in to the frequency of revelation in each voice we hear and spy it in each face we encounter? This is no small task. But if we bear in mind that to receive is not simply to submit but also to struggle, then perhaps we can treat every street corner as if it were pregnant with revelation.

Each year on Pesach, the holiday commemorating the exodus from Egypt, when called upon to open the door for Elijah the Prophet, herald of the messiah, I stand at the portal to our home and imagine my ancient forebears smearing lamb's blood over their lintels so that the angel of death might "pass over" them. I think also of the Egyptian soldiers who drowned so that we could have our miracle. And I wonder: Does redemption always come at a price? If so, is it really redemption? Can we really celebrate? A Hasidic rabbi conjured in Martin Buber's dialogue *For the Sake of Heaven* admits that he would wade up to his neck through blood to bring about the end of days. Trotsky once said that if one can be guaranteed of redemption, all things to bring it about are justifiable. For me, the Passover Haggadah provides a powerful response to what can only be called overweening radicalism. Before blessing the second cup of wine at the seder, the Haggadah instructs us to dip a finger into our cup and remove a drop for each of the ten plagues, as we recall that while they catalyzed our liberation, the same plagues also caused Egyptian suffering. We also read from a midrash, according to which, when the angels began to praise God for his miracles, God silenced them and began to weep, saying, "The Egyptians are my children, too."[18]

That the holy one cries at the very moment in which God's powerful hand is most manifest in the world's affairs testifies that even the creator of the world does not enjoy perfect peace and is not exempt from the ethical dilemma. Indeed, like the angelus novus in Klee's painting and

Benjamin's commentary, God must be cock-eyed. We must work to build a better world, all while knowing that our constructive and inspired labor is not without its destructiveness, too. The ancient Greeks used the same word—*pharmakon*—for both medicine and poison. When Gandhi and his followers fasted and boycotted for an independent India, as Reinhold Niebuhr highlights in *Moral Man and Immoral Society,* their actions caused factories in Birmingham and Manchester to lay off thousands. Can we ever be certain about our beliefs and actions? As Hannah Arendt wrote during the Adolf Eichmann trial, one who cannot judge is lost. We need to summon some degree of certainty to judge. But at the same time, whenever we take a stand for something or someone, we are also taking a stand *against* something or someone and therefore always causing hurt by our actions.

What then, are we to do?

Recognizing our limitations without accepting our imperfections, which is what Moses does, we must love. Only by loving do we summon the courage to act, to enter into worlds with others, to seek harmony amid pandemonium, and to find humanity amid what Arendt calls "the holes of oblivion." Only by loving did Abraham bargain with God over the fate of Sodom and Gomorrah, extracting the pledge that they should be saved for ten righteous souls. When it comes to particular questions—whether we should bail out irresponsible companies whose bankruptcy would cause thousands of employees to lose their jobs; or whether we should strike at terrorists in their homes; or whether we should spend scarce resources to stop the spread of AIDS in Uganda or to serve soup and provide shelter to homeless children in the Bronx—in the end, we must respond. Yet when we admit that the choice is difficult, when we consider the moral input of others, and when we turn our hearts toward each possibility, we are acting ethically. If with humility we heed our duty as cock-eyed angels, then we shall take flight, not away from the world, but irresistibly into the future.

Notes

Epigraph: Walter Benjamin, Thesis IX, "On the Concept of History."

1. My thanks to Nauman Naqvi for his insights regarding this aspect of the painting.

2. According to tradition, each angel possesses but one leg, a sign of unity and total balance. During the *Amidah*, the "standing" prayer at the core of Jewish worship, custom dictates that one pray with feet together in imitation of the angels.

3. According to midrashic legend, the finger of an angel touches each baby coming through the birth canal on the spot above the center of his or her upper lip. The physical impact of the touch is there for all to see on one another's faces; the purpose of the touch is to erase the truth held by the pure soul in the womb just before entry into the world.

4. In Hebrew, the word for image, *tzelem,* and the word for shadow, *tzilum,* share the same root. In ancient Greek, the word for image—*eidolon*—also signifies phantom. While Genesis 1:27, "And God created man in his image (*b'tzalmo*)," celebrates our likeness to God, it also reminds us that we are only semblances of God.

5. According to Menachem Mendel of Kotzk, the "Kotzker Rebbe" (1787–1859), a person should carry a piece of paper in each of his two pockets. One scrap should read, "I am but dust of the earth." The other should say, "The world was created for me alone."

6. In Søren Kierkegaard's existentialist interpretation of the "binding of Isaac," Abraham chooses the teleological over the ethical.

7. Antigone's choice is complicated by the fact that her duty to bury her brother, whose status as an enemy of the state forbids his burial, is a matter not simply of familial but of religious obligation. The gods demand that she bury her brother. Additionally, Creon, the tyrant forbidding her to bury her brother, is also her uncle.

8. The word *decide* derives from the French *de-cider,* literally meaning "to cut off," and often meaning "to kill." Deciding, by its very nature,

means eliminating all other options, closing doors, *killing* the alternate possibilities.

9. Babylonian Talmud, *Eruvin,* 13b.

10. Franz Kafka, *Parables and Paradoxes,* ed. Nahum N. Glatzer (New York: Schocken, 1975), 31.

11. Deuteronomy 16:20.

12. Exodus 4:10.

13. Exodus 32:7–20.

14. Exodus 20:1.

15. Mishnah, *Avot* 1:1.

16. Babylonian Talmud, *Menachot,* 99a.

17. Rabbi Yitzchak Hutner (1906–1980), *Pachad Yitzchak (The Fear of Isaac),* volume on Chanukkah (section 3), from a posthumously published lecture.

18. *Midrash Exodus Rabbah,* 23:7.

God in Our Ethics

MAE GIBSON
2008
University of Wisconsin–Superior

And what about God? Once we sang
"There is no God like ours."
Now we sing "There is no God of ours."
But we sing, we still sing.
—Yehuda Amichai, *The Jews*

WHEN I WAS THIRTEEN years old, I started attending church in my
small Southern town. I would like to believe that I had begun my church-
going in an effort to seek out God and Goodness, but I do not think this
is true. If my memory serves me correctly, I went to church because it
was a place where I was liked—not for my scholastic abilities, not for
who my sister was, but for myself. And I'm sure that I also comforted
myself with the notion that I was doing a supremely Good thing by in-
dependently attending church each week, something that most of my
peers did only out of necessity initiated by their parents.

There was a fellow independent churchgoer who was my age. His
name was David Wyatt. Under earlier circumstances, I probably would
have reached out to David, who was a misfit of the same order to which
I had once belonged. But the situation was different now—I had transformed from an ugly duckling into a slightly-more-attractive duckling.
No longer an outcast, I was coveted, rather than rejected, by my peers.
Did I dare risk this newly won position? Did I dare risk taking a grave
misstep and tumbling from my pedestal, only in an effort to be kind to
someone who didn't really seem to matter? I did not. However, I was

also not deliberately cruel; I chose indifference to David as a means of assuaging the guilt in my gut and convincing myself that I was honoring my ethically sound upbringing, which emphasized kindness to and acceptance of all others.

There were moments when David would speak and I would feel revulsion—mostly because I felt an empathetic understanding, and I hated the knowledge that I was somehow linked to this outcast. I also hated him for his foolishness. Didn't he see that we didn't want him? Even the adult leader of our youth group engaged in subtle mockery of him. One night, David stood up and told us how much he loved us. He said that the times he was happiest were when he was with us and that was why he came to church on his own each week, even though his parents did not attend. I think we all laughed.

The next day, David died. He had been in church that morning, and I remember we were both left waiting for our rides after everyone else had gone. For some reason I can't recall, David had a kitten with him. He asked me if I'd like to hold it. I pretended not to hear him. Three hours later, he was hit by a car and died.

This is a small thing in the grand scheme of the world. It is the unintentional death of one boy. It is not genocide, it is not a holocaust, it is not the terrible oppression of a people. It is a boy riding his bicycle on a Sunday afternoon and getting hit by a car. But in my world, it was everything. And fifteen years later, it is still so much. I want to make sense of the world, I want to make sense of myself in the world, and the axis I keep turning on is the death of David Wyatt.

There are moments when I can't breathe because of my shame. I think this is where danger begins in the world of morality and ethics. It begins as a spark of indifference to someone who appears meaningless. Where do hatred and destruction grow if not from the soil of indifference?

I remember lying in the fetal position on the floor of my bedroom, mournfully weeping amid the countless trophies of my adolescent accomplishments. Why hadn't I looked at him when he spoke to me that morning? I hadn't even acknowledged his existence, and there is no remedy for cruelty once death has arrived. And it *was* cruelty. We deceive ourselves when we believe that cruelty and indifference are two separate things. Although there is no way to measure this, I believe indifference killed as many Jews as outright cruelty did in the Holocaust.

We are implicated by our mere existence in this world. We have a responsibility in life to extend ourselves to our fellow creatures rather than sit idly by as we dwell in our own comfort. It is not enough to look the other way; rather, we must look head-on at injustice (of any type and severity) and commit ourselves to its eradication.

This is not about guilt. I want to make that clear. I acknowledge that there is guilt there—of course there is—but the guilt is not what terrifies me. It is the fear that I am continuing to feed the beast of indifference inside myself. On paper, I have learned not to make again the mistake I made with David Wyatt. On paper, I have learned to be kind to the poor, unfortunate souls in the world. But in life, I am removed and often still indifferent. I am so afraid for myself that I see everyone else as the enemy, and I cannot afford to share kindness with them.

I stopped going to church that day. Barely a teenager, I was faced with the huge, overbearing concept of hypocrisy. I certainly no longer believed in God. If God were real, surely he wouldn't have led me into his house of worship only to seduce me into indifference.

He would not have taken the life of a boy who was kind and genuine, leaving behind gross hypocrites to feign sadness at his death. Church became a dark place in my mind. B. H. Fairchild elaborates on a similar experience in his essay "Credo," as he recalls a boy who was orphaned and disabled by a drunk driver: "Scarcely a day has passed since then that I have not at some point thought about the redheaded boy. I have thought about him and not returned to the church I attend for months. One Sunday this memory flew into my head and I left before communion and did not return for a year. But I returned. This could be interpreted as weakness. But that's what Christians do when they attend mass or services: they admit that they are weak. They talk to God."[1]

Clearly, I feel a kinship with Fairchild through our similar loss of faith. But he handled his loss differently: it seems that he was not quite able to let go, and he kept returning to God. While he was merely enraged at a God in whom he still believed, I took my anger a step further and ceased believing altogether. I became almost intolerant of devout religious folks. Instead of sitting in judgment of people like David Wyatt, I sat in judgment of faithful churchgoers. This was not a step toward self-improvement. It seems that I picked an easy time to disbelieve in God, as Wim Wenders writes in his essay "Interrogation": "Sometimes, surrounded by technology and man-made objects, people have difficulty experiencing faith. They feel so self-sufficient that God can only be a second-hand experience for them. It's stunning how people have gotten used to living practically without self-acquired knowledge, without any apparent need for a first-hand life."[2] I was able to keep busy enough that any notice I took of God's absence was an afterthought. There is a song by the band Death Cab for Cutie that resonates with me on this subject:

> In my head, there's a Greyhound station
> where I send my thoughts to far-off destinations
> so they may have a chance of finding a place
> where they're far more suited than here.

It would seem that I packed God up and sent him off on a Greyhound bus.

I deluded myself that I was still finding ways to be spiritual, when really my spirit was simply being shoved aside in the name of tangible accomplishments that I thought would be nourishment enough. My attempts at "spirituality" were no more than infrequent reiterations as to why I did not believe in God, coupled with a few yoga lessons. By not finding (let's face it: not even trying to find) any legitimate way to nurture my spirit, I lost any foundation for my own ethical behavior. There was nothing to keep my own morality in check. Our ethics are not meant to be created in our childhoods and shoved in a box somewhere; they must be reshaped daily, as we encounter scenarios that challenge our beliefs. If we ignore these scenarios, we lose our moral center and our understanding of our responsibility to humanity.

I moved to New York City in my early twenties, believing that being immersed in one of the world's foremost cultural centers would compensate for my lack of spirituality. I believed that the diversity there would be eye-opening, a warm initiation into other ways of life. What I found was dismaying. There is no such thing as a melting pot, and if there ever were one, it would likely be a tragedy. We are not meant to all be boiled down into sameness, but we *are* meant to seek out each person's individual value as our common denominator. The problem is that people are terribly afraid. What I discovered in New York is that birds of a feather really do flock together. People are accepted among those who are most similar to them. This most often reveals itself racially, which is a sad reality. I also discovered that stereotypes exist because they are based on some amount of truth. And when we encounter people who are different from us, who are disinterested in us, we rely on these stereotypes in a feeble attempt to understand them.

The part of my heart that was David Wyatt became engulfed in hatred during my time in New York. I grew tired of rejection. I grew tired of fear. I grew tired of constantly being pushed, physically and emotionally. And so I shrank. I decided not to bother trying to understand people anymore, as they were sure to disappoint me anyway. I envisioned myself as a character in a video game—everyone around me was simply a nameless, faceless obstacle in my life. I commuted an hour by bus every day, and I realized that if anything ever happened during my commute, I would have no idea who the person sitting next to me was. I would not even know if my seating partner was male or female. I stopped *seeing* people, and I closed myself off to feeling the presence of life be-

side me. It is so much easier to hate when no one has a face. Isn't this
how soldiers are able to endure war? Don't they convince themselves
that their enemies are not people? To us civilians, this seems a tragic
way of regarding life. But if we closely examine our own quotidian existence, I think many of us will find that we live most of our days as if we
are engaged in battle.

What happened to me upon my own loss of ethical understanding
was that a void seemed to grow inside my center. My comprehension of
who I was ceased to be anything more than a compilation of the perceptions of those around me. Chameleonlike, I faded into becoming whatever I was judged to be. If I was liked on any given day, I liked myself
and thought myself worthwhile. If I had experienced some small loss
in my life, I subsequently lost everything.

Upon a particular job not panning out the way I had hoped, I ceased
to get out of bed for three months. I felt that I truly had no center, no
grounding in the world. How could I have inherent self-worth? Weren't
we all meant to be judged, and didn't our very identities rely on this
outside judgment? When David Wyatt died, he ceased to be anything
other than what we remembered him to be (or so I thought). Did it matter if he liked himself? Our interpretations of him lived on even when
he did not. Life for me became the endless chasing of my own worth as
defined and accepted by others.

I got lost. Everything was blurred inside me. I knew I wanted to be
Good, but I started to lose sight of what that even meant. Making strong
moral choices became a catch-22. My loss of spirituality led to my loss
of moral grounding, which in turn led to my loss of self. And having lost
my sense of self, I had no hope of regaining a strong moral center without help.

But help is hard to come by. I found that therapy did not improve my
situation. Therapy served only to define my flaws, which I had already
done; I had no problem diagnosing myself. Therapy addresses the mind,
not the soul, so we hyperintellectual automatons are unlikely to benefit.

Gnawing at the back of my mind was the thought that I needed some sort of regular spiritual nourishment to really work through this, because, as Blaise Pascal states in his *Pensées,* "It is the heart that perceives God and not the reason."[3]

But I remained loath to go to church. Not only did I still believe that church was for the weak, but this belief was supported by everyone I had come to know. In her essay "The Renewable Vow," Doris Betts refers to it as the "voice whispering that belief in God is not only naïve but a defect of both character and intellect."[4] Major metropolitan areas in America have an intense focus on strength, intelligence, and competitiveness. It seemed an almost ridiculous notion to attend church regularly, and many of those who do must keep it to themselves. After all, I lived in New York for six years and never met anyone who was a churchgoer, yet there are hundreds of houses of worship in the city, and most are filled to the brim every weekend. As my dad would say, "That just don't compute."

It's a slippery slope to start mixing religion with ethics, as we don't want to believe they rely on each other. And I don't necessarily think they have to. But I believe most of us turn to religion for our ethics because we don't know where else to find them. It seems that the only places where it is acceptable to discuss our morals and ethics are school and church, so our options are rather limited unless we wish to engage in the offensive faux-pas of forcing our beliefs upon others (which happens quite often and is even encouraged in some religions). As Sydney Lea writes in "The Pragmatist's Prayer," "I don't usually talk about my faith except to people who share it. . . . It is not something that lends itself to ratiocination; it is at once too profound and too simple. It doesn't make good controversy, because controversy, to me, runs against its grain."[5] It seems that speaking about God, religion, and ethics outside of church is perceived as an invitation for heated argument rather than heartfelt discourse. We in America are not geared to think about our souls and our relationship with God outside of church. Any questions

about our beliefs beyond the safety of those four walls feel too provocative, and so we either shut down or jump up onto our soapboxes, rather
than taking the opportunity to create a path between ourselves and the
human being staring us in the face.

I recently moved away from New York City, back to a small town, but
this time in the Midwest. People are shocked when I tell them I've
moved here from New York. Most of the time, they ask with bewilderment, "Why on earth would you move *here?*" They do not comprehend
that I moved here specifically for these moments—to be looked in the
eye and spoken to as though I matter. It is because the moment they
look me in the eye, I become a person to them, and I must answer for my
thoughts, my deeds. I moved here because I was tired of hiding among
the masses and excusing my poor behavior because no one seemed to
care. I moved here in search of accountability, in search of my ethics.

While visiting my family home last year, my agnostic mother presented
me with an article in the local newspaper written by a minister about his
specific religion, one with which I was previously unacquainted. This
religion has no creed, but its principles state that "it affirms the worth
and dignity of every person, advocates freedom of belief and the search
for advancing truth, and tries to provide a warm, open, supportive
community for people who believe that ethical living is the supreme
witness of religion." Hope reared up inside me as I felt a flicker of faith
that there was a place to seek out my ethics without shame, guilt, or fear.
If I had been someone who prayed, it would seem as though my prayers
had been answered.

I do not want this essay to be a promotion of organized religion, because that is not only disrespectful but generally ineffective. As I ended
a speech I gave ten years ago, "It really doesn't matter what any of us do
with our lives, as long as we inspire love rather than hate." These words,
though simple and straightforward, somehow manage to elude me more
often than not. But I think they are the truth—I think they are the root
of it all. I think these words are the summation of the ethics by which I

want to live my life. And it turns out I need to draw a spiritual community into my life to help me with the *how* of this dictum, a notion that Richard Chess speaks to in his essay "What About God?":

> Story and song. Story joins me to a past, what I'll call *my* past. Song joins me to a community of singers, my voice one among many, sometimes in harmony, sometimes not, but always with the intention of creating out of many one, a beautiful, whether wistful or joyful, wholeness. . . . Story and song help me overcome a feeling of isolation and alienation from others. When I am shattered into many pieces . . . each with its own needs, its own demands, story and song help me gain a little distance from these noisy, often competing pieces. And when . . . I feel powerless, unable to ease suffering or adequately address injustice, story and song—Torah and prayer— help me renew my dedication to work toward justice and peace. . . . I am restored, for a moment, to wholeness.[6]

I know this feeling of which Chess speaks. It is the reason I cry every time I sing a hymn in church. It is one of accountability as a means to living holistically. It may seem obvious, but after years of confusion, I have determined that ethics rely on accountability. In order to become the best versions of ourselves, we must see others and also be seen. For my part, I rely on a newfound belief in an as-yet-undefined God to help me face the darkness within.

In his essay "Interrogation," Wim Wenders writes of his own search for lost religion: "I remember how tentatively I started to pray again. I remember how that slowly changed me. I remember how I wept when I realized I had finally come home, when I felt that I was found again."[7] When I am brave enough, I speak to God out loud, and it is in hearing my own prayers that I come to understand myself and my place in the world. My prayers tend to be straightforward and elementary, but they make my point. Others take a more eloquent path on their way to articulation, as does this one, from Saint Francis of Assisi: "Lord, make me an instrument of thy peace. Where there is hatred, let me sow love. Where there is injury, pardon. Where there is doubt, faith. Where there is despair, hope. Where there is sadness, joy. O Divine Master, grant that I may not so much seek to be consoled, as to console; to be understood, as to understand; to be loved, as to love; for it is in giving that we receive, it is in pardoning that we are pardoned, and it is in dying that we are born to eternal life."

I love this prayer because it is a call for ethical behavior. It is a prayer to turn our attention outward and to have faith that this giving of ourselves will be the thing that fills us up. Yet even though Saint Francis could express so acutely how he wanted to live, he still needed to ask God for the power to manifest this in his own life. For him, human ethics required God's support. Does this mean he was weak? Atheists might say yes, Christians might say no, and I would say it makes no difference really, so long as he knew what he needed to get by.

A few months after I timidly set foot in church for the first time in fourteen years, I was back in New York on business. My last day there was a cold, windy, rain-soaked Sunday. I had planned to go to church but was contemplating skipping it in favor of comfort and rest. Thankfully, I fell back on a valuable lesson I learned in school: we make decisions in times of leisure so that they will serve us in times of stress and fear.

Two hours later, I walked into serenity. A grand, beautiful building welcomed me with open doors, exuding warmth and peace. I made my way to the front of the church and settled into an empty pew, where I promptly began to weep upon picking up the hymnal—here was the very same book of treasured words and songs that we have in our little church in my small Midwestern town. Suddenly, and for the first time in my life, I understood that I was part of something bigger than myself. There in that cold, gray, overwhelming city, where I had once felt so much loneliness, I discovered a place where souls gather in search of love, humanity, and community. What a wonder it was that there, on that restless island, a crowd of people had come together to literally sing out their fears and their hopes. What a gift I received that day! It was as though I'd found my place in the world.

That service included a reading of Ralph Helverson's "Impassioned Clay," which may well have been pouring forth from my own soul:

> We have religion when we stop deluding ourselves that we are self-sufficient, self-sustaining, or self-derived. We have religion when we hold some hope beyond the present, some self-respect beyond our failures. . . . We have religion when we look upon people with all their failings and still find in them good; when we look beyond people to the grandeur in nature and to the purpose in our own heart. We have religion when we have done all that we can, and then in confidence entrust ourselves to the life that is larger than ourselves.[8]

I like to substitute "we may seek out sound ethics" for "we have religion" in the above reading, because to me, that is what religion is. In understanding this, something profound has happened to me. Rather than continuing to spin wildly around his memory, I have quietly ushered David Wyatt to his much-deserved resting place within my heart. It has become a little easier to breathe each day.

Notes

1. B. H. Fairchild, "Credo," *Image* 55 (Fall 2007).
2. Wim Wenders, "Interrogation," *Image* 55 (Fall 2007).

3. Blaise Pascal, *Pensées,* no. 424.
4. Doris Betts, "The Renewable Vow," *Image* 55 (Fall 2007).
5. Sydney Lea, "The Pragmatist's Prayer," *Image* 55 (Fall 2007).
6. Richard Chess, "What About God?" *Image* 55 (Fall 2007).
7. Wenders, "Interrogation."
8. Ralph N. Helverson, "Impassioned Clay," in *Singing the Living Tradition* (Boston: Unitarian Universalist Association, 1993), no. 564.

Muhammad Is Not

ALAMDAR MURTAZA
2009
University of Rochester

Love, says Bloom. I mean the opposite of
hatred.

—James Joyce, *Ulysses*

I SOLD MY SOUL FOR THE liberal arts. I came to America to study
what I could not have learned in my home country. But before I got on
the plane to attend Kenyon College in Gambier, Ohio, I had chosen to
sign a piece of paper, the contents of which continue to haunt me to this
day. The voluntary act of my signing that document, however, is much
more of a nightmare to live through than the printed subject matter itself. In signing under that print, I gave up my soul's right to breathe, to
move about freely in the world, to take part in all the joys of life, and,
most important, to worship God as I choose fit. How did I manage to so
incarcerate my soul? Without guilt and without fear of persecution, I
denied these important rights to others. But at the time, this was the
only way to arrive on the shores of your country. I hope one day to restore those rights to myself and to whom I once denied them by rectify-
ing my mistake. I plan to do this with what I have gained through my
education.

When the college admission letter was finally in my hands, I read:
"Congratulations on your admission to . . . ." I believed I had achieved
a great victory for myself. I knew I was on the right path. That everything I had done up to that point was perfectly in line with what had
been expected of me, Alamdar, as a grandchild, a son, a brother, a Mus-

lim, and an upright citizen of the Islamic Republic of Pakistan. It was by that name, and through those roles after all, that people would know who I was. When they would inquire about my origins, I would tell them, "I am Pakistani." Now the rhetoric has changed in the concluding months of my college career, and since I first came to study in the United States. The shame is too great to bear, the struggle of the people in my country seems endless, and the land of my father stands for all those things I have come to thoroughly despise. "I am from Pakistan," I say, cowering behind the "Pa," "k"-hissing, and then cringing as if I have posed a question to myself about the last syllable "-ssstaaaan?" All the while I hope and pray that I only have to answer such a question at loud intersections, in overcrowded coffee shops, and at undergraduate philosophy council meetings. Why should a graduating senior, who has been given great opportunity and support, been shown love and deep sympathy for his ignorance, think with such embarrassment about where he began his journey?

After accepting my admissions offer, the time had come to acquire the appropriate documents for my travels. I needed to show I existed in some official capacity for government records. That is how they made sure who I was. And who was I? Unsure. It turned out that I would discover the answer very soon. I was with my father when I went to receive my Pakistani passport in the offices in Islamabad. People are more likely to take you seriously if you are accompanied by an adult in federal buildings. There is a very good chance you will be thrown out of line, sent home, or be forced to beg at the main gate if they find out you are too unconnected and unimportant not to have to pay small tokens to everyone on your way in, from the guards and gardeners to the desk clerks and the minister of the interior himself. It is not a curious matter as to why none of the poor have passports or identification in Pakistan. They simply move about like driftwood, in a vision of perfect disparity.

Once you have been measured, and weighed, and found to be a living entity by the proper authorities, you may walk out the way you came in, with your electronic passport that meets all of today's global standards. You have finally secured an identity for yourself. However, at the door on the way out, there is one more thing you must do to call yourself a Pakistani. My father had begun to move down the stairs. He said he would bring the car around while I finished up. There was a paper that needed signing. Easy enough, I could sign it and leave. The lady handed the piece of paper to me with gusto. "Sign here please."

Page title, Annex IV, "Preformation" with an "O": "Proformation for Obtaining a Pakistani Passport." The "O" stares out. Something is wrong. Perhaps this is a mistake. A quick glance makes everything better. The "O," just a typographic error. The bureaucratic language. So very clear and straightforward. "To the best of my knowledge . . . the information given here." Truthful? Yes, of course. "Surrender all previous documents." Glad someone thought of it. What is this? A Declaration? "Declaration in Case of Muslims." And certainly proud of it. "(i) I am a Muslim and believe in the absolute and unqualified finality of the prophethood of Muhammad (peace be upon him) the last of the prophets." Amen. The poor without passports roaming the streets outside. "(ii) I do not recognize any person who claims to be a prophet in any sense of the word or of any description whatsoever *after* Muhammad (peace be upon him) or recognize such a claimant as prophet or a religious reformer as a Muslim." But . . . Where is Baba? Gone to get the car. I need to speak to my father and ask him a question. "(iii) I consider Mirza Ghulam Ahmad Quadiani to be an imposter nabi and also consider his followers whether belonging to the Lahori or Quadiani group to be Non-Muslim."[1] Who? A trickle of sweat. The "O." This is a mistake. The poor outside. Their dignity intact, but yours about to be slashed. A quick glance makes everything better. Quadiani? Ahmad The Imposter? Never heard of him. That is not us. Thank God. "Signature & thumb impression (with name in block letters of applicant in indelible ink)." Thumb and paper.

"Thank you, sir, here is your passport."

I walked out of the building in Aabpara Market and gazed up at the federal section lodged in the forehead of the plaza. I sat in my father's car, a Shi'ite Muslim who had declared Ahmad Quadiani an imposter, and all the Ahmadiyya sect to be apostates. Two Shi'ites in a Sunni majority state with their seatbelts fastened, driving home in silence, having cleansed the world of its demons. Had my father left early because he knew what I was about to do? Maybe he could not bear to see it done again, this time by his own son. I, Alamdar Murtaza, an apostate (in the eyes of those who label apostates), declare these apostates apostates. Though I have never met you, because you will never reveal yourself to me for fear of your life. And though you must have a family, and were born of a mother and father who love you immensely, and brothers and sister who look up to you, today I consented to the government of Pakistan denying your right to Islam. You are no longer a Muslim. One of us now has a passport and will receive an education. The other will sit and think about what they did to deserve their place in the world or will sell themselves just as I have. "Signature & thumb impression." Indelible scar, a soiled conscience, indelible, indelible. Signed APOSTATE.

There is a story that is known to every Muslim boy and girl, in every Muslim household, whether the members of that household be Sunni, Shi'ite, Ismaili, Wahhabi, Ahmadi, Bahai, or Druze. It has been told a thousand different ways, and each tongue has redacted its meaning for their own audiences. I hope to tell it here in a way that is most acceptable to each of those groups, and why I believe it holds a distinction among the traditions of the Prophet that no other story shares. It is recited aloud, and with great pride, due to the sublimity of the moral that it carries. This tradition relates that in Mecca, after the ill-received proclamation of his prophethood, Muhammad, peace be upon him, would have garbage flung at him from a neighbor's window each time he would walk from under it. When no garbage fell on his head one day he went up to the garbage flinger's quarters and asked politely if he could attend to her, and if she was well. It turned out that she was very unwell.

Tradition relates much about the ways in which our antagonist's emotions transformed after Muhammad's visit to her quarters. Much weight in the story is put on how ashamed the woman felt, how humiliated she was that none of her own kith or kin had come to aid her, but the only one who sat beside her in her last hours on this earth was the man she had so vehemently despised. In some accounts the woman is Jewish; in Shi'ite accounts, she is a member of the clan of Umayya, the enemies of the progeny of Muhammad. Some Bahai attribute this tradition to their leader and not to Muhammad, as do other sects to their leaders. But all these ways of relaying the story have very little to do with the reason that we tell the story to our children. Perhaps we have forgotten why the story is told altogether. I believe it is told because each Muslim boy and girl must be instructed to believe that even the exemplars of their respective faiths, the ideologues of their beliefs, had no capacity within themselves to cultivate hatred. That hearts and minds can only be conquered by love. We tell the story to remember that those greater than us drowned out the sound of their own insignificant voices to make room for others. Where there is I, there can be no definitive victory. If we take the message of the story to heart, if we truly believe that the ones whom we deem far greater than us lived by marks of such self-effacement, then the following must also be true: In Islam, there can be no one who is a blasphemer or a heretic, and there can be no law that considers "blasphemy" or "heresy" a just law. To believe this premise, we only have to remember the reason we tell the story to our children.

This premise must also apply to world-renowned authors and artists whose heads many Muslim leaders have been crusading after for the past few decades. Although few to none have read Salman Rushdie's *Satanic Verses,* and even more in the Muslim world cannot read and write to begin with, there are numerous protests that take place in the Muslim capitals of the world throughout the year, advocating Rushdie's decapitation. In Islamabad this past year, banners spelling a call to this action were strewn from shops in crowded markets all over the city by mobs of the Red-mosque madrassa students. It is no surprise that what we know the least about excites our uneducated, illiterate masses the most. In *The Divine Comedy* Dante Alighieri confines Muhammad to the deepest level of Hell. He also provides the most unbearable descriptions of his condition there. The twenty-eighth canto of *The Inferno* reads,

> ... as one I saw torn open from the chin
> to the farting-place.
>   Between his legs dangled his intestines; the pluck
> was visible, and the wretched bag that makes shit
> of what is swallowed ...
> ....
> ... with his hands opened up his
> breast saying: "Now I spread myself!"
>   See how Maometto is torn open! Ahead of me
> Ali goes weeping, his face cloven from his chin to
> forelock.[2]

If today, I brought these words before some of our religious figureheads and convinced them Dante was a living Italian, I am certain some of them would most likely believe me. They would issue fatwas against Dante Alighieri, the Italian poet, and seek to decapitate him. Their followers would bomb and attack Italian embassies and consulates, threatening the safety of Italian citizens around the world. What I could never convey to those figureheads, however, would be that Muhammad would not have taken such measures or allowed anyone to take them on his behalf. Dante believed that Muhammad was a Nestorian Christian who denied Christ's divine nature. He also believed Muhammad and Ali to be dissenters of the Christian church with large followings and so, in the space of ink and paper, sequestered them to one of the lowest levels of Hell.[3] It is safe to say that Dante will never be taught to high school and college students in Pakistan. At the same time, they will never chance upon the descriptions and imagery of heaven created by the Italian that have no match in any other language or work of verbal art.

There is a prayer that is known to each Muslim boy and girl, man and woman, in every Muslim household, whether the members of that household be Sunni, Shi'ite, Ismaili, Wahhabi, Ahmadi, Bahai, or Druze. It is one of the last sections of the holy Qur'an. It can be recited within one's heart, and like many other parts of scripture, it is believed to provide relief from any calamity that may befall a Muslim. It is adorned on walls and tapestries in houses and mosques alongside three other shorter prayers that hold the distinction of providing protection from the evils of the world to those who recite it. The last verse of this section, titled *Kafirun,* "Those Who Reject Faith," is translated, "Say Muhammad [to the *dis*believers]. . . . To you be your Way, and to me mine."[4] I have known this part of scripture for twenty-two years. I learned its translation in my second year of college. On uncovering its meaning, I believe, as with the tradition of the garbage flinger, that we have forgotten why we recite this verse more often than 90 percent of the rest of the holy Qur'an. The reason I did not bother to learn the translation of this verse all these years is because like many non-Arab Muslims, I was taught that there is a hidden power in the very words and letters of the Arabic language. That because this was the language of Muhammad, if I continued to glance at it, and rehearse the phonetic correspondences of its forms, the hidden power in the verses would unleash itself. Indeed, there is no denying that the sonic space created by the sound of the Qur'anic Arabic is so rich in its poetic form that one feels deeply moved by its recitation. But that is not why we recite these verses so frequently. The reason we frequently recite these verses, and why we internalize them, is because their meaning shows that when disagreement arises in matters of faith, a Muslim can make no better offering to the opposition than the words themselves. In that sense, the letters and the words, and their sound, do carry an unspoken strength. They acknowledge that each individual must be given the opportunity and time to acknowledge the views of another. Yet our ayatollahs, our sheikhs, the rectors of our universities, and the caretakers of our neighborhood mosques do not offer these words when their beliefs are challenged. Instead they lash out with such deep rage, cursing the very name of their neighbor, that such fury cannot be matched even in the fieriest pits of hell. Men in *mimbars* seldom translate these words for their followers, and we in turn do not challenge them with these words. For this reason, their influence has become so strong that they can even transform the policies of governments. But when the laws of a nation come to uphold the ridicule and humiliation of any single group of people, those laws become unworthy of being followed. When laws negate the very existence of a religious group, those laws fail to deliver justice.

Muhammad, the prophet commanded by God to speak to the Muslims on the issue of those who did not share his faith, *Kafirun,* offered the most basic of human rights to those groups. In addition to deference, Muhammad offered disagreement with and (all Muslims place their hands over their ears) the rejection of his religious beliefs.

We are taught to believe in the hidden strength of the particular letters of a particular script, and the sounds that correspond to them, without knowing the meaning they carry. However, what occurs before us in the world seems too simple and too uncomplicated to attract our attention. The God of all Muslims, as it is said in the holy Qur'an, "will choose for His special Mercy whom He will—for God is Lord of grace abounding."[5] The strength of God's choice to elevate in status whomever he wills includes those people whom nation-states, their legal systems, and their religious scholars consider to be non-Muslim, impostors, or heretics. To this effect, the same God that asked Muhammad to promulgate his message to the *Kafirun* taught the people and government of Pakistan an important and harsh lesson in the practice of their Islam. It showed them they were in unmistakable and undeniable error not to make the same offering as the Qur'an to their fellow Muslims. The right to disagree in matters of one's religion and to worship God free of humiliation or persecution. The God of all Muslims, Beneficent, Merciful, raised a man from the sect of the Ahmadiyya—passport-less, mistreated, declared apostates and impostor Muslims—to such great heights that the whole world learned of his name. His name was Doctor Abdus Salam. He was the first and only Muslim Noble Prize-winning physicist. When the Ahmadiyya were denied their right to Islam by the government of Pakistan in 1974, Doctor Salam left for London.

Of all the sects of Muslims on God's earth, why did God choose a man from an impostor race, a group of lowdown blasphemers, to raise, in the eyes of the outside world, the perception and esteem of a nation that did not and continues not to acknowledge his beliefs? The lesson learned here moves beyond irony and informs us blatantly of how misguided we are as a people.

The Qur'an teaches us that the negation of another's faith is often the negation of his or her personhood and that such a discriminatory act is the only blasphemy there can be. Today the word "Muslim" is missing from the gravestone of our great national hero Doctor Salam, but God has carved it into eternity. No one will remember the name of the *qadi*-judge who had it erased from his tomb.

The history of the Pakistani nation is filled with similar teachings from the God of all Muslims. The most renowned institute in Pakistan for its contribution to medicine, public health, and education was founded by the Agha Khan, who is the leader of the Ismaili faith, another minority in Pakistan. The institution is attended only by the brightest and most elite class of students in Pakistan. Abdul Ghaffar Khan, the man the world knows as the "frontier Gandhi" (frontier referring to the North-West Territories of Pakistan), realized Mahatma Gandhi's dream of a nonviolent army. He was imprisoned and eventually murdered for being seen as a Hindu sympathizer but is still loved by all Pashtuns for his lionhearted bravery, his compassion, and his kindness. In the earliest years of its conception, Pakistan did not recognize the pious Khan's cause for his people. It was to simply educate them. Now they contribute in large numbers to the Taliban. Despite our failures and shortcomings, in the hopes that we will open our eyes, the God of all Muslims continues to raise, from the races of the persecuted, under-represented groups in Pakistan, the recipients of his Mercy and Grace.

Across the road from one of the most frequented barbeque restaurants in the "modern" capital of Islamabad, "Tandoori" in the G-7 Sector's Sitara Market, there is the boundary of a ghetto. A long mud wall sits next to a wide and deep sewage channel teeming with rubbish and city trash. The wall is crowded with young boys and girls, men and women of all ages. The scene is shadowed by large trees, and little can be made out of what is behind the wall. A table away from ours, there is a family locked in such a rare sight that one would say their ritual seems even a little pagan. The old father and mother, the son and the daughter, their wives and husbands, and all their children are holding hands. Their eyes are shut, and their heads are bowed before the food on their table. Their elbows rest in the air just above the tabletop. A whisper, something they recited aloud, but hardly, reaches our ears. Did you catch it?

"Amen." Amin. God of all Muslims. God of the Universe, "So be it."

The Christians of Pakistan live among trash heaps and in ghettos. We pile the trash up and around and right on top of their broken-down, sullied, uninhabitable lives. They walk by us every day, cleaning and sweeping our streets. Up in the early hours of the morning and out of sight by the time the workday starts. They occupy only the lowest tiers of life. The days they see we have no trash for them, they come knocking on the back door, or come into our house through a side entrance, wondering if we are well, and if there is some reason we did not have anything for them to collect for the day. Yet if you see them, assembled around warm food at night, with their families by their sides, they display a dignity in their demeanor, a pride and love so strong in their eyes, that no Muslim in their position could carry. In Pakistan, the example of Muhammad is being followed most closely by non-Muslims. It seems

abundantly clear in such glimpses who God has selected among us for
His Mercy. That is again, "whomever He chooses."[6]

Muhammad. The man whose name we seek to protect so vehemently,
with such vigor and such uncompromising stringency, would not stand
with us on this day. He would visit the houses of all those we have injured and upset, and he would inquire about them. He would apologize
on our behalf. Instead of receiving the pledge of allegiance from the
multitudes, recognizing him as the Messenger of God on earth, he would
be pleading for our forgiveness in the eyes of the world. We should defend him from performing such acts of pardon on our behalf with the
same vehemence, such that no such disgrace should befall his sacred
name. But that day is yet to come.

There is a passage of the Qur'an that should to be taught to all Muslim boys and girls, men and women from the minute they can read and
understand the words of their own language. It will instruct them properly in their faith. It is a passage that is frequently paraded in journalistic
columns and apologist pieces by both secularists and moderates. It is
however, very much a part of the religion of all Muslims who do not
adhere to those labels, whether those Muslims be Sunni, Shi'ite, Ismaili,
Wahhabi, Ahmadi, Bahai, or Druze. It should be commented upon
from every mimbar in the Muslim world. To speak it as one who stands
within the tradition and not as an apologist for the faith is to occupy
a station of Truth. To speak it whether anyone hears it or not, whether
the world is present or absent when you sincerely believe it, is to have
chanced upon one of the greatest secrets of the Qur'an's words, their
graphic form, and their extraordinary sound. In the Name of God, The
Beneficent, The Most Merciful. "Let there be no compulsion in religion: Truth stands out clear from Error . . . And God heareth and
knoweth all things."[7] If we are convinced that we possess something
that stands out clear from error, then we must insist on its validity without compulsion. I believe these words can be taken further to mean that
one must hold the validity of one's claims even without persuasion. The

last line of the Qur'anic passage above suggests that even persuasion retracts from God's purpose. He is the Hearer and the Knower of all, and we are not. What good is the assertion of our claims if God already knows the heart and mind of all. He is the only One who can move us to the quick. The God of all Muslims does not grant us the right to compel or persuade others in matters of religion. He also does not grant any group power to deny another group the right to their Islam. Instead the God of all Muslims prescribes "Say Peace."[8]

Muhammad is not "a mercy for all creation" if we do not allow Muhammad to be a mercy for all creation.[9] If we continue to stand in the way of our prophet's message, neither our own lives nor the lives of those around us will ever amount to anything more than the dust of this earth. God will continue to raise in reward whomever He chooses, and to us, the most unlikely of His servants will continue to uphold the standard of Islam. Because we could not learn to offer peace, we will remain utterly separated from Him and His message.

When I arrived in America, the man who signed on to be my legal guardian in the United States was Mansur Arain. He was my father's old college friend from Karachi University. He welcomed me, the son of his old friend, whom he had never seen or ever spoken to, with open arms. I know today why my father left the passport office before I signed the piece of paper declaring myself a Muslim and others non-Muslims. He had spoken to Mansur Arain earlier that day about my guardianship. Mansur Uncle, as I called him, was an Ahmadi Muslim who must have left Pakistan for a better life in the United States. When we returned home from the passport office my father told me about how his old buddy from his school days, Mansur Arain, had agreed to serve as my legal guardian for the duration of my college study in America. However, a semester into college, I was given word that Mansur Uncle had passed away in a car accident. I went to Freehold, New Jersey, to pay my respects at his *janaza*. Then, a part of my life I believed I would never get the chance to repair was brought again into my present. There, assembled in a congregation of Ahmadi Muslims, alongside free, proud men and women of God, I pressed my forehead into the ground before our unseen God. Allah. The greater holder of truth, the greater knower of the unknown. They spoke, as I did, "Amin." So be it. Lord of Heaven and Earth. So be it.

Notes

1. Nabis are prophets different from Rasuls; Rasuls are known to receive, record, and extend the divine word of God. For example, Aaron, Solomon, and David are Nabis, whereas Abraham, Jesus, Moses, and Muhammad are considered Rasuls.

2. Dante Alighieri, *Inferno,* 28:23–33, trans. Robert M. Durling (New York: Oxford University Press, 1996).

3. Dante, *Inferno,* 28:33.

4. Qur'an, 109:6.

5. Qur'an, 2:105.

6. Qur'an, 2:105.

7. Qur'an, 2:256.

Raising the Shield of the First Amendment

REBECCA SHELTON
1994
University of Missouri–Kansas City

"YOUR CHILDREN ARE GOING to burn in hell," a woman said to me. I didn't think so. But it was not the time to argue with more than five hundred people shouting and ranting biblical phrases at me.

"I get my dander up when one or two people decide they can rule the world," a man said over the microphone. "If Congress can make rules to give the rights to one, and take away from the majority, then it's time to stand up."[1]

That night, in Adrian, Missouri, the high school gym was packed to the hilt with angry people demanding that the school board continue religious activities in the school. I watched the next woman step to the podium.

"It is time, whether you are a Christian or not, to stand up now," she said. "If we don't, we'll lose more rights. I say to the school board, make the right decision. May God guide your decision. And you have the majority to back you up."[2]

For three hours, this crowd pleaded, booed, wept, and clapped in standing ovations whenever someone mentioned the name of God. Here, in this small rural town of sixteen hundred people, the First Amendment was being tested.

This is the story of one voice against many, an autobiographical case study of a dissenter. Neither lofty platitudes nor a string of legal arguments, it is a story that depicts the most trying moral dilemma I have ever faced. As one who spoke out against those in power, who willfully ignored and refused to adhere to the First Amendment, I will describe the events that propelled me into a situation that I could never have imagined. I will tell what it feels like to be pitted against religious zealots who believe they are fighting for God. I will tell what it costs to become a dissenter.

Furthermore, this case raises a critical question in today's society. Do the rights of one outweigh the wishes of a majority? The answer will reveal why the First Amendment is so difficult to preserve. My story begins ten months before the September 10, 1992, Adrian school board meeting.

One afternoon, my eight-year-old son told of a classmate who had asked their teacher why people around the world speak different languages. She answered with a Bible story about the Tower of Babel. According to the Bible, the ancients built a high tower in an attempt to reach God. But God was angered, and punished the people by causing them to speak different languages. On hearing this, I was upset because I did not want my son taught the Bible literally.

During the eight years I lived in Adrian, I was aware that the school led the audience in prayer over the loudspeaker before football games, annually distributed Gideon Bibles to the elementary children, used Christian themes for Easter, Thanksgiving, and Christmas, and regularly invited local ministers to speak at pep rallies, offering all children a chance to "be saved." Yet these religious activities in the school only reflected the community's overall Christian spirit. For instance, the editor of the newspaper once called for a boycott of non-Christian businesses, including Procter and Gamble, which was accused of using "satanic" trademark symbols. During a summer drought, the town held prayer meetings, asking God to send rain. Once, the city council delayed issuing a liquor permit to the owner of the grocery store to give one local minister ample opportunity to dissuade the store owner from stocking his shelves with "the devil's drink."

Nevertheless, the town and school's religious fervor had not directly affected or bothered me until my son was taught that the Almighty's wrath was the origin of languages. To me, the problem with the Bible story was twofold. On one level, my son respected the authority of his teacher, and, when taught the literal interpretation of a Bible story, he accepted it in the same way that he accepts multiplication facts. On another level, I realized that the school, as an extension of the government, was clearly promoting a particular religion. I called the superintendent and described the earlier Bible lesson. I asked if there was a policy concerning religious activities in the school.

"We've never had much problem about it," the superintendent said. "We don't have a large Jew element in town."[3] He added that if a parent objected to their child participating in a Christmas program, the child was welcome to sit out. In the past, he explained, a few Christian parents had complained about offensive language found in some of the library books, such as *The Grapes of Wrath*. To satisfy their complaints, he had pulled the books from the shelves. His decisions were made arbitrarily, he said, on a case-by-case basis, because in Adrian "we all think alike." If I wanted a policy, he suggested that I request one from the school board.

I was shocked to hear his words. What I had perceived as merely harmless overindulgence in religion actually carried with it a deeper connotation. I saw the underlying meaning of the phrase "we all think alike." This is the inherent danger of allowing majority opinion to supersede an individual's civil rights. On the surface, a group consensus appears harmonious. They say you do not have to conform. You are not forced. You are free to believe whatever you want. But in reality, to believe contrary to the majority is to become isolated and set apart.

At this point I faced a dilemma. I could let the matter go, or I could go to the school board and request a policy. The first option was easy. The second option would involve my taking some action. But I had never felt the need to speak out on an issue. I was not an activist. Neither did I feel a moral duty to uphold the First Amendment or to protect others, including "the Jew element." I was just a parent. Still, I knew that the school's religious activities had more than crossed the constitutional line of separation between church and state.

At the next school board meeting I nervously asked the members to establish guidelines concerning religion in the classroom. The board promised to review the matter and thanked me for coming. For months I waited, called, and sent letters, asking if any progress had been made on the policy. The board members never even discussed it. Meanwhile, religious activities increased. Missionaries came to class, speaking of their work in Africa to convert the natives. And my son came home with another Gideon Bible.

Then I wrote to the American Civil Liberties Union, described the incidents, and asked for information about other schools' policies. In subsequent phone conversations, the ACLU director said that many public schools in Missouri engage in varying degrees of religious teaching and holiday programs with Christian themes. Having received a number of complaints similar to mine, the ACLU was looking for a test case. They sent a letter, with my approval, to the Adrian school. It listed my complaints, and read: "Each of these incidents constitute[s] significant abuses of the Establishment Clause of the First Amendment.... We trust there will be no repeat of these alleged activities."[4] The ACLU's letter made its way into the hands of some community leaders. Soon, hand-drawn posters appeared on the front windows of the hardware store, the laundromat, and the corner café. One depicted the Supreme Court justices and the ACLU dressed in hooded black robes, like the Grim Reaper, poised to cut off the head of a man labeled "prayer." In the local newspaper, a letter to the editor called for all "believers" to attend the upcoming school board meeting and voice their concerns.

That's how I ended up in the high school gym facing a mob of irate Christians. To show their defiance, the meeting opened with a minister leading a prayer as the entire room stood and bowed their heads. The gas station owner, sitting next to me, waved his hand and said, "Come on, stand up. You used to be one of us." But I did not stand up. Instead,

I looked into the faces of my neighbors. They did not smile or acknowledge me.

"I don't think any of this is right," a high school student said over the microphone. "Nobody should have the right to come to our town and change the way we do things."[5]

My request for a policy had exploded into a holy war. The Christians were outraged because they felt that their right to pray was being taken away. But their argument is not accurate. Both children and parents can pray, anytime, anywhere, even at school, whether in the hallway, the classroom, or in the cafeteria before eating lunch—as long as the school does not sponsor it. When the Adrian school sanctions Christianity, it tramples the religious freedom of non-Christians. Thomas Jefferson had this in mind when he wrote the Establishment Clause. However, he could not foresee that the same Establishment Clause that prevented the government from setting up a religion would one day prevent Christians in Adrian from setting up their religious practices in the government. Indeed, the tables have turned.

When the meeting ended, I made my way to the door. But the Adrian ambulance driver stopped me. Clenching his fists, he demanded to know why I was doing this. I left quickly. That night, the school board tabled the matter, hoping the passage of time would ease the tensions. But they underestimated the town's emotional intensity. The pastor of Adrian's Assembly of God church said, "This is Missouri. There's a lynch-mob mentality here."[6] What was happening in Adrian is similar to a trend occurring nationwide. Televangelist Pat Robertson sees the battle lines drawn. "Christians have let other people set the agenda. Those days are over. It's a war . . . I think we can prevail."[7] Claiming a membership of half a million Americans in his Christian Coalition, Robertson said it was time for "civil disobedience" by believers against laws that do not conform to the Bible. He, like the citizens in Adrian, felt that God and prayer must be present in the schools to prevent "cultural and family decay." This theory is also flawed. The public schools'

purpose is to teach children to read and write. It is the parents' job
to teach morality to their children. If morality has declined, it is not
the schools' fault but the fault of parents who have neglected their
responsibility.

As weeks passed, the Kansas City newspapers and television stations reported the controversy. Immediately, I began to receive letters
and phone calls. Some supported me. "This country, in my opinion,
needs to maintain and adhere to separation of church and state."[8] A
waitress who worked in the restaurant on Main Street said, "A lot of
people say it's not right for one person to change things for a whole
town. Well, in 1954 in Topeka, it only took one little black to change
racial segregation."[9] But more letters disagreed. Many wrote that if I
"found God," I would not need to pursue this issue any further. Still
others wrote harsher suggestions. "This country needs to get back to
God.... We will get back to God or else suffer the consequences. If you
don't agree with the people in the school system of Adrian, you should
move, because as long as you are defiant it will hurt your children."[10]

Ironically, by advising me to move out of town, this writer was engaging in the same type of oppression that her Christian predecessors suffered. The Pilgrims were forced to leave England, and Roger Williams
was exiled in 1635 as a "dangerous agitator" for saying that church and
government should not be entangled. He later founded Providence and
Rhode Island, granting, for the first time, religious liberty for "the most
paganish, Jewish, Turkish, or antichrist consciences and worship."[11]
These are two of many instances in American history that reflect a
"go-along-or-get-out" attitude. As weeks passed, the town of Adrian
organized a group called "Wake-Up." They tied white trash bags, as
ribbons, to trees, street signs, and fence posts, to symbolize the return of
school prayer.

At school, my children were teased and called names, such as "antichrist." Parents forbade their children to associate with mine. One morn-

ing, my husband arrived at work to see a swastika painted on his tool box and a noose drawn on his locker. Now I was scared. Seeing my family suffer made me wonder if I had made the right decision.

Then one evening, a parent in Adrian called to say she was glad that I had spoken up because she was tired of her children being forced to listen to the Christian messages in school. The leader of a Kansas City Jewish organization called to personally invite me to see their exhibit on the Holocaust.

"You are a hero to the Jewish people," she said. I told her I did not understand. She explained that if more people had stood up in Hitler's time, it might have made a difference. She thought that more people must stand up in America to prevent the same thing from happening again. Her words were reassuring. I felt that I could hold my head up and not fear because I had the First Amendment, the ACLU, parents, and citizens to support me. However, my newfound strength was quickly dashed when six hundred people attended the next Wake-Up meeting. This time, local political candidates showed up to publicly support the Christians.

And Missouri's attorney general, Bill Webster, sent a letter that read, "I believe that if the citizens of Adrian have traditionally had pre-game prayers that do not offend anyone or promote a particular religious agenda, then it is not proper for the ACLU to replace the community's values with their own liberal agenda."[12] On the surface, his letter sounded good. Adrian, like the entire nation, has many Judeo-Christian traditions. American currency reads "In God We Trust." Congress opens with a prayer. The Ten Commandments are listed on a plaque at the Supreme Court. Still, the issue is not about erasing tradition from the school or government. The issue is about the Adrian school's non-compliance with the law. Missouri's top law enforcement official was implying that as long as no one was offended, the Constitution he had sworn to uphold need not be adhered to. His premise is wrong on two counts. First, one person did object. Second, offensive or not, all laws must be obeyed to ensure that the civil rights of each individual are not violated.

Wake-Up also hired an attorney to represent them. He was willing to obey the law as long as the outcome was to his group's liking. "Our rights, our practices, are being trampled and stopped. Now is the time for God's people to say, 'Enough'! As long as we can work within the system, and effect change, we will. But if it comes to a point, as a last resort, then it will come to a revolution."[13] The attorney was saying that it was going to be their way—or else. The Puritans took the same position in 1630. They banished "Whosoever shall revile the Religion and Worship of God."[14] And those who participated in idolatry and blasphemy were put to death. Although this is an extreme case, it illustrates how strongly some believe and to what lengths they are willing to enforce their beliefs on others.

Another widely held opinion was summarized by the Wake-Up member who said, "We have a right to have the school we want, after all, we pay for it through our taxes."[15] Again, this is a fallacious argument. Although taxpayers and parents do play an important role in the school system, the Constitution prohibits them from turning a public school into a Christian school.

The leader of Wake-Up gave another reason why he thought the Christians should succeed. "One person stopped prayer in school, so surely many people with God can bring it back."[16] This implies majority rule. The majority does rule with respect to electing representatives, raising taxes, or whether to fund new sewers, but there is no majority religion.

During the Wake-Up meeting, the members prayed, read scripture, and talked about a "battle plan" to circumvent the First Amendment. They wanted the graduation ceremonies turned over to local ministers, and the booster club, instead of school officials, to lead the pregame prayer. Pressure was mounting. The Christians had grown in number and were now backed up with heavy political muscle. I felt truly alone, overwhelmed, and outnumbered.

At home, I thought about the writing of the Bill of Rights. It was as if the authors of the First Amendment had created a silver shield engraved with these words, "Congress shall make no law respecting an establishment of religion, or prohibiting the free exercise thereof; or abridging the freedom of speech, or of the press; or the right of the People peaceably to assemble, and to petition the Government for a redress of grievances."

The silver shield of the First Amendment was shiny, beautiful, and held up for all the world to admire. And through the years, ordinary people like me have had occasion to take up that shield. Without it, one would be trampled under the feet of the majority. In my mind, I took a closer look at my shield. I saw pockmarks where, like rocks, the negative letters and phone calls had hit my shield. I worried that it would not withstand the pounding. But when I looked on the underneath side of my shield, I saw that the Supreme Court had added reinforcing layers of silver. In 1962, the court said prayer in public schools was unconstitutional.[17] Next, the court said only objective teaching of religion was allowed. In 1980, the court said holidays could only be observed on both a secular and a religious basis. And recently, the court struck down the inclusion of religion during baccalaureate services.[18]

In the end, despite Wake-Up, the state attorney general, local politicians, business leaders, parents, and students in Adrian, when faced with a possible lawsuit by the ACLU, the Adrian school officials backed down and enforced an earlier a memo that "advise[d] all staff members not to lead or encourage any type of religious practices or discussions that are not directly related to a specific lesson. The staff is to be instructed that they are not to lead or encourage prayer."[19]

Immediately, the pregame prayers were halted. However, Wake-Up members stood outside the fence surrounding the football field, shouting prayer over a bullhorn before the game, and some students formed a group called "Christians in Action," CIA for short, to pass out religious tracts and material on school grounds. Both of these were short-lived. The Easter program was changed to a "Spring Celebration." The manger scene was eliminated from the Christmas program. My children's classmates got tired of calling names. And the trash bag ribbons blew away.

Indeed, my battered and worn shield had withstood yet another battle. Looking back, I faced what I believe to be the most important moral dilemma an individual can ever encounter when confronted with injustice. That dilemma is, Do you look away, or do you speak out? This question is nothing new; it's as old as humankind. But it places one at a precipice.

Speaking out against injustice, especially when it involves religion, carries a cost. For a time, I became an outcast. A whole town turned against me. I was physically threatened. My husband and children were also threatened with ridicule and vandalism. Before this ordeal, like many Americans, I took my First Amendment rights for granted. I never thought that one day I would have to fight for my right—not to *worship*. But had I kept silent, the religious activities would have continued. Books would still be pulled from the shelves. Jewish children would have to "sit out" of the Christmas program.

The children would have only two options—go along and receive favor or sit out and be labeled "different." What kind of choice is that? It is not freedom, it is coercion. As Anne Nichol Taylor said, "There is no religious freedom without the freedom to dissent."[20] Beyond my personal experience, the Adrian case has significance in a broader context. The school board and townspeople had always practiced religion in the school. It was tradition. No one had dared question their religious activities in the school. As James Madison wrote, in the face of "overbearing majorities . . . a Bill of Rights would prove to be little more than a parchment barrier."[21]

Yet, when I exercised my First Amendment rights, it worked. But not without the moral support of my family, and other citizens, as well as the money, resources, and attorneys of the ACLU to see it through if necessary. By speaking out, I gained freedom for myself and for others.

Notes

1. Sharon Keisel, "Prayer in Adrian R-III Challenged," *Adrian Journal,* September 10, 1992, 1+.
2. Keisel, "Prayer in Adrian."
3. Victor Kretzschmar, telephone conversation, December 19, 1991.
4. Letter from Carla Duggar, associate director of the American Civil Liberties Union of Kansas and Western Missouri, August 25, 1992.
5. Donald Bradley, "Prayer in Adrian Schools Is a Constitutional Issue," *Kansas City Star,* September 27, 1992, A1+.
6. Bradley, "Prayer in Adrian Schools."
7. Pat Robertson, "God and the Grassroots," television program, aired November 4, 1994.
8. Letter from Phyllis Campbell, Anderson, Missouri, September 18, 1992.
9. Bradley, "Prayer in Adrian Schools."
10. Letter from Clara Force, Springfield, Missouri, September 16, 1992.
11. Milton Meltzer, "Roger Williams: Bloudy Tenent of Persecution," in *Milestones to American Liberty: The Foundations of the Republic* (New York: Thomas Y. Crowell, 1965).
12. Donald Bradley, "Small Town Gets Big-Name Help in Fight with ACLU," *Kansas City Star,* September 27, 1992, A1+.
13. Sharon Keisel, "WAKE-UP Group Formed and Ready to Fight for Their Rights," *Adrian Journal,* September 23, 1992, 1+.
14. Meltzer, "Roger Williams."
15. Keisel, "WAKE-UP Group Formed."
16. Keisel, "WAKE-UP Group Formed."
17. "Religion and the Public Schools: A Summary of the Law" (American Jewish Congress, 1977).
18. Lynn Decker, "As the ACLU Cries 'Censorship,' the ACLU Cries 'Foul,'" *Civil Liberties* (Fall 1993).

19. Adrian R-III Administration, memorandum, September 1, 1992.
20. Quoted in "1993 Women of Free Thought Wall Calendar" (Black Cat Enterprises, 1993).
21. Ira Glasser, "Democracy and Equality Are Both Good Things, but They Are Not the Same Thing," *Civil Liberties* (Fall 1993).

WINNERS OF THE ETHICS PRIZE

2009

ZOHAR ATKINS
"The Duty of Cock-Eyed Angels"
First Prize
Brown University

ALAMDAR MURTAZA
"Muhammad Is Not"
Second Prize
University of Rochester

ALEXANDER ENGLERT
"Asserting One's Presence: Exploring Moral Responsibility"
Third Prize
Gettysburg College

RITA CHANG
"Blood, Sweat, and Tears: My Experience in Human Rights and
    Workers' Rights"
Honorable Mention
University of Delaware

DANIEL MING
"Between Spectacle and Engagement"
Honorable Mention
Vassar College

2008

MAE GIBSON
"God in Our Ethics"
First Prize
University of Wisconsin–Superior

HEATHER HELDMAN
"Independence"
Second Prize
Yale University

NIKOLAS NADEAU
"The Ethics of Reclaiming"
Third Prize
St. John's University (MN)

ELAINE LAI
"Colorblind America and the Death of Affirmative Action"
Honorable Mention
Wesleyan University

JESSICA RICHMAN
"Truth and Reconciliation"
Honorable Mention
Stanford University

2007

MAGOGODI MAKHENE
"The Ethics of South African Identity"
First Prize
Neumann College

KATHRYN EDWARDS
"Guilty and Exonerated: Growing Up with the Death Penalty"
Second Prize
University of Texas–Austin

REBECCA KRAUS
"Morality and Memory: Schindler's List and the Ethics of
    Representation"
Third Prize
Boston College

SOPHIA PARASCHOS
"An Inculpable Love"
Honorable Mention
Carleton College

LYNETTE SIEGER
"Torture: The Bleeding of Universal Human Rights"
Honorable Mention
Westminster College

2006

TRACY KE
"Memory, Loss, and Revitalizing Democracy: The Mothers of the
  Plaza de Mayo"
First Prize
Duke University

AMIA SRINIVASAN
"The Sun Once Shone on Auschwitz: Ethics and the Threat of the
  Aesthetic"
Second Prize
Yale University

TRISTAN FISCHL
"Speaking for Themselves: Aphasia and the Poetry of Witness"
Third Prize
Western Connecticut State University

CHRISTOPHER ALLISON
"The Ethical Role of History: Towards a Proper Understanding of the
  Role of History in Human Life"
Honorable Mention
Olivet Nazarene University

SIRI DAVENPORT
"A Crash with Humanity: Prejudice Rooted in Identity, Fueled by Fear"
Honorable Mention
University of Louisville

2005

SARAH STILLMAN
"Made by Us: Young Women, Sweatshops, and the Ethics of Globalization"
First Prize
Yale University

CHRISTINE HENNEBERG
"The God on My Grandfather's Table"
Second Prize
Pomona College

CATHERINE BOSLEY
"L'Oiseau du Paradis"
Third Prize
George Washington University

LOGAN PLASTER
"Surprised by Suffering"
Honorable Mention
Northwestern University

KATHARINE WILKINSON
"The Last Will Become First: Liberations of Race, Gender, and
    Sexuality in Renee Cox's 'Yo' Mamma's Last Supper'"
Honorable Mention
The University of the South

2004

LESLIE BARNARD
"Forty-three Cents"
First Prize
Pomona College

PETER ERICKSON
"The Burden of Lightness"
Second Prize
University of Chicago

DAN CARLIN
"Chasing Images of the Dead: The Unreality of the Iraq War in American Media"
Third Prize
Washington University

AYELET AMITTAY
"The Problem of Empathy: Over-Identification in Claude Lanzmann's 'Shoah'"
Honorable Mention
Brown University

LAUREN SMITH
"Looking Out of a Cubicle—and Finding a Conscience: The Independent Moralist in Bosnia and Modern America"
Honorable Mention
University of Texas–Austin

2003

ALEKSANDR (SASHA) SENDEROVICH
"Tatyana's Glory, or the Birth Pangs of a Civil Society: The Ethics of Normalcy in Present-Day Russia"
First Prize
University of Massachusetts–Amherst

SARAH WATKINS
"Healing the Wounds of Genocide: A Case Study of the Gacaca Court System in Rwanda"
Second Prize
Indiana University Southeast

KATHERINE BAIR
"From Nurturing Terror to Raising Hope"
Third Prize
Youngstown State University

ALEXANDRA RAHR
"Are Holocaust Memorials Ethical?"
Honorable Mention
Dalhousie University

BRITTANY PERHAM
"The Statue of Grief"
Honorable Mention
Tufts University

2002

COURTNEY MARTIN
"The Ethics of Transformation"
First Prize
Barnard College

YVETTE CABRERA-ROJAS
"Questioning the Arrival at the Station of Departure"
Second Prize
University of Louisville

IAN JANKELOWITZ
"From Oppressed to Oppressors: The Ethical Issues of Post-
    Holocaust Jewry in Apartheid South Africa"
Third Prize
University of Nevada–Las Vegas

JAMES ADOMIAN
"From Carthage to the City of God: Augustinian Free Will and the
    Romance of Aeneas and Dido"
Honorable Mention
Whittier College

AARON MACLEAN
"On the Combing of Hair in Herodotus"
Honorable Mention
St. John's College

2001

JAMES D. LONG IV
"Deaths in Paradise: Genocide and the Limits of Imagination in Rwanda"
First Prize
The College of William and Mary

KELLY A. DALEY
"Suicide and Public Speaking"
Second Prize
Mount Saint Mary College

ARIELLE S. PARKER
"The Moral Need to Regard the Extraordinary Nature of Humanity"
Third Prize
Brandeis University

KELIN A. EMMETT
"If This Is a Man"
Honorable Mention
Michigan State University–East Lansing

JENNIFER C. SLAGTER
"Acknowledging the Wounds: Sethe's Ethical Dilemma in *Beloved*"
Honorable Mention
Trinity Christian College

2000

ALEXA R. KOLBI-MOLINAS
"The Secret of Redemption—Memory and Resistance: A Lesson for
   the Twenty-First Century"
First Prize
Smith College

MATTHEW D. MENDHAM
"Replication and Repugnance: Leon Kass on Human Cloning"
Second Prize
Taylor University

MINH P. DOAN
"To Make Boundaries Converge"
Third Prize
Berea College

DANIEL A. BROOK
"Beyond Teaching Tolerance"
Honorable Mention
Yale University

BRETT E. GROSS
"The Ethical Challenges of the New Millennium"
Honorable Mention
University of Minnesota–Twin Cities

1999

SAMI F. HALABI
"The Bosnian Women"
First Prize
Kansas State University

F. JASON COSTA
"The South African Truth and Reconciliation Commission and the
    Case of Stephen Biko"
Second Prize
Emory University

ANGELA LEDDY
"Papa's Medals"
Third Prize
State University of New York–Cortland

ABIGAIL KRAUSER
"The Ethics of Contradiction"
Honorable Mention
Columbia University

STEFAN SCHULZ
"Challenging the Innocence of the Scientific Mind"
Honorable Mention
Sonoma State University

1998

LAURA OVERLAND
"Their Lives in Our Hands: Fulfilling Our Ethical Obligations to the
    Terminally Ill Enrolling in Research Studies"
First Prize
University of Missouri–Kansas City

QUANGANH RICHARD TRAN
"To Bridge the Divide"
Second Prize
University of California–Irvine

MEGAN ZUERCHER
"Recovering Radical Innocence: Ethical Reflections on *To Kill a
    Mockingbird*"
Third Prize
College of the Ozarks

LINCOLN PENN HANCOCK
"Bad Faith and the Ethics of Truth"
Honorable Mention
Guilford College

RICHARD KEMP
"Enforcing the Darkness: Ethics and War"
Honorable Mention
University of Maryland–Baltimore County

1997

TAMARA DUKER
"Ethics and One February Morning"
First Prize
Duke University

BRIDGETT TAYLOR
"Lost in the Maze: The Ethics of the Labyrinth in the 'Garden for
    Forking Paths'"
Second Prize
Castleton State College

MARK REEDER
"Defending Morality? Ethics Through a Cracked Windshield"
Third Prize
University of New Hampshire

MATTHEW DONOHUE
"The Journey to the Rim of Tomorrow"
Honorable Mention
Oregon State University

JANET LIN
"Stu and the Ethics of Humanity"
Honorable Mention
Amherst College

DAVID SIROKY
"On Morals and Moralists: The Case of Professor Smiricky"
Honorable Mention
Boston University

1996

KIM KUPPERMAN
"Of Borders, Infidels, and the Ethic of Love"
First Prize
University of Maine–Machias

DAVID GREVEN
"The Wanderer in a Dark Wood: An Ethical Dilemma"
Second Prize
Hunter College of the City University of New York

JEANETTE ROSENFELD
"'Love Your Neighbor as Yourself': Nonviolent Resistance in Le
    Chambon"
Third Prize
Barnard College

VIRGINIA HENRIKSEN
"Silence"
Honorable Mention
Buena Vista University

CHONG-MIN HONG
"The Fragility of Goodness"
Honorable Mention
Harvard University

1995

ANDREA USEEM
"Toward a Civil Society: Memory, History, and the *Enola Gay*"
First Prize
Dartmouth College

COURTNEY BRKIC
"In the Times of Darkness: The Responsibility of the Individual"
Second Prize
The College of William and Mary

NADIA YAKOOB
"The Horizon"
Third Prize
University of California–Los Angeles

MONICA EILAND
"The Legacy of Anne Frank: An Ethical Perspective"
Honorable Mention
University of North Carolina–Chapel Hill

MARJORIE HUANG
"Overcoming Obstacles to Creating an Ethical Society: The Moral
    Responsibility of 'Humanitarian Intervention'"
Honorable Mention
Tufts University

1994

WIN TRAVASSOS
"Tearing Down the Lazaretto"
First Prize
Harvard University

ROBERT WESTERFELHAUS
"Dancing with Shadows: The Dangers of Responding to Evil"
Second Prize
Ohio Dominican College

REBECCA SHELTON
"Raising the Shield of the First Amendment"
Third Prize
University of Missouri–Kansas City

JULIE CANTOR
"Women's Rights as Human Rights: A Discussion of Violence from
    Philosophy to Policy"
Honorable Mention
Stanford University

RACHEL MADDOW
"Identifiable Lives: AIDS and the Response to Dehumanization"
Honorable Mention
Stanford University

1993

JENDI B. REITER
"Who Killed Superman?"
First Prize
Harvard University

AARON THOMPSON
"Technology, Literature, and Ethical Growth"
Second Prize
Otterbein College

CARRIE MILLER
"American Community and the 'Eclipse of the Public'"
Third Prize
Claremont McKenna College

THOMAS MURPHY
"Justice—For Whom? Reflections on the Persian Gulf War"
Honorable Mention
University of Iowa

JUAN M. PLASCENCIA, JR.
"Letters from Prison: The Ethics of the Political Prisoner"
Honorable Mention
Harvard University

1992

KIMLYN BENDER
"The Mask: The Loss of Moral Conscience and Personal
   Responsibility"
First Prize
Jamestown College

KAREN HO
"Ethics Education Toward a More Moral Society"
Second Prize
Washington University

THAO DINH VO
"To Remain Unique: Identity, Memory, and Ethics"
Third Prize
Dartmouth College

DAVID EATON
"The Dialectic of Autonomy and Paternalism"
Honorable Mention
Trinity University

ALLISON HANDLER
"Bridges"
Honorable Mention
Williams College

DONNA MCKEREGHAN
"Teaching Morality in Our Pluralistic Society"
Honorable Mention
Eastern Washington University

1991

PEGGY BROPHY
"Public Sins and Private Needs"
First Prize
Colby-Sawyer College

MEREDITH L. KILGORE
"Ethics and War in the Persian Gulf"
Second Prize
University of Hawaii–Manoa

JASON HODIN
"Ethics"
Third Prize
Wesleyan University

CHRIS NEWMAN
"Individual Rights and the Common Good: Conflicts and Solutions"
Honorable Mention
St. John's College

LAURA ELAINE POGLIANO
"Ransoming Morality: The Problem of Language"
Honorable Mention
College of St. Francis

STEVEN CHRISTOPHER WRENN
"The Moral Significance of the Story"
Honorable Mention
Santa Clara University

1990

AMY JESSICA ROSENZWEIG
"Choices and Challenges: Issues of Conscience in Jewish Literature"
First Prize
Northwestern University

STEVEN JEFFRY ALLEN
"The Meaning of Ethics Today: A Critical Structure for Evaluating
    Modern Ethics"
Second Prize
Edgewood College

STEPHEN FAIRCHILD
"Implementation of Corporate Ethics in America: Choices and
    Challenges of Our Leaders"
Third Prize
Claremont McKenna College

PAULA C. RHODE
"The Relationship Between Ethics and the Law"
Honorable Mention
University of Tampa

JONATHAN D. SPRINGER
"Black and White in the Land of Israel/Palestine: Toward an Ethic of
   Care"
Honorable Mention
Harvard University

DANIEL P. THERO
"Human Destruction of Tropical Forests and the Consequent
   Extinction of Species: A Modern Ethical Challenge"
Honorable Mention
Siena College